A SHORT HISTORY OF REVOLUTIONARY CUBA

Short Histories are authoritative and elegantly written introductory texts which offer fresh perspectives on the way history is taught and understood in the 21st century. Designed to have strong appeal to university students and their teachers, as well as to general readers and history enthusiasts, *Short Histories* comprise novel attempts to bring informed interpretation, as well as factual reportage, to historical debates. Addressing key subjects and topics in the fields of history, the history of ideas, religion, classical studies, politics, philosophy and Middle East studies, these texts move beyond the bland, neutral 'introductions' that so often serve as the primary undergraduate teaching tool. While always providing students and generalists with the core facts that they need to get to grips with, *Short Histories* go further. They offer new insights into how a topic has been understood in the past, and what different social and cultural factors might have been at work. They bring original perspectives to bear on current interpretations. They raise questions and – with extensive bibliographies – point the reader to further study, even as they suggest answers. Each text addresses a variety of subjects in a greater degree of depth than is often found in comparable series, yet at the same time in a concise and compact handbook form. *Short Histories* aim to be 'introductions with an edge'. In combining questioning and searching analysis with informed historical writing, they bring history up-to-date for an increasingly complex and globalized digital age.

For more information about titles and authors in the series, please visit: https://www.bloomsbury.com/series/short-histories/

A Short History of . . .

the American Civil War	Paul Anderson (Clemson University)
the American Revolutionary War	Stephen Conway (University College London)
Ancient China	Edward L Shaughnessy (University of Chicago)
Ancient Greece	P J Rhodes, FBA (Durham University)
the Anglo-Saxons	Henrietta Leyser (University of Oxford)
Babylon	Karen Radner (University of Munich)
the Byzantine Empire	Dionysios Stathakopoulos (King's College London)
Christian Spirituality	Edward Howells (Heythrop College, University of London)
Communism	Kevin Morgan (University of Manchester)
the Crimean War	Trudi Tate (University of Cambridge)
English Renaissance Drama	Helen Hackett (University College London)
the English Revolution and the Civil Wars	David J Appleby (University of Nottingham)
the Etruscans	Corinna Riva (University College London)
Florence and the Florentine Republic	Brian Jeffrey Maxson (East Tennessee State Republic University)
the Hundred Years War	Michael Prestwich (Durham University)
Irish Independence	J J Lee (New York University)
the Italian Renaissance	Virginia Cox (New York University)
the Korean War	Allan R Millett (University of New Orleans)
Medieval Christianity	G R Evans (University of Cambridge)
Medieval English Mysticism	Vincent Gillespie (University of Oxford)
the Minoans	John Bennet (University of Sheffield)

A SHORT HISTORY OF REVOLUTIONARY CUBA

Power, Authority and the State since 1959

Antoni Kapcia

BLOOMSBURY ACADEMIC

LONDON • NEW YORK • OXFORD • NEW DELHI • SYDNEY

BLOOMSBURY ACADEMIC
Bloomsbury Publishing Plc
50 Bedford Square, London, WC1B 3DP, UK
1385 Broadway, New York, NY 10018, USA
29 Earlsfort Terrace, Dublin 2, Ireland

BLOOMSBURY, BLOOMSBURY ACADEMIC and the Diana logo are trademarks of
Bloomsbury Publishing Plc

First published in Great Britain 2021

Cover design: Terry Woodley
Cover image Cuban leader Fidel Castro speaking to people of Santa Clara in the town square.
Photo by Grey Villet/The LIFE Picture Collection via Getty Images.

A catalogue record for this book is available from the British Library.

Library of Congress Cataloging-in-Publication Data
Names: Kapcia, Antoni, author.
Title: A short history of revolutionary Cuba : Power, Authority
and the State since 1959 / by Antoni Kapcia.
Description: New York : Bloomsbury Academic, [2021] | Series: Short
histories | Includes bibliographical references and index. |
Identifiers: LCCN 2020037982 (print) | LCCN 2020037983 (ebook) | ISBN
9781788312158 (hardback) | ISBN 9781788312165 (paperback) | ISBN
9781786726414 (epub) | ISBN 9781786736475 (ebook)
Subjects: LCSH: Cuba–Politics and government–1959-1990. | Cuba–Politics
and government–1990- | Cuba–History–Revolution, 1959. |
Nationalism–Cuba–History. | Socialism–Cuba–History. |
Cuba–Relations–United States. | United States–Relations–Cuba.
Classification: LCC F1788 .K355 2021 (print) | LCC F1788 (ebook) | DDC
972.9106/4–dc23

ISBN: HB: 978-1-7883-1215-8
PB: 978-1-7883-1216-5
ePDF: 978-1-7867-3647-5
eBook: 978-1-7867-2641-4

Series: Short Histories

Typeset by Deanta Global Publishing Services, Chennai, India
Printed and bound in Great Britain

To find out more about our authors and books visit www.bloomsbury.com
and sign up for our newsletters.

Contents

Glossary of Spanish terms

Balsero	Rafter (literally), or boat person (after 1994)
Bonche	Armed political gang (thus also: *bonchismo*) in 1934–52
Burocracia	Bureaucracy (thus also: *burócrata*, bureaucrat)
Caballería	Traditional unit of land measure
Caja de cambio	Currency exchange kiosk
Casa particular	Bed and breakfast accommodation (after 1993)
Coletilla	Disclaimer (by workers in right-wing newspapers)
Colono	Sugar grower (largely before 1959)
Combatiente	Guerrilla fighter
Conciencia	Consciousness
Contra	Against
Criollo	Cuban-born white during the colonial period
Cuenta propia	Self-employed (thus also *cuentapropista*, someone self-employed)

Glossary of Spanish Terms

Dentro	Within
Encomienda	The Spanish colonial system in the Americas of entrusting local indigenous populations to the care of an early colonist, allowing him to use their labour in exchange
Funcionario	Bureaucrat
Ideario	Body of ideas (especially philosophical or political)
Imaginario	The imaginary (imagined 'world')
Jineterismo	Hustling or prostitution (after 1993)
Libreta	Ration-book
Logros	Achievements
Lineamiento	Guideline (used of reform programme from 2011)
Mambí (plural *mambises*)	The name given to the (mostly non-white) independence rebels of 1868–78 and 1895–8
mambisado	The name given after 1902 to the (largely white) political elite, associated with the 1895 rebellion against Spain
Martianismo	Belief in, reverence for, Martí's ideas and meaning (thus also: *martianista*)
Microbrigada	Voluntary construction brigade (1960s and 1970s)
Moneda nacional	Cuban peso
Paladar	Private restaurant (after 1992)
Parametración	Restriction (between defined parameters)
Peninsular	Spanish-born white during the colonial period

Antoni Kapcia

Permuta	Exchange of housing
Peso convertible	Special internally exchangeable currency from 1993
Piratería	Pirating (of books)
Poder Local	Local power (1960s local government body)
Por la libre	Anything goes, or freewheeling
Quinquenio gris	Grey Five Years (period of cultural restriction 1971–6)
Rebelde	Rebel
Rendición de cuentas	Rendering of accounts (OPP accountability meeting)
Solidarismo	Sense of solidarity
Triunfo	Triumph
Voluntario	Voluntary (as in *trabajo voluntario*, voluntary labour) or volunteer

Acronyms and initials

ACRC   Veterans' Association (Asociación de Combatientes de la
          Revolución Cubana) from 1993

AJR   Association of Rebel Youth (Asociación de Jóvenes
          Rebeldes), youth wing of the 26 July Movement until 1960

ANAP   Small Farmers' National Association (Asociación Nacional
          de Agricultores Pequeños)

CIA   (US) Central Intelligence Agency

PCC   Cuban Communist Party (Partido Comunista de Cuba),
          both 1925–39 and from 1965

CDR   Committee for the Defence of the Revolution (Comité de
          Defensa de la Revolución)

CNOC   National Confederation of Cuban Workers (Confederación
          Nacional de Obreros de Cuba)

CSD   Democratic Socialist Coalition (Coalición Socialista
          Democrática) of 1939–44

CTC   Confederation of Cuban Workers (Confederación de
          Trabajadores de Cuba) (1939–61) *also* Confederation of
          Cuban Workers (Central de Trabajadores de Cuba) from
          1961

CUC   Internally convertible peso (from 1993)

DEU	University Student Vanguard (Directorio Estudiantil Universitiario)
DR	Revolutionary Vanguard (Directorio Revolucionario) (1957–62)
DRE	Revolutionary Student Vanguard (Directorio Revolucionario Estudiantil) (1955–6)
EIR	Revolutionary Training Schools (Escuelas de Instrucción Revolucionaria)
FEU	University Student Federation (Federación Estudiantil Universitaria), from 1923
FMC	Federation of Cuban Women (Federación de Mujeres Cubanas) from 1960
ICAIC	Cuban Film Institute (Instituto Cubano del Arte e Industrias Cinematográficos)
INRA	National Agrarian Reform Institute (Instituto Nacional de Reforma Agraria)
ISA	Arts University (Instituto Superior de Arte)
JUCEI	Coordinating, Executive and Inspection Boards (Juntas de Coordinación, Ejecución e Inspección)
MNR	National Revolutionary Movement (Movimiento Nacional Revolucionario), 1953–5 *also* National Revolutionary Militias (Milicias Nacionales Revolucionarias) from 1960
MTT	Territorial Militias (Milicias de Tropas Territoriales), from 1981
OPP	Organs of People's Power (Órganos de Poder Popular), from 1976
ORI	Integrated Revolutionary Organizations (Organizaciones Revolucionarias Integradas), 1961–2 revolutionary coalition
PNR	Policía Nacional Revolucionaria (National Revolutionary Police)

PPC	Cuban People's Party (Partido del Pueblo Cubano), known as the *Ortodoxos*
PRC	Cuban Revolutionary Party (Partido Revolucionario Cubano), 1892–9 (Martí's Independence party)
PRC-A	Authentic Cuban Revolutionary Party (Partido Revolucionario Cubano Auténtico), known as the *Auténticos*, from 1934
PSP	People's Socialist Party (Partido Socialista Popular), the name of the Communist Party from 1944 to 1962
PURS	United Party of the Socialist Revolution (Partido Unido de la Revolución Socialista), 1962–5
SDPE	Economic Development and Planning System (Sistema de Dirección y Planificación Económica), after 1975
UJC	Union of Communist Youth (Unión de Jóvenes Comunistas), from 1960
UNEAC	National Union of Cuban Writers and Artists (Unión Nacional de Escritores y Artistas de Cuba)

Preface

Since so much has been written about the Cuban Revolution over the years (especially about the 1960s, the system's remarkable survival in the 1990s or now as the historic generation nears its final act in power), what more can be said? Essentially, what this study intends is to correct the common tendency to squeeze something called 'the Revolution' into pre-existing paradigms, which have rarely corresponded to what was, or is, really happening.

What will be argued here is based on almost five decades of research on Cuba and four decades of travelling around sixty-five times to Cuba, giving me much material for trying to shape that 'correction'. That material has been garnered from years of conversations with Cuban friends, acquaintances, interviewees, academics and politicians (former and current), from conversations with (and reading the work of) numerous non-Cuban experts of various kinds, and sometimes simply from observing the many different ways that things work (and don't work) in Cuba. It has also arisen from mind-numbing personal experiences of Cuban officialdom (the mythical *burocracia*) at all levels. All of this has led to conclusions about the overall system, then weighed up against the theories and conventional explanations.

Finally, several different research projects have slowly built up a reservoir of findings and suppositions about the system and its workings: from the mid-1980s analysing the implications of policy and personnel changes in successive Communist Party Congresses for the *Journal of Communist Studies*; in the early 1990s, interviews with former government colleagues of Che Guevara from the early 1960s; from the mid-1990s, trawling daily through different Cuban and US newspapers and assessing the implications of news, usually bolstered by double-checking with Cuban colleagues 'in the know'; in 2004–9, during a collaborative project on cultural history, unearthing revelations about the workings of the system, past and present;[1] in 2012–20 another collaborative project in the Granma province enabled me to refine some of the earlier ideas and judgements against the background of the real grassroots political and administrative structures;[2] and finally, discoveries arose from consultancy work on the ins and outs of the whole national structures of policymaking. Hence, this is very much the work of a life-long historian (working backwards empirically towards a possible theory from the evidence gathered), rather than that of a political scientist, a profession to which I make no claim at all.

Over all of those years, and specifically for this book's long preparation, I owe a great many people a great many debts, including countless Cuban friends and colleagues, from whose personal experiences and perspectives I have learned much; I will not name them here, as (1) there are too many and (2) some may well prefer not to be named in a work with which they may not fully agree, but, if they read what follows, they will all probably recognize themselves as particular sources of information or judgement. I will, however, name one who, above all, helped me to shape, refine and deepen my ideas throughout: my very good and dear friend Fernando Martínez Heredia, much missed since his sad death in 2015 and on whose always balanced wisdom and encyclopaedic knowledge I relied and valued so much.

Those I will name from outside Cuba include, first and foremost, my partner Par Kumaraswami, with whom I have worked so productively and enjoyably since 2004 and from whom I have also always learned so much, not least how to think differently from the ways I had become used to. She has always given me new insights, deep understanding and great empathy with the subject; more importantly, she has long been by my side, sharing much with me and helping me to develop. Without her, this book might not have been written. Beyond that, I would also like to acknowledge the very specific help gained from all the thirty-odd postgraduates whom I have the real pleasure to supervise and with whom I have worked: I have learned much from them, as they always brought new ideas, perspectives and information, helping me to develop my understanding of Cuba. I especially cite here more recent ones whose research has informed many of the insights in preparing this text: (in alphabetical order) Anna Clayfield, who opened up the unresearched 1970–5 period for me; Lauren Collins (whose insights into the workings of the Cuban 'dense web' I have found so deep and illuminating); Emily Kirk (who opened my eyes to some of hidden thinking in Cuba on health and sexuality); Rosi Smith (whose work on Cuban education has been so outstandingly different from everything that went before); and Isabel Story (whose work on Soviet cultural influence forced me to rethink my own rather outdated thinking on the Cuban–Soviet links).

1

THE EVOLUTION OF A
RADICAL NATIONALISM

To start with the past misreadings of the Cuban Revolution to which the preface referred, we can see fairly quickly that, in its first decade, the conventional approach was often reading the process through the prism of the widespread focus on the person (and personality) of Fidel Castro, usually seeing him as the latest, if the most unusual, manifestation of a 'typically Latin American' personalist or populist regime (Draper 1965). As the Revolution then moved into communism and the global Cold War (from 1961–2), the alternative tendency was to read 'the Revolution' (by then capitalized, as in Cuba) as a 'typical' communist state, as a Caribbean version of the 1948–90 Socialist Bloc: monolithic under a dictator, like East Germany's Ulbricht or Romania's Ceausescu (Gonzalez 1974; Horowitz 2008). Sadly, both approaches remained all too visible in 2016 when the media focused on the death of Fidel (given the importance of both Castro brothers within the narrative that follows here, we have little choice but to distinguish between them henceforth by either 'Fidel' or 'Raúl'). In one BBC News television interview on 26 November, after having meticulously explained his historical significance, this author was asked: 'so would you say Castro was a typical Latin American dictator or a typical Communist dictator?' Evidently, nothing had changed since 1968.

Therefore, what this study aims to do is to focus on what can be argued is the essence of the six-decade-long process: a long-delayed (and thus radicalized) process of post-colonial and decolonizing nation building which, given the 'templates' then available to such processes across the post-colonial world and based on the radicalism of many

Cuban traditions, moved inexorably towards some version of 'socialism' as the means to achieve that goal. The importance of that alternative perspective is that it recognizes fully the strength and depth of the nationalism originally underpinning the Revolution, and also the depth and character of the transformation which that nation-building project intended, or which developed. Put simply, what we might call 'Cuban socialism' was always somewhat maverick, even at its most apparently 'Sovietized', and (despite what we are often told) was not simply attributable to Fidel but rather reflected the ideological patterns of those traditions and a range of other factors that this study addresses.

This means that, rather than forcing 'the Revolution' into the straitjacket of unhelpful paradigms, we might be better advised to consider it in a different context of the many post-colonial regimes of Africa and Asia in the late 1950s and early 1960s, often driven by the same priorities which preoccupied the Cuban leaders. They included an overwhelming (and often stifling) emphasis on unity; a frenetic drive to 'catch up' by rapid, often industrial, development; a single-party system to unite different elements of the preceding anti-colonial radicalism; and a welfare state to ensure rapid social development and popular support.

In other words, we should think of the Cuban Revolution less as a static, monolithic and 'typical' communist system and more as a contested, often empirical, nation-building process. Importantly, that process was initially restricted within (and often shaped by) an underdeveloped economy and then (for three decades) shaped and restricted by the Cold War, bringing prolonged isolation and active external hostility (most evidently, the US embargo and in periods of outright subversion). Of all the factors shaping the patterns and thinking of those six decades, the external context is perhaps one of the most crucial, whether that applies to sugar's world price and market, to the role and attitude of the United States, to the role of the Soviet Union (1961–91) or to the politics and growing interpretations within the 'Third World' in the 1960s and 1970s. That context has served more to set the parameters for nation building than to be simply the stage on which the process has evolved.

The point here is to explain not just the Revolution's historical context but also one of the Revolution's most perplexing characteristics for outside observers: the system's remarkable survival over six decades. Most obviously, it has survived six decades of US hostility: the US embargo (the longest – and, probably, the least successful – sanctions in history, formalized fully in February 1963 and still in existence in 2020), one US-backed invasion (1961), sustained funding of external sabotage (1960s and 1970s) and subversion. Secondly, it has survived repeated economic crises: in 1962–3, 1970, and, most traumatically, the disappearance in 1989–91 of the whole edifice of trade and of economic and military support which Cuba's alliance with the Socialist Bloc and Soviet Union had meant from 1961, but especially from 1972. That crisis, which hit Cuba more severely than either the crises and recessions of 1920 or 1929–33, should have proved terminal, as predicted by many (Oppenheimer 1992). Finally, the Revolution has survived twelve years after Fidel's retirement.

The question of survival brings us back to the literature on Cuba, which has attributed it to a range of possible explanations, often depending on the interpreter's political position. These include the obvious assumption of systematic coercion (through either monolithic repression or Fidel's personal(ist) control). In reality, the Fuerzas Armadas Revolucionarias (FAR, Revolutionary Armed Forces) were reduced by half in the early 1990s' economic crisis and have never since recovered their former funding (Klepak 2005: 61), while the government briefly ceased to function effectively. Meanwhile, Fidel himself relinquished any personal control in 2007. This common explanation is related to another: the Cuban population's presumed fatalism or passivity, assumed to result either from years of indoctrination, repression and isolation, which led to resigned acceptance, or from a grudging pragmatism (as welfare levels were partially protected) or from simple fear of the alternatives. The latter did have some justification in 1990–4, as Cubans returning from the Socialist Bloc and Soviet Union brought accounts of post-collapse falls in living standards and welfare; that argument would become less tenable after a few years, as those former Bloc countries saw economic growth and stability in the 2000s. One more obvious and convincing explanation offered was the power of Cuban national pride, and the government's ability to exploit it, whenever US presidents acted in ways that sparked nationalist responses in Cuba, by tightening the embargo (1992, 1996 and 2004) or by raising the levels of hostility (as with Reagan and Bush).

While some of those common explanations have convincing elements, they all have flaws or only hold water for certain moments or periods. This author, in addressing survival, has elsewhere suggested other possible factors. The first is the persuasive and cohesive role of ideology: not so much Marxism–Leninism as a more complex organic, dynamic and always adaptable belief system (*Weltanschauung*), which succeeded in driving, uniting and offering solutions to enough Cubans most of the time (Kapcia 2000). Another is the cohesive effectiveness of what was described as a quasi-corporatist (but a post-colonial revolutionary corporatism) system, with its inclusive tendencies and comprehensive processes and mechanisms of participation and involvement (Kapcia 2014: 119–23).

In fact, summarizing all of the more convincing explanations, we can see that the most sensible approach is probably to combine several elements into an explanation rather than seek one impossible single cause. Broadly, we can summarize these as economic, social, ideological and political. The economic factors most often mentioned focus on the comprehensive rescue programme from 1992, especially measures such as the decriminalization of the US dollar (which allowed urgently needed remittances to flow to families – and the system); the imposition of a dual currency system which (for all its later problems of inequality and inaccurate accounting) ensured that the state garnered most of the hard currency, enabling it to purchase imports; the shift to tourism, soon to become Cuba's mainstay; an agrarian reform that ensured farmers' loyalty and better provision of food supplies; and the permission to form joint venture enterprises with foreign capital. The social factors were often related: the guarantees of free education and healthcare and the strengthening of the ration book. The ideological factors were the residual sense of solidarity among enough Cubans (often expressed as a system of low-level reciprocity between friends and neighbours) and the strength and depth of nationalism (long shaped by a sense of anti-imperialism and regularly boosted by successive US policies). Finally, the political factors were the cohesion and reconstruction of the participatory system (ensuring a degree of communication and involvement, even in the workplace); the long-standing emigration of any potentially organized and substantial opposition; the role of the churches in ensuring access to external supplies and in preventing social disintegration; and the effectiveness of new layers of local governance.

This study, however, offers yet another possible factor, related to the quasi-corporatist explanation by examining the evolution (partly based on ideology and substantially based on empirical evidence) of what will be presented as a complex and overlapping matrix of power (and within that of different kinds of power) within a constantly evolving state. In other words, it is the systemic analysis of the corporatism that was described in 2014 (with its focus on personnel and group dynamics), full of complexity but remarkably effective, characterized by multiple vertical structures of power, participation and governance, all interlocking with horizontal processes of negotiation and consultation. It will be argued that this reflects, and in turn has shaped, the evolution of the Cuban state as something less monolithic than a highly complex infrastructure for those structures and processes.

THE HISTORICAL CONTEXT

However, before embarking on that, we need to outline the very particular historical context which so shaped modern and contemporary Cuba and the post-1959 system, a task which most observers see as essential to any understanding of why Cuba experienced such an unlikely and improbably durable radical transformation after 1959. For, while Cuba shared many of Latin America's wider historical experiences, certain processes made Cuba's political culture unique. It is, of course, a truism that every country is 'unique', no matter how similar any two might appear; moreover, recent scholarship has moved away from the traditional focus on Cuba's apparent 'exceptionalism' (Hoffmann and Whitehead 2007), a reassessment that has usefully reminded us of a similar radicalized nationalism witnessed across Latin America in 1900–60. Equally, many developing countries after 1960 faced some of the same challenges as Cuba, while Cuban emigrants from the early 1980s were often little different from millions of economic migrants in search of material improvement in developed countries (Duany 2011; Krull and Stubbs 2018).

Two concepts are used repeatedly throughout this study – radicalism and nationalism – and this is an apposite moment to clarify the way that both are defined here. Broadly, when the term 'radical' is used, it usually refers to a political stance going beyond whatever was the norm at a given time or in a given way of thinking; that 'beyond' could be either on the Right (towards corporatism or fascism, or an exclusive nationalism) or towards the Left. In the latter case (more common in Latin America), radical postures usually proposed deeper or more rapid changes than reformist or gradualist stances, or, in comparing with pro-Soviet communism, seeking more fundamental and more immediate approaches to revolutionary change.

WHAT WAS MEANT BY NATIONALISM?

Consideration of nationalism, of course, opens Pandora's box, given its multiple and changing global meanings and manifestations, let alone in

Cuba. As we will see, what can be broadly termed 'Cuban nationalism' has actually had many different shapes, bases, platforms and targets over some two centuries, some more recognizable for North Americans or Europeans but others either particularly Cuban or shared with other Latin American societies. Lilian Guerra has helped us considerably by convincingly examining the several different nationalisms in the early Cuban Republic, broadly distinguishing between a pro-imperialist, a revolutionary and a popular nationalism (Guerra 2005: 8–21, *passim*), although two other books by her have effectively taken that typology further into more dimensions (before and after 1959), but always focusing on the imagining of 'the nation' (Guerra 2012, 2018). Indeed, her emphasis on the essence of Benedict Anderson's path-breaking approach, to understand nationalism as 'imagined communities' (Anderson 1983), takes us to the heart of the different understanding of the multiple layers and types of meaning applied to the term in Cuba over the decades.

Although Anderson's approach insisted on taking the concept's origins further back than the conventional starting point of the French Revolution, it is less that dimension that interests us here (since several of Cuba's nationalisms did broadly follow from 1789) and more the imagining process. That is because the Cuban manifestations that emerged in the 1800s were all focused on imagining something new: while one might posit some nationalisms as essentially nostalgic (harking back to a real or an imagined lost identity, either a sovereignty supressed by an outsider or a cultural identity seen as threatened by 'the other'), the many versions of *Cuba Libre* which we will see in this study all shared the novelty of what they imagined, since there had never been a separate or independent Cuba since the early Spanish colonization. Hence, all versions that emerged were imagining something as yet unformed, perhaps inevitably leading to the many variations. In some respects, Cuban nationalism was thus like the Left's familiar tendency to divide since it is always easier to create a consensus on what *is* (the status quo) or on what *used to be*, based on a broad (but rarely universal) consensus, than on what *should be* in an as yet unrealized future.

However, this study will trace the evolution of several conflicting nationalisms (Guerra 2005) that all changed over time, according to the hegemonic powers' ability to convince. While Spanish colonialism more or less worked (for enough interests in the emerging *criollo* – Cuban-born white – elite), any proto-nationalism was limited to a small intellectual minority or those driven by external ideology (often freemasonry). Once it was more widely seen as no longer effective, a reluctant separatism (rather than, yet, any clear nationalism that assumed a separate Cuban nation) posited US statehood; only when that failed as a prospect did a still reluctant separatism metamorphose into the pro-imperialist nationalism (Guerra 2005) that characterized significant parts of the white rebel constituency of 1868–98, and indeed beyond that. However, we will also see the emergence of an increasingly popular nationalism (perceiving *Cuba Libre* as racially equal and multicultural) which, as each rebellion evolved (and two were supressed) and as external ideas entered the equation to shape the 'imagining' more ideologically, became more coherent in some basic respects (the shared principles for shaping the future *Cuba Libre*) but still necessarily imagined, rather than rationally conceived. Guerra's third (revolutionary) nationalism can be seen in the creation and character of the Partido Revolucionario Cubano (PRC, Cuban Revolutionary Party), infused always by explicitly leftist principles and interpretations of history, past and future.

Thereafter, we will see those nationalisms then diverge further, as the relationship with the United States complicated Cubans' awareness of what an independent Cuba needed and could achieve, but also as one strand of nationalism began to reflect the wider radicalization of anti-US sentiment elsewhere in Latin America. Finally, of course, the quasi-redemptive nationalism (Guerra 2012) that evolved in the 1940s (confused by the 1933 'revolution' and then a populism that promised much but signally failed to deliver) helped to create the context for the 1959 Revolution, which, of course, would become divided irreparably by the rapid radicalization of a more explicitly socialist form of the fusion of revolutionary and popular nationalisms, whose institutional expression over the following decades (as national pride and enforced collectivism shaped a defiant survival of a perceived imperialism) brought a deeper, but much less recognizable, version of nationalism, one that was rescued in the early 1990s and which then drove redefinitions. However, this overview of these different nationalisms remains just a summary; their fuller elaboration must await the appropriate moment of the narrative.

MODERN CUBA'S UNIQUE CONTEXT

Returning therefore to this chapter's central thread, it seems unquestionable that Cuba's pre-1959 history saw a genuinely unique *combination* of processes, experiences and challenges that made the 1959 revolutionary moment at least unusual and, in many respects, remarkably unique. No other Latin American country experienced an upheaval, and then an enforced isolation and sustained external hostility, on the Cuban scale, while Cuba's communism survived the collapse of the Berlin Wall and even that of the Soviet Union.

What then were the processes, experiences and challenges that made Cuba so different, shaping the Revolution? The answer lies essentially in an unusually prolonged Spanish colonialism (continuing almost eighty years longer than in other Spanish colonies), a subsequent US military occupation leading to a three decade legal neo-colonialism under US hegemony and then a less obvious economic hegemony for a further two and a half decades. Furthermore, Cuba's sugar (long its major export commodity) outproduced and outexported most similar competitors but eventually suffered from global overproduction, transforming sugar from one of the best possible commodities in the early 1800s into one of the worst in the 1940s. It was also sugar that determined Cuba's late, but seminal, entry into the mass slave trade, which attracted growing US interest and eventually Soviet interest. Meanwhile, Cuba's geographical position, straddling the Caribbean and the Gulf of Mexico, made the island commercially, geopolitically and strategically crucial.

Spain's colonial rule lasted so long, principally, because of the unusual reluctance of Cuban *criollos* to contemplate rebellion compared to other Spanish–American *criollos* who had led their independence rebellions in 1808–26, a reluctance motivated by a pragmatic recognition that the already lucrative sugar economy (partly generated by the brief British occupation of 1762–3 (Thomas 1971: 42–71), from which they benefited and which was fuelled by massive imports of African slaves), was threatened after 1807 by British and US abolitionism. While Spain remained in Cuba, their wealth and protection (against the slaves) were guaranteed.

Two other factors also contributed. First, an implicit consensus between Britain and the new United States (each fearful of the other's potential occupation of an independent Cuba) ensured that continued Spanish rule was tolerated, discouraging any Cuban independence movement. Secondly, after 1826, Spain's determination to hold the line in Cuba against further loss of colonies was bolstered by thousands of Spanish refugees from Louisiana and the independence rebellions, turning Cuba into a more decidedly loyal bulwark.

However, over the following decades, Spain's weakness became patent and the US sugar market's value to Cuba's *criollos* grew (by the 1840s taking close to half of Cuba's sugar exports), convincing many *criollos* to consider possible US statehood rather than outright independence, to continue the slave trade, slavery and sugar exports. That annexationism flourished in the 1840s and 1850s, shared briefly by powerful interests in the US southern states and based on the 1845 Texan example, generating several conspiracies and rebellions (Opatrný 1990; Pérez 1988: 104–15; Thomas 1971: 207–32). However, with the outcome of the American Civil War, that possibility ended, forcing many frustrated planters to contemplate rebellion, especially as abolition of the slave trade had already made slave prices prohibitive, impoverishing many planters.

On 10 October 1868, a planter-led rebellion began in eastern Cuba (near Manzanillo), under Carlos Manuel de Céspedes, leading to a ten-year bitter struggle (the *Guerra Grande* or the Great War) based on unremitting guerrilla warfare mostly waged by black *mambises*, many of them slaves or ex-slaves, seeing independence as their path to freedom and equality (Ibarra Cuesta 1967). However, the rebellion was weakened by internal divisions over strategy and Cuba's future, with or without slavery, inside or outside the United States. Those divisions – enhanced by the resistance from tens of thousands of uncompromising Spanish volunteer militiamen (*voluntarios*) – led to the rebel surrender in 1878, followed by a short defiant prolongation of the rebellion (under Antonio Maceo) and then a second, more isolated, rebellion in 1879–80 (the *Guerra Chiquita* or the Little War).

By the 1880s, however, Cuba had changed fundamentally. Spain's abolition of slavery in 1870 (postponing full implementation until 1888 to protect slaveowners' prosperity) removed that issue from Cubans' considerations, and around 80 per cent of Cuba's sugar went to the US market, making Spanish rule even less convincing. Meanwhile, the colonial authorities penalized Cubans for their rebellions, with punitive taxation and the obligation to pay Spain's war debt (Pérez 1986: 5–10) that predictably antagonized many hitherto pragmatic loyalists. Meanwhile, US corporate interests were steadily buying up Cubans' land in the east, creating modernized semi-industrial refineries, acquiring a stake in the Cuban economy and changing the nature of sugar cultivation and production (López Segrera 1981: 126; Pino-Santos 1983: 213)

Finally, two new elements entered the equation: the emergence of the poet and activist José Martí and the radicalization of the Cuban emigrant tobacco workforce in Florida (Poyo 1998). Mostly exiled from Cuba since 1871, Martí was central to the development of Cuban separatism through his persistent writings on, and campaigning for, Cuban independence and the 1892 creation of a single united PRC.

The radicalism of that highly unionized and politicized workforce led the party to recognize the need for the future *Cuba Libre* to be both socially equal and politically independent. Since previous rebellions had already demonstrated a popular social and racial base for that idea, most non-white rebels seeing independence as a path to equality, this new character made at least one strand of Cuba's emerging nationalism one of Latin America's most popular and radical. However, there was, as yet, no real separatist consensus on what nationalism (or 'nation') meant in terms of its definition or future programme. While the grassroots interpretation might be radical in its egalitarian social vision for a *Cuba Libre*, many middle-class whites and elite *criollos* still saw 'nation' as racially limited and hierarchical, with them supplanting the *peninsulares* at the top. They essentially echoed the political sovereignty focus of their 1808–26 counterparts in the other Spanish colonies.

The final rebellion began in February 1895, but Martí's death on 19 May, only three months later, deprived it (and an eventually free Cuba) of a popular leader. However, this new revolt was more powerful, popular and militarily successful than in 1868–78, soon reaching the west and forcing the Spanish to bring tens of thousands of reinforcements and adopt extreme measures, including the notorious concentration of civilians into camps, with a death toll of over 100,000 (Martí 2017; Tone 2006: 193). In April 1898, however, the United States entered the picture, driven by fears among US commercial interests (about the conflict's potential damage) and by a campaign by both influential US political and strategic interests (seeing Cuba as crucial to US security) and press barons, all demanding intervention. When the USS *Maine* mysteriously exploded in Havana harbour in February 1898, the government was forced to declare war on Spain in April, turning the last Cuban War of Independence into the short Spanish–American War. After Spain surrendered (July 1898), the Treaty of Paris (January 1899) gave all Spain's remaining non-African colonies to the United States, including Cuba.

What followed was a seminal forty-month US military occupation, shaping much of Cuba's subsequent independent development and overseeing major changes to Cuba's economic, social and political patterns. First, the already substantial US financial and commercial presence grew; secondly, alongside welcome social reforms (health and hygiene), a cultural 'Americanization' began, education being reshaped along US lines and with an influx of Protestant US religious missionaries and would-be settlers (Leimdorfer 2008); thirdly, the unity constructed by Martí and the PRC fractured, as the military authorities (preparing for some sort of self-rule) created a pluralist party system, dividing the PRC into two separate parties, vying for office. Meanwhile, many Spanish civil servants were retained, while Spanish financial and commercial interests were protected.

Finally, in May 1902, wary of a potential for anti-US nationalist resentment, the US government and occupation authorities gave Cubans their independence (by now from the United States, not Spain), but only on condition that the wording of the controversial Platt Amendment be incorporated into the still draft Cuban Constitution. That Amendment (to a US Navy Appropriations Bill then before the US Congress) was seen as the perfect means to create a Cuban protectorate, with formal independence but an effective US hold without the need for troops. Eventually accepted marginally and reluctantly by the Constitutional Assembly, it included several things: a US veto on Cuban foreign treaties and loans, the lease of territory for US naval use (eventually meaning only Guantánamo Bay) and the US right to intervene militarily to restore public order (Pichardo 1969: 119–20). Hence, after fourteen years of struggle, Cubans now saw their independence constrained and undermined by the Amendment forced into their new constitution, and 1903 saw two treaties cementing that further: the Permanent Treaty (enshrining the Amendment) and the Reciprocity Treaty (guaranteeing Cuban sugar preferential access to the US market in exchange for preferential access to Cuba for US manufactures). Hence, the new Republic began with independence and legitimacy questioned.

However, resentment was temporarily quelled by the Reciprocity Treaty's benefits, that is, a two-decade boom in sugar sales and prices which overshadowed doubts, although the growing frustration of Cuba's black population (after fighting in all three rebellions, they found themselves denied equality, political representation and employment), which erupted in 1912 into mass protest, provoking an army massacre of perhaps 3,000 people (Castro Fernández 2008; Helg 1995). Meantime, the evident corruption, patronage and electoral fraud of the Republic's politics provoked rebellions in 1906 and 1917 (Ibarra Cuesta 1992), worrying the US government into dispatching troops, under the Amendment, occupying Cuba once again in 1906–9.

In 1920, the dam broke. After a spectacular boom in 1919–20 (the *Danza de los Millones*, or the Dance of the Millions), responding to the First World War's market-closing and sugar-producing effects, which saw investment and borrowing swell, the world sugar price plummeted, bringing widespread unemployment and wage cuts and weakening government finances (Thomas 1971: 544–63). The collapse also damaged Cuban sugar and banking interests, creating a vacuum into which US capital soon moved, by 1925 accounting for 81 per cent of all Cuban loans and 69 per cent of deposits in Cuban banks (Pérez 1986: 188). By 1921, therefore, many Cubans doubted the wisdom of the 1903 treaties and Cuba's close dependence.

The result was a rapid awakening of a temporarily quiescent nationalism and a rise of radicalism, both fuelled by new political ideas and events in Europe and Latin America. The period 1923–5 saw student demonstrations and activism, the 1925 creation of the Partido Comunista de Cuba (PCC, Cuban Communist Party) hereafter using English initials to avoid confusion with the *Ortodoxos'* PPC) and an intellectual questioning, all combining to change Cuban politics. In particular, nationalism and radicalism began to fuse, represented best in Julio Antonio Mella, the student leader who led many initiatives and co-founded the PCC.

However, it is important to understand what this new nationalism actually meant: for it was a Cuban manifestation of the wider emerging current of ideologically shaped anti-Americanism. Stimulated by the visible entry of, and increased regional military and economic domination by, the United States in Latin America (especially in 1898–1934), and then given coherent ideological force by Lenin's theory of imperialism (as the highest stage of capitalism), this became a sort of 'continentalism': perceiving US hegemony as imperialist and capitalist, it was a much broader 'nationalism', seeing Latin America as sharing a common identity under and against US imperialism, and drew many young people (especially students from 1922) into a changing Left, 'nationalizing' the Left and radicalizing nationalism.

Meanwhile, more traditional nationalisms (more firmly based than this always minority new interpretation) still prevailed in Cuba: 'pro-imperialist' nationalism (Guerra 2005) could be seen from the first president Tomás Estrada Palma and compliant governments of the Republic's first two decades, while the traditionally nationalist liberals echoed the rhetoric of 1895–8 but were reluctant to challenge the new empire. One such pragmatic nationalist, Gerardo Machado, was elected popularly in 1924 on a platform of 'co-operativism', which hinted at a degree of nationalism. However, as he became increasingly authoritarian from 1928 and the economy again collapsed after 1929, a virtual insurrection began from 1930, student protests generating armed activism and an increasingly militant unionized workforce engaging in strikes and occupations (Soto 1985).

The outcome was the army's removal of Machado (August 1933), a short-lived student and soldier-based five-man government (the Pentarchy) and what was called 'the 100-day revolution', under one of the five – Ramón Grau San Martín. The 'revolution' (actually lasting 134 days) was in fact hardly revolutionary in aim or effect, characterized more by constant upheaval, increased radicalism – best represented by the Interior Minister, Antonio Guiteras (Cabrera 1974) – and a range of different nationalisms, ranging from the corporatist radical Right (ABC) to several unorthodox varieties of the Left. Worries among business sectors and US interests led to a coup on 15 January 1934 by Fulgencio Batista (one of the leaders of the September 1933 mutiny), welcomed by the US embassy. Thus ended the tormented and questionable 'First Republic'.

The 'Second Republic' (1934–58) saw a mixture of rising hopes and frustrating demoralization undermine the system's fragility. It was characterized by the hegemony of the 'generation of 1933' (key protagonists in the 1930–3 insurrection), Batista's authoritarian tendencies in two separate periods (indirectly in 1934–40 and directly in 1952–8) (Argote 2006; Alcántara Janeiro 2019) and the structural weaknesses revealed by the hegemonic but variable populist nationalisms prevailing in 1940–52 and manifested in the *Auténticos*, *Ortodoxos*, Batista, Guiteras's Joven Cuba and some of the more ideologically coherent *bonches*, and a growing, but unfocused, sense of disillusion. The *bonches* were the pseudo-political armed gangs that had inherited the mantle of the once 'heroic', often student-based 'action groups' of 1930–3, but which essentially engaged in gang warfare, extortion and violence. In 1948, the *Auténticos* infamously sought to quell them by incorporating some leaders into senior police posts but also by using them to strong-arm known communists from the labour unions. The *bonches* thus contributed to the growing disillusion (Aguiar Rodríguez 2000).

However, one of the First Republic's main characteristics was absent, the US role disappearing from political discourse in 1934 after Franklin Roosevelt 'abolished' the Platt Amendment by abrogating the US intervention rights under the Permanent Treaty, part of his non-interventionist 'Good Neighbour' policy towards Latin America. Henceforth, nationalists of all types were less able to claim convincingly that Cuba was a US neo-colony.

The Second Republic's steady disintegration is easily traced (Whitney 2001). Batista's first period of authoritarianism (1934–40) was neither open nor unpopular. He exercised power from behind the scenes, controlling six successive 'puppet' presidents: some ruled briefly, Carlos Hevia serving for only fifty-six hours in January 1934 and his successor Manuel Márquez Sterling for only six hours (18 January); others proved unable to challenge Batista, notably Carlos Mendieta (twenty-three months, 1934–5), José A. Barnet (December–May 1935–6), Miguel Mariano Gómez (May–December 1936) and the longest-serving, Federico Laredo Bru in 1936–40. Through them, Batista ensured enough stability to deter further US involvement, generate some economic recovery, and quell the unrest of 1930–3. He targeted the Right by marginalizing them or (as with the small ABC terrorist group) incorporating them into government and respectability. The Left was attacked bloodily: the March 1935 general strike was brutally repressed and Guiteras (Batista's main rival for popularity) was murdered that year.

Thereafter, Batista embarked on his version of Latin America's contemporary populism, such as Brazil's Getûlio Vargas, Mexico's Lázaro Cárdenas and (later) Argentina's Juan Perón. Initially, he protected Cuba's sugar producers (large and small, the latter being the most publicly courted) and encouraged a partial economic 're-Cubanization', as US interests withdrew partially. He also launched a rural education campaign (using army officers as teachers), demonstrating continuity from his 1933 'revolutionary' image. In 1937, he engineered a curious electoral alliance with the PCC (then following the new Comintern policy of 'popular frontism') in the Coalición Socialista Democrática (CSD, Democratic Socialist Coalition) of 1938–44. That alliance performed well in two 1939–40 elections: for the Constitutional Assembly and the presidency and congress, Batista emerging victorious in the latter (Alcántara Janeiro 2019).

The 1940 Constitution was remarkable for its often radically nationalist character, rejecting the discredited 1901 charter – that ideological mix reflected the emerging dissidence. While the CSD partly shaped its character, it also incorporated elements of Grau's 1933 programme, reflecting the other newly powerful force: the Partido Revolucionario Cubano–Auténtico (PRC-A, Authentic Cuban Revolutionary Party) created in 1934 by Grau and other student veterans of 1930–3, its name expressing its declared *martianista* heritage. The *Auténticos* soon attracted a wide range of progressives and centrists, winning a majority in the Constitutional Assembly and in 1944 winning the presidency and congress, on a programme of revolution, morality (against corruption) and nation(alism) (Grau 1934).

However, the *Auténtico* performance in office (under Grau till 1948 and then his chosen successor, another 1933 'veteran', Carlos Prío Socarrás) was a severe disappointment: they proved distinctly unrevolutionary, tolerant of widespread corruption and pro-US during the Cold War from 1948. Given the circumstances (Cuba being heavily dependent on the US sugar market and investment, and still constrained by Washington's preferences), *Auténtico* populism could achieve little more than rhetorical success (Ameringuer 2000). However, their failure then generated another, more radical (and more redemptive), version of nationalist populism, in the post-1947 Partido del Pueblo Cubano (PPC, Cuban People's Party), always known as the *Ortodoxos*. The party was a splinter from the *Auténticos*, led by another 1933 'veteran' Eduardo Chibás, whose main target was corruption. The *Ortodoxos* struck a chord, their appeal enhanced by Chibás's public suicide on radio (making him a popular martyr), and they seemed destined for electoral success in June 1952, until Batista again seized power (10 March 1952), launching a new authoritarianism.

Initially, the political parties' response was somewhat rhetorical, with little solid organized opposition (Ibarra Guitart: 2000; López Civeira 1990); moreover, public disillusion with corruption and memories of Batista's reforming past made the coup less unpopular than it might have been. However, opposition did come immediately from the Havana and Santiago students and sectors of the *Ortodoxos*' eastern and youth wings, soon coalescing into a loose alliance of discontented radicals and nationalists under a young lawyer and former student activist (now a would-be *Ortodoxo* congressional candidate), Fidel Castro. Failing to challenge the coup legally, he developed *Ortodoxo* and student contacts: in January 1953, he led a mass student protest on the centenary of Martí's birth (contrasting Martí's image, principles and ideas with Cuba's present condition) and then plotted a spectacular action to stimulate wider opposition.

That action came on 26 July 1953 when 133 mostly young men, from western Cuba, attacked two military barracks, Santiago's Moncada garrison (Cuba's second largest) and the much smaller Bayamo garrison. Although the attacks were repelled, the episode became one of the fuses to spark rebellion. The bloodshed was considerable: nineteen soldiers were killed, but sixty-one attackers died, either in the assault or after arrest and torture. Fifty-one survivors (including Fidel and his brother

15

Raúl) were tried in October 1953, an event which gained considerable publicity and gave Fidel the opportunity to begin a propaganda war against Batista by a characteristically long eloquent defence speech, whose final words ('History will absolve me') became the title of the resulting rebel movement's first manifesto (Castro, F. 1961).

The 26 July Movement (M26J) was born in the Isle of Pines prison where the rebels planned their strategy. Released in a June 1955 amnesty, they created the M26J in Havana, and then left for Mexico to prepare an expedition for late 1956 which would resurrect the Moncada plan of guerrilla war in eastern Cuba's Sierra Maestra. In Mexico, they were joined in late 1955 by the peripatetic Argentine rebel Ernesto Guevara (soon christened 'Che' by his Cuban colleagues).

On 25 November 1956, eighty-two rebels left Mexico on a small motor yacht, the *Granma*, to reach the Oriente shore south of Manzanillo; arriving seven days later, two days after the planned landing (planned to coincide with a distracting uprising in Santiago) and slightly further south than intended (ending up in a more impenetrable mangrove swamp), they remained undetected for three days until Batista's forces attacked them in the open at Alegría del Pio, killing twenty-one and dispersing the rest, who either escaped, were arrested or retreated in small groups heading for the Sierra. Finally, on 16 December, sixteen rebels formed one single group, the basis of the eventual Rebel Army.

Over the following two years, several processes ensued. First, the Rebel Army gradually built up its bases, numbers and military skills, tying down the less mobile (and largely conscript) army, while undergoing a rapid political radicalization through contact with the increasingly supportive local peasantry and under the influence of radicals like Guevara and Raúl Castro (the latter eventually leading a second guerrilla front in another eastern Sierra). Meanwhile, the M26J's urban wing engaged in a highly effective strategy, distracting the army and police by sabotage acts, targeted assassinations and skilful propaganda, while continually supplying the guerrillas with arms, funds and recruits; that effort (largely under Armando Hart in Havana and Frank País in Santiago until his death in 1957) contributed fundamentally to the insurrection's success, provoking Batista into a random repression that alienated many erstwhile passive or neutral Cubans, helped by the press's faithful recording of much of the daily violence. By mid-1958, it was Batista who seemed more besieged than the (now relatively safely ensconced) guerrillas, leading him to launch one final, unsuccessful offensive on the rebel bases in May 1958 (Sweig 2002).

The Rebel Army's counteroffensive then liberated the Sierra's west and dispatched two separate rebel columns (under Guevara and Camilo Cienfuegos, each commanding around 150 men) to advance on Cuba's west, tipping the strategic balance. When the US government, embarrassed by the media's favourable coverage of the guerrillas and condemnation of Batista's repression, then halted the supply of arms and aircraft, Batista's political and moral position was further undermined. By mid-December 1958, Guevara and Cienfuegos had reached west-central Cuba, at which point a new rebel element came into play, helping Guevara on 30–1 December to defeat Batista's army in Santa Clara, Batista's last redoubt, using tactical skills and benefiting from the army's demoralization.

That new element was the small student-based Directorio Revolucionario 13 de Marzo (DR, Revolutionary Vanguard). Like the M26J, the DR grew out of the 1950s' student radicalism, created in 1956 by the official Federación Estudiantil Universitario (FEU, University Student Federation) under José Antonio Echeverría, a charismatic leader whose Catholicism drove his political radicalism towards a moralistic stance against inequality and tyranny. As an FEU leader, he declared rebellion against Batista through the FEU's new armed wing, the Directorio Revolucionario Estudiantil (DRE, Revolutionary Student Vanguard). Echeverría's popularity led the M26J leaders to negotiate with him over both pre- and post-victory strategies (Álvarez Blanco 2009); however, on 13 March 1957, a DRE attack on the Presidential Palace came close to assassinating Batista but resulted in several rebel deaths, including Echeverría (Chomón 1969; Zito Valdés 2016). The residual group under Faure Chomón and Eloy Gutiérrez Menoyo then rechristened itself the DR-13-3 (after the Palace attack) and in 1958 created a guerrilla force under Menoyo, in the central Sierra del Escambray; it was duly joined by others (under Chomón) in February 1958, forming the Second Front of the Escambray (Hurtado Tandrón 2005). When, in late December 1958, Chomón's group joined forces with Guevara, that group proved crucial in shaping the revolutionary coalition after January 1959, while Menoyo's group remained apart.

Meanwhile, another action group had been created in 1952 by Rafael García Bárcena, the Movimiento Nacional Revolucionario (MNR, National Revolutionary Movement). It was also born out of Catholic Action ideas, but never engaged in military action, as its planned assault on Cuba's largest army garrison (Havana's Campamento Columbia) in April 1953 was halted by the secret police. Nonetheless, the MNR affected later developments: first, their plan may well have influenced Fidel's Moncada ideas, and, secondly, their collapse saw members join the new M26J.

The December 1958 Santa Clara battle was decisive: a sizeable, but demoralized, army was outwitted and outfought by a much smaller but battle-hardened rebel force, and the defeat led Batista to flee Cuba for the Dominican Republic, allowing the rebel columns to march on Havana on 2–3 January, Cienfuegos seizing Campamento Columbia and Guevara occupying the Cabaña fortress on Havana Bay's eastern shore. Meanwhile, a last-ditch military attempt to seize power on 31 December had been defeated by the M26J's three-day general strike. By 1 January 1959, therefore, the 'old Cuba' had come to an end.

THE REVOLUTION IN JANUARY 1959

The 'new Cuba' seemed brighter but its character was still unclear. While the Rebel Army (possibly numbering around 2,000 in January 1959) enjoyed a unique popularity and legitimacy, based on their leading role in the rebellion, their newly radicalized ideas were not necessarily shared by many inside and outside the M26J. Those dissenting included the residual political forces of the 'Second Republic', especially the *Auténticos* and *Ortodoxos*, whose hegemony in 1944–52 had shaped the character and frustrations of the evolving political radicalism and multifaceted nationalism, but whose relatively weak response in 1952, together with some leaders' willingness to negotiate with Batista (1955–7) or to participate in his two questionable elections (1954 and 1958), discredited them widely. Moreover, both parties' leaders had spent the *Batistato* abroad, plotting and financing rebellions, while the M26J were seen to have stayed to fight Batista head-on, becoming significantly more credible than the traditional 1930–50 'action groups' and *bonches*.

However, one representative of the 'old politics' remained intact, albeit with a slightly tarnished image, given its recent opposition to the emerging rebellion: the communists' renamed Partido Socialista Popular (PSP, People's Socialist Party). Long enjoying residual prestige among unionized workers for their locally effective advocacy and also among those on the Left who recalled their role in shaping the 1940 Constitution, despite being banned by Batista they retained a disciplined and committed core membership of between 6,000 and 10,000.

However, any M26J collaboration with the PSP was problematic. First, the PSP's 1938–44 alliance with Batista, however progressive his presidency then, sat uncomfortably with younger Cubans who only knew the Batista of 1952–58. Secondly, the PSP had never fully opposed Batista after 1952, leading some to suspect a desire to resurrect an understanding. Thirdly (most resented by the M26J), the PSP had openly criticized both the Moncada and *Granma* episodes, only shifting towards greater support in mid-1958. That criticism partly reflected fears of suffering from Batista's reprisals but also the party's support both for the Soviet line of 'peaceful coexistence' with the United States (i.e. discouraging any communist association with revolutions in the US 'sphere of influence' to avoid US suspicions). It also stemmed from the Soviet (and PSP) approach to the theory of revolution: faithful to Marx, they viewed socialism as only possible in advanced capitalist societies where capitalism's internal contradictions had created a revolutionary proletariat. They, therefore, opposed any revolutionary action to accelerate something that historically and 'scientifically' could not accelerated. It had shaped their attitude to the 1933 'revolution' and remained a firm view.

It was the guerrillas' growing success which changed the PSP leaders' minds, along with pressure from the PSP's *Juventud Socialista* (JS, Socialist Youth), which was aware of the M26J's challenge to youth recruitment, and pressure from former student colleagues of Fidel. Nonetheless, the PSP shift was welcomed by some rebels, notably Guevara (willing to collaborate with PSP groups during the westward march) and Raúl Castro, who had joined the JS in 1953 until his participation in the Moncada and *Granma* ventures. Equally, within the PSP, one respected leader, Carlos Rafael Rodríguez, was more sympathetic, aware of Fidel's popularity and political skills. Hence, in 1958, the PSP made overtures to the rebels, publicly encouraged members to support and even join the rebellion and sent two leaders (including Rodríguez) to the Sierra.

This proved crucial: in January 1959, the emerging 'Revolution' was clearly being shaped by a tripartite alliance of the M26J, the PSP and the DR. While the first government was a coalition of social democrats, liberals and a few M26J activists, it was that alliance (and especially the Rebel Army under Fidel) which drove the early decisions. However, even that alliance did not boast a consensus. On the one hand, the most radical element was evidently the Rebel Army; enjoying a unique legitimacy in Cuba (Buch and Suárez 2009), they mostly wanted the future Cuba to be more than a clean version of the pre-1952 political landscape. Moreover, they did not even share that radical perspective with all their urban counterparts (called the *Llano*, or 'plain', to distinguish them from 'the Sierra') who, not radicalized by the same factors as the guerrillas, often espoused more moderate and mixed goals. Some in the M26J (like David Salvador, the union leader) were decidedly anti-communist, opposing the growing collaboration with the PSP; some of Chomón's DR faction were unenthusiastic and cautious, resenting the M26J's and PSP's access to power. Meantime, Gutiérrez Menoyo's dissident DR faction remained separate, awaiting clarity on the Revolution's direction before committing themselves. However, the PSP's attitude to the alliance differed substantially: while others imposed conditions on their loyalty, the PSP gave unconditional support to Fidel's leadership, offering their members as 'foot-soldiers' in the post-victory tasks. Given the PSP's discipline, organization and radical view of a future Cuba, this offer could not be refused. Hence, given these differences, initial post-victory unity was always likely to fragment, preventing any lasting consensus on the shaping of the new Cuba.

DEFINING THE STATE

Before recounting the early reforms towards that reshaping, it is apposite here to address the question left hanging earlier: the nature of the structures in which a 'new Cuba' might be shaped. This task also demands analysis of the state structures of the 'old Cuba' that had collapsed by late 1958. It is apposite precisely because one of this study's central arguments is that to understand what 'the Revolution' was (and still is), one has to understand the nature and functioning of the infrastructure around its political processes. It will be argued that this infrastructure should be seen as a framework constructed steadily over the six decades since 1959, consisting of parallel and sometimes overlapping vertical structures of either power, participation and governance, with an evolving character and purpose over time and interlocking with each other via at least three different levels of crosswise and horizontal processes of consultation and negotiation. Those structures have always varied between two processes: one has channelled decisions downwards through all the different vertical structures, especially for formal consultation and debate, the results of which have then notionally been passed back up for final decisions-making; in the second, every vertical structure has been obliged to engage in a constant process of negotiation and inclusion with all the other parallel structures, at all levels. As will be seen, while this constant process of consultation and negotiation has varied in scope and effect and always slowed decision-making (often stultifyingly), it has also often ensured decision-makers' awareness of concerns, complaints, sentiments, pressures and demands from below, especially as some of those structures have collectively included all Cubans at some stage, apart from explicit 'refuseniks'.

To elaborate a little, we can firstly identify the vertical structures of power, governance and participation as consisting of different kinds of power: political decision-making power and influence, ideological power (essentially one key basis of any ideological authority), participatory empowerment through popular involvement and mobilization, and legislative and executive power (and governance). The first of those classifications of power has been manifested in two different sets of structure. The first are what have been identified as the concentric (inner, intermediate and outer) circles of power and influence, until 2019 consisting especially of key participants in the 1953–8 rebellion and selected elements of the pre-1959 PSP; those circles remained long in existence (albeit with personnel changing over the decades), providing a vital continuity of ideology, commitment, loyalty (to the group and the 'project') and a pool of talent and capacity (Kapcia 2014).

Ideological power refers to the single party: from 1965, the PCC (Cuban Communist Party), whose unique position was confirmed in February 2019 by the referendum on the new Constitution. However, one fundamental truth here (often overlooked by those who see post-1959 Cuba in terms of the old 1948–89 Socialist Bloc) is that a single party in Cuba did not emerge until 1961, and even then lacked a full-fledged national structure until at least 1965, after which it still suffered from internal differences about its purpose, internal mechanisms and effectiveness until its first congress in 1975. Hence, there was no dominant controlling single party for the first decade and a half of the Revolution's existence.

Selective in membership, the PCC has always been paralleled by its youth wing, the Unión de Jóvenes Comunistas (UJC, Union of Communist Youth), seen as the PCC's seedbed. Both organizations currently with similarly sized memberships (around 500,000, i.e. one million together). As this study will demonstrate, in the 1960s and early 1970s, personnel in the successive parties' governing councils matched almost exactly the concentric circles, making them part of decision-making and a vehicle for power. However, from the mid-1970s, the PCC changed slowly, becoming more powerful at all levels (especially the grassroots), but, after going through several reassessments, streamlining and purges in 1985–96 and a period of stasis until 2011, it then changed significantly, eventually returning to its official role of ideological guidance: from 2012, it was inside the PCC that a significant level of ideological authority was seen to rest.

Participatory power and mobilization will mostly be seen here to refer institutionally to the seven (or perhaps eight) Mass Organizations, the most important of which were created *before* the single party, filling the existing gap between government and population in ways that, even later, a party could not do, and which (it will be argued) essentially constituted the (human) infrastructure of the emerging revolutionary state, until post-1975 institutionalization. Much underestimated or neglected in the literature on the Revolution, these organizations have often played a fundamental role in mobilizing 'the willing' to take a degree of ownership of *their* Revolution and in capitalizing on that popular commitment and enthusiasm, initially to enact the projected social revolution cheaply, by using human labour and voluntarism. They still exist, their role still revealingly undefined but recognized by the 2019 Constitution. Crucially, unlike the selective PCC, they are defined as 'mass' because they have always included everyone qualifying through gender, workplace, age, study or residence (as appropriate), between them therefore always theoretically including all Cubans, although not all groups perhaps expected to be so defined have had their own Mass Organization.

Finally, the evolution of both the legislative power and the patterns and principles of governance and representation has been largely empirical and dynamic. In 1976, the two post-1962 experiments (JUCEI and *Poder Local*, Local Power) were replaced by the current system of Órganos de Poder Popular (OPP, People's Power), until 2019 at municipal, provincial and national levels. The national level (the National Assembly and its Council of State) has been widely viewed outside Cuba as an uncompetitively elected, rubber-stamp legitimizing body, which until 1992 only met for two fortnight-long sessions a year. However, changes enacted under the 2019 Constitution may well have breathed new life into those bodies (outlined later). Finally, executive power has rested with the government and the cabinet (Council of Ministers), seen universally until 2008 as the executors of the decisions passed down (usually from the PCC's *Buró Político*, Political Bureau); however, under Raúl Castro, the government suddenly began to acquire a life of its own, exercising a power separate from the other structures, something likely to continue from 2019.

However, these vertical structures have long been complicated and enhanced by a series of constantly operating horizontal processes of negotiation, consultation and inclusion of all parallel structures at each of three levels: national, provincial (after 1976) and local, although the latter has three levels – municipal, *barrio* and block or street. It will be argued here that it is these 'horizontalist' processes that force us to question the usual assumptions about the Cuban state, since the need to ensure horizontal negotiation might suggest that, contrary to our expectations about personalist or autocratic power or about any communist system's totalitarianism (Horowitz 2008), the powers identified in these structures have been contingent, conditional and negotiated. This therefore forces us to address less the reality of 'power' per se than the importance of political *authority* within the system, an authority earned or conferred by any one of a number of experiences, sources or purposes, but always transcending the simple and naked exercise of power in terms of decision-making and decision-executing.

This is not to enter into a long and complex discussion of the many theories of power (or indeed of the state) since this study is not a political science text; rather, because this is a history of processes, events and the evolution of a system and a way of thinking, the question of power here is reflected upon from the point of view of the observed reality of what actually happened, of what actually evolved and of what was actually intended at any given time, and within that, of how the decisions have been taken over decades, of who took them and of why they were taken as they were. In other words, the study's interpretations and methodology are those of historiography, reflecting on the evidence found and offered, not least because, for all the theories to explain either power or the state as an idea or as a practice within many or even most societies, this account of the evolution of something called the 'Cuban Revolution' shows that power, authority and the state (its nature, scope and purpose) have always been 'works-in-progress', constantly debated, negotiated, reshaped and rethought, to adapt to the changing needs, external environment and society.

However, all three terms (power, authority and state) do need to be defined as they are used in this study, especially as they have all changed over the decades. First, what is meant by political power is the capacity to make and enforce decisions that influence the way a territory and its society are governed, regulated, taxed and protected, or decisions that are equally influential further down the system. All such power is therefore necessarily relative since 'national' decisions can, and mostly do, determine the parameters of power and action at those lower levels, unless there is a power vacuum at the top.

Authority is more amorphous, however, but it is seen here as the power to influence, which is held by generalized respect for the person or the institution exercising or enjoying that authority, a respect which can have any number of sources: experience, success, military strength, deference, hierarchy (of any kind), age, pragmatism, charisma and so on. Thus, while a person or group may not exercise decision-making powers in a given territory, certain factors may endow them with an authority which obliges their views, status or representative capacity and role to be respected, and which may influence – or even veto – decisions without actually determining them and imposing them. Hence, a prime minister may well command respect because of the authority of that role within the accepted political hierarchy but may not enjoy the power to persuade his or her government or party to accept their judgements or policies; that respect, therefore, may mean the need for those below to show deference, respect the written or unwritten rules or the etiquette about how to challenge. Ultimately, that person has the authority to sack and appoint those below. While this concept may well conjure up familiar ideas of the essentially unstable charismatic authority identified by Weber (Adair-Toteff 2005) and used for Cuba by Richard Fagen (1965) and Edward Gonzalez (1974), it is suggested here that authority in modern Cuba is more institutionally earned, defined, defended and sustained than personal attraction and loyalty; indeed, its inherent importance for the cohesion of popular support and the political system suggests that authority in Cuba may have a more lasting impact.

Finally, what is the state? That question is central to this study since post-1959 Cuba has long been the object of criticism and arguments about the power of 'the state', as in the dichotomy between the state and civil society, or talk of the repressive state; many Cubans, for example, talk of *el estado* (the state) as something 'up there' controlling their lives, preventing them from doing what they want or what they might think is best for Cuba, or as a dead weight on normal life and any progress. However, currently around 80 per cent of those same Cubans are employed by the state, in what outside Cuba would be called the public sector (education, welfare, defence, health, civil service, etc.) and the nonprivate commercial or productive enterprises. Hence, the logical questions to pose in the face of such complaints are the following: Are those ordinary

Cubans part of the state, by being employed by publicly run bodies? At what point in an institutional structure does a state employee become a state *funcionario* (bureaucrat) or, indeed, an employer rather than a line manager? Where does 'the state' start and end?

This issue has been complicated by the shift in the global political consensus about the state. From the 1930s, the state was widely seen as something necessary and beneficial (to protect, feed, employ, generate recovery and defend), as seen in the widespread evolution of welfare states in Europe, Latin America and (albeit less so) the United States. However, by the 1970s, the prevailing orthodoxy was inexorably moving towards a neoliberal concept of the state as an inefficient, anti-progressive and even inherently repressive block on individual and market freedom. The notion of totalitarianism, theorized most prominently by Hannah Arendt (1951), contributed to this, by conflating Nazism and communism, defining a monolith repressing a free society; thereafter, the state increasingly became something more likely to repress than be benevolent.

Meanwhile, historians and political scientists continued to talk of 'strong states' and 'weak states', often synonymous with the capacity either to defend or impose strict systems of security, or simply survive threats to overthrow governments or to allow a civil service to continue regardless of changes in elected governments, that is, not subject to political whims of those in power. Thus, a supposedly strong state could be one where the armed forces ran the state and imposed political decisions (O'Donnell 1973) but also one where the elected government controlled the armed forces ensuring their non-intervention.

Hence, the notion of 'the state', like 'civil society', has often become whatever individuals have wanted it to mean, for good or bad. Given this, and given the central, but evolving, nature and role of the Cuban state over six decades, it may be more useful to seek a nuanced description of what 'the state' might be. That is particularly pertinent if one considers the evolution of academic thinking about the state in Latin America: until the 1960s, the common tendency was to base analyses of Latin American politics on conventional European or North American models, the state being an entity rarely being rethought (Lipset 1960; Lipset and Solari 1967). With the rise of the military-run state from 1964 (followed by the wholesale process of militarization across the continent in the 1970s), a wave of revisionist but indirect theorizing of the state itself began. Although often bringing new insights into a little-studied area, these theories often arose from a prime focus on political sociology or the military. One outstanding example was O'Donnell's notion of bureaucratic-authoritarianism, seeking to explain the relationship between elites and a new military (and militarist) approach (O'Donnell 1973). David Collier's equally path-breaking edited collection (Collier 1979) saw other country-specific studies follow a related approach to theorizing the new military-run states. Few, however, really questioned the consensus on the Latin American state itself. Even Miguel A. Centeno's many contributions to the theorization of strong and weak states in Latin America, and his notion the inclusive purposes of what he called capable states (Centeno 2009), drew substantially on Charles Tilly's many sociology-based comparative-politics works on societies across the world, a perspective which had invariably assumed a commonality in 'the state'.

As these new approaches were largely stimulated by political processes across Latin America which, though rooted in post-1930 import-substitution experiences, responded to Cuba's challenge, Cuba was logically excluded from their scope of analysis. Only a few political scientists (including Centeno himself) turned their attention to the Cuban state (rather than focusing on 'the party' or '*caudillo*'); one outstanding exception was Jorge I. Domínguez's study of the post-1959 political structures of governing within a historical perspective (Domínguez 1978), a work which has contributed to this study's approach by reflecting on a state that had evolved over many decades.

Returning briefly to the bigger picture, this different approach is deemed necessary precisely because of the bewildering range of theories of the state as a concept, ranging from Machiavelli, Hobbes, Spinoza and Hegel to modern and contemporary reflections by 'end of history' advocates. Indeed, the length of time over which the notion has been theorized and debated has probably contributed to the declining usefulness of some of those classic writings: 'the state' as an entity (if that ever existed outside the thinker's consciousness) and, certainly, the many different states that have emerged over the centuries have changed so fundamentally in character, strength, scope, purpose and function since those theories were created that it seems logical to constantly readdress a concept that necessarily must also change, not least as our perspectives and knowledge of our respective states have also changed.

Since the 1940s, three different approaches to the state have emerged as convincing paradigms. The first is the hegemonic view in the liberal tradition, generally assuming a degree of commonality among different democratic and capitalist societies and systems, sufficient to see the state as neutral. The second is the neoliberal and Hobbesian godchild of that tradition, seeing the state as inherently obstructive, negative and antimodern, as a restriction on individual freedom. The third is the leftist tradition (based largely on Lenin and Antonio Gramsci) of seeing the capitalist state as a decidedly un-neutral part of the apparatus of capitalist domination, enshrining and institutionalizing the capitalist class and the 'naturalness' of the ideas and values associated with free market or monopolistic capitalism.

Curiously, however, compared to the plethora of theories of the capitalist state, the socialist state – where Gramsci's counter-hegemony succeeds in overthrowing a failed hegemonic system and elite to become the new hegemony – has been nothing like as well and as extensively theorized, despite the prevalence from the early 1920s of regimes and democratically elected governing parties defining themselves as socialist. Indeed, one might observe that many 'theories' of the state under socialism (almost always focused on the Soviet Union, post-1948 Eastern Europe or post-1949 China) have actually been descriptive narratives rather than detailed analyses of institutions and structure, descriptions often underpinned by assumptions about the states' totalitarian nature, usually seeing the state as an authoritarian amalgam of a ruling single party, a party-dominated governing structure with limited popular involvement, a heavily overloaded bureaucracy, institutions of state repression and systematic restriction of expression and education.

This brings us to Cuba, for one of the arguments to be made here is the need to go beyond simple assumptions, based on conventional readings of the Socialist Bloc and Soviet Union, and to look instead at the specifics of a very unusual case of socialism: one which came to power in a territory where the state was first created and distorted by colonial authority and rule (for almost four centuries), then converted into a decidedly neocolonial apparatus (explicitly and then implicitly), then, even after the move towards socialism (however defined), to a situation with at least two sustained periods (1960s and 1990s) where the inherited state was in permanent crisis of fluidity, contestation, haphazard formation and even fragility, on a base of organizational weakness. Hence, Cuba does seem to merit particular attention, not necessarily because of its exceptionalism, but because it does not seem to 'fit' pre-existing theories.

This brings us back to the theories. For recent variations of leftist analyses (led by Poulantzas (1978) and shaped by Gramscian approaches and ideas) have suggested new approaches to the state on a more case-by-case basis. One notable contribution has come from Bob Jessop, whose work (2002, 2007, 2016) has increasingly gravitated towards a study and a theory not of 'the state' but instead of (plural) 'states', given that more can be learned from individual cases (and their possible lessons for a wider explanation) than from applying potentially clumsy overall theories. Jessop has suggested that we add to Weber's conventional inventory of the elements of the state (territory, population and the apparatus of rule) the notions of 'the state idea' and the 'state project', the latter often the hegemonic material of the emerging elite. Even he, however, has essentially examined the capitalist state and not the state under a socialist 'state project'.

This is where this book attempts to point hesitantly in the direction of a possible reading of such a state, albeit one whose specificities are so unusual as to risk being unhelpful. What is proposed here, therefore, is that we should think of the Cuban state not as something divorced from people and/or society but as the changing, adapting and organic infrastructure of the structures, processes and systems which ensure the security, stability, provision, well-being and continuity of society, that is, that makes a society function as a society, within rules, parameters and possibilities. Hence, the state is also the necessarily evolving framework for political power and authority (of the new socialist hegemony), of governance, participation and decision-making, in a different way from what preceded socialism; it is 'necessarily evolving' because a state that does not adapt organically to changes in society, the international context, technology, ideological consensus and so on will soon lose legitimacy and be challenged or will have to resort to coercion.

TRACING THE EVOLUTION OF THE CUBAN STATE

What this means now is a need to reflect on what exactly 'power' and 'the state' meant before 1959. More precisely, what was the platform that was either rejected after 1959 or became (at least partly) the base for the new structures of power and the new state?

Starting early in the Spanish colonial system, we can make some relatively easy observations about the state and some more complex observations about power, since colonialism was never a simple structure or process of imposition and domination but most frequently a network of hegemonic power, persuaded consent and subordinated collaboration. For the first three centuries (between early sixteenth-century colonization and the early 1800s), the colonial state in Cuba referred to several structures and one main purpose: to maximize income and resources for the Spanish Crown, which eventually meant protecting the trade between the mainland colonies and the metropolis. Those structures had several dimensions as Cuban society changed, but they essentially meant the infrastructure to ensure the flow and regulation of that income and those resources, the protection of the Spanish population, the colony's defence and the hierarchy of authority. In Spain, authority was generally judged to emanate from heredity (protecting the monarchy and aristocracy as ideas), property and blood; however, colonial authority in all Spain's American colonies rested less on heredity (since the Crown always sought to limit the potential power of a hereditary aristocracy, even if the emerging elites were soon de facto hereditary) than on property and ethnicity, or more precisely notions of colour. Hence, power was exercised formally by the Spanish authorities but, in reality, by the elites emerging on the ground, a power based on property (which mostly included the unregulated ownership or use of labour through the *encomienda*) and on their economic value to the Spanish Crown. Therefore, in the sixteenth century, authority depended on those structures but, as the Cuban colony developed, it became nuanced by differences within the caste hierarchy, with a pyramid structure: white authority prevailed at the top (divided hierarchically between Spanish-born *peninsulares* and Cuban-born (white) *criollos*, always implying assumptions about possible ethnicity), mixed-race *mestizos* (also called *pardos*) were below them, but above *mulatos* (mixed black and white), and below them the few surviving indigenous (despite their theoretical protection and occasional classification as white). At the bottom were always the black slaves.

In this system, the relationship between power and authority was that power might well have been exercised at the base by colour, origin and property, but those exercising that power were often content to concede authority to the colonial administration, since it suited their purposes to have those officials on their side, ensuring their protection and turning a blind eye to breaches of financial and economic regulation, thereby effectively endowing them with the local power that they enjoyed. Hence, 'authority' meant recognizing necessary hierarchies and notionally respecting the law and force.

Talk of authority introduces another dimension, fundamental to Spanish imperialism at any time or place: the role of the Catholic Church. Given its role in education (especially of the elite), in formalizing the registering rituals of 'belonging' (baptisms, marriages and deaths) and in establishing an overall ideological authority (to confirm the colonizers' primacy), the popular mottos for Spain's conquest of the Americas (and the preceding Reconquest of Spain) rang true: *cruz y espada* (cross and sword) for the conquest and *oro y almas* (gold and souls) for its purpose. Simply, without the church's active role the colonization process might not have been completed and sustained so effectively. Even one aspect separating Spanish colonialism from others (the general toleration of the indigenous population's and African slaves' formal – rather than deep – adherence to the imposed religion) may well have reinforced colonialism's efficacy, while contributing to the survival of indigenous and African-origin cultural beliefs and practices.

In Cuba, the church's presence and activity were broadly much less visible or significant than in colonies whose plentiful resources (silver or plantation crops) demanded the use and control of the indigenous population or slaves, while ensuring their relative quiescence or subordination. Although the size of Cuba's pre-1492 indigenous population (now thought to be 110,000–120,000) and the scale of its rapid decline (long seen as reduced to a few hundred within fifty years, but now believed to be greater) are constantly under review, Cuba certainly had relatively few indigenous people or resources requiring a high level of religious-ideological authority and control. Once Mexican and Peruvian silver began to flow to Spain, Cuba (particularly Havana) had one simple but important imperial role: to gather, protect and ship the bullion to Spain. For two centuries, Cuba's economic and social development was thus subordinated to that role, remaining largely undeveloped, attracting few Spanish settlers and with no large-scale economic activity requiring the massive slave imports. Hence, the church remained relatively invisible, largely limited to cities and the Spanish or *mestizo* populations, and focused on education, charity and small-scale agricultural production.

However, as elsewhere in the colonial system, some forced syncretism did take place at the grassroots, with indigenous (and slave) religious practices continuing, especially in more isolated communities. As modernization began after the 1760s (chiefly sugar-driven), two social effects resulted: mass slave imports (over 600,000 by the mid-1800s) made the slave, free-black and *mulato* population the majority by the 1840s; and the white population grew, stimulated by the 20,000–30,000 refugees after 1803 and then by the officially encouraged Spanish immigration (over 100,000). Cuba now needed a church-led structure of religious-ideological authority, especially as the non-white population had steadily brought several new religions, engendering varying degrees of syncretism. However, thanks partly to the Enlightenment's ideological influence in *criollo* thinking, the church was poorly prepared institutionally to meet that challenge; hence, its invisibility remained a Cuban characteristic, proof seen in the relative absence of church buildings and clergy in rural Cuba, outside large towns and cities.

Therefore, the colonial Cuban state was always negotiated, but often proved resilient, witnessed in the willingness of *criollo*, *pardo* and *moreno* militias in 1762 to resist the British invasion (Keuthe 1986: 16–18; Rueda Jomarrón 2009: 13), and then in the authorities' willingness to negotiate with the British. Did that reflect faith in the Spain's authority, pragmatic loyalty or the dichotomy of colonial rule, that is, accepting Spain's authority to control Cuba because of the fundamental 'problems' inherent in the colonial population?

All this changed gradually by the 1830s due to several pressures: Spain's loss of colonies; the influx of, and reliance on, mass slave labour; the colony's rapidly growing sugar-based wealth; the external threats from Britain (especially the pressure to abolish the slave trade) and the United States' early designs on Cuba. Most obviously, while the motives for *criollo* loyalty changed (becoming more pragmatic, i.e. to preserve the slave trade and protect white society), the old self-image of the colonized as 'the problem' remained (especially the imagined political unreliability of the black population), as did a consensus well beyond the patterns in other Spanish colonies.

However, Spanish power and authority had been seriously weakened by the loss of those other colonies; after Spanish American independence, few *peninsulares* sought to return to a Spain that they saw as weaker, preferring instead to move to, or remain in, a more 'Spanish' Cuba. Moreover, the evidence of weakness was clear in Spain's unequal relations with Britain and the United States: Spanish control of Cuba was allowed to survive partly because those two 'powers' preferred that. It was also weakened by Cuba's declining economic value to Spain: its old fleet-based value had disappeared by the 1740s, and its new sugar-based importance brought Spain relatively little income, going instead to the island's growers (Cuban and Spanish, the latter still exercising local power and influencing Madrid's colonial policy) and, increasingly, US interests.

Therefore, the colonial state's purpose and nature also changed. No longer was it to protect revenue, but now to preserve the colony at all costs. These costs included allowing its own laws and treaties to be flouted with impunity, especially in the contraband slave trade; turning a blind eye to corruption since Spain lacked the wherewithal to run the two remaining American colonies (Cuba and Puerto Rico) efficiently or with adequate remuneration to colonial officials; and the burden of sending hundreds of thousands of Spanish troops in 1868–78 and 1895–8 to quell rebellions. That drive to preserve also gave the state a new function: fostering Spanish immigration to strengthen the *peninsulares* and outweigh a nascent separatism. However, the state retained some military power, although both rebellions showed the army's relative weakness against popular guerrilla-based struggle; it was largely the Spanish settlers (through the civilian *voluntarios*) who demonstrated real power by imposing their collective will on successive governors.

Meanwhile, Spain's political turmoil steadily undermined its already flawed authority, just as in 1807–20 when many *criollos* elsewhere, worried by Spain's unreliability, decided reluctantly on self-rule. By the 1890s, Spanish colonial authority was therefore in crisis, severely challenged by the United States' growing attraction (and ideological authority) and economic benefits for the Cuban elite. US authority was confirmed by the number of Cuban exiles, in the absence of any Cuban citizenship, choosing to take US citizenship as a gesture against their previous Spanish citizenship (Pérez 1983: 289; 1988: 107; 1999: 44). Those exiles included hundreds who gravitated from the 1880s towards Protestantism, rejecting the old church–state associations and attracted by Protestantism's nonconformism and deeper popular roots.

Ultimately, rebellion and US military intervention finally demolished Spanish colonial power and authority, beginning a new phase, with new sources (and wielders) of power and a new state. The latter was the explicitly neocolonial state that, under the Platt Amendment and Reciprocity Treaty, lasted until 1934. Although independence was only granted in 1902, the future new state was in gestation throughout the 1898–1902 US military occupation, only its form and sources of authority changing in 1902.

The new state's characteristics were clear enough: power rested in the United States, channelled firstly through the occupation authorities and thereafter through the US ambassador, until Sumner Welles's failed 1933 mediation (between Machado and a non-existent moderate opposition) proved inadequate. Authority by then had two separate layers. Real decision-making power was clearly held by the United States, on trade, political systems (established by the post-1899 occupation authorities and then modified under the second US military occupation of 1906–9), on banking (the US government's refusal to countenance a Cuban national bank) and, ultimately, through the Platt-permitted authority to intervene unilaterally and overrule Cuban decisions on loans and treaties. Neocolonial power was explicit in all those respects.

However, below that was a subaltern political authority, vested in the 'generation of 1895', popularly called the *mambisado*: former high-ranking officers of the rebel Liberation Army whose service (and not necessarily success) gave them entry to the processes of political (or at least electoral) contestation. All the First Republic's presidents were such veterans, while a similar military record also legitimized armed rebellions (1906, 1917 and 1931), allowing them try to capture the government, if not the state. However, that power was limited to winning elections and enjoying the fruits of office, never meaning any real decision-making power that might change anything.

Meanwhile, alongside the new elite sat the church, its authority enhanced by the US occupation authorities' willingness to work with it (to ensure social peace and public morality). While the 1901 constitution separated church and state, the church still enjoyed an ideological authority, reinforced by its social prestige. By allying itself politically and socially with the urban elite and the Spanish population (the latter contributing significantly to the size of Cuba's clergy), it wielded an authority above the many Protestant churches and sects that had taken root in the rural and urban working class. While the latter enjoyed a popular (counter-hegemonic) ideological authority that helped shape a current of moralism in political thinking, the church's authority came from talking directly to those wielding power. That distinction would later shape the different denominations' responses to the Revolution. While many Protestant churches supported or tolerated radicalization, the Catholic hierarchy moved rapidly from formal welcome to outright hostility.

Cuba's new independent state was from early on more clearly structured than its failing predecessor. Mostly, this reflected the US military's efficiency in realizing their assigned role to lay the basis for an independent Cuba: establishing the rules, structures and curriculum for a national education system along US lines, for a national electoral structure in a multiparty system (dismantling Martí's carefully constructed PRC), for a legal system that nailed US elements and principles onto the pre-existing Spanish legal processes, and a Rural Guard to police the countryside, large enough to be effective but small and limited enough to prevent any propensity for political intervention (Pérez 1988: 334–44). However, its apparent effectiveness also came from crucial decisions under the occupation: to retain the existing experienced Spanish bureaucracy in the civil service (rather than using 'less reliable' Cubans) and to allow the Spanish population's presence in the commercial world to continue. Moreover, the 1901 Constitution defined as Cuban citizens those Spanish residents choosing to stay after Spain's withdrawal, legitimizing their position as new Cubans (Pichardo 1986: 76), while often still enjoying the same privileged social and economic positions. Indeed, the Spanish population's numerical strength in Cuba was enhanced over the next three decades, as more Spanish migrants entered Cuba (albeit many as non-settling seasonal labour), adding to the *peninsular* population. Unlike in the colony, however, the Spanish commercial presence was steadily dwarfed by the economic power of the US capital.

There were two flaws in the new system and state. The first was an essential contradiction. However strong and resilient the new state might seem (in continuity, force and economic power), the implicit authority given to dissident veterans of 1895–8 to rebel built in a destabilizing element, enhancing the Amendment's contradictory reality: although designed to ensure stability and (by deterring unrest) prevent the need for US military intervention, it proved counterproductive since all three of that generation's rebellions were launched precisely to *bring about* such intervention, hoping that intervention would effect change to include those rebelling. Hence, the Amendment was an instrument for destabilization rather than stability. Indeed, the lack of a strong army (until the 1906–9 occupation persuaded the US government of the need for a larger army) helped keep the new state weak.

The second flaw was the whole edifice's reliance on the benefits of US dependence, overcoming frustrations over the hopes of independence. In 1920–1 that legitimacy was undermined by the economic crisis and the ensuing replacement of Cuban-owned enterprises in many sectors by US interests. Given the latent (if diffuse) nationalism, quietened, divided and disarmed since independence, this questioning of the relationship engendered a new source of authority: of a more coherent nationalism, radicalized by new political ideas, as seen in the emergence of student and veterans' protest (1923), the Communist Party and the anarcho-syndicalist–led CNOC labour confederation (Shaffer 2005), leading to the 1930–3 insurrection.

What followed 1933, therefore, was the urgency of a new structure of power, authority and the state, since the discrediting of the old system, the 1895 generation and the old external relationship, together with the effects of the Depression and new ideas from Mexico and Russia, had seriously weakened the Republic's legitimacy. Therefore, 1934–58 saw that new structure emerge. The most obvious difference was that the US hold over the Cuban state was less evident, obvious because Roosevelt's 1934 unilateral abrogation of the US intervention rights removed the 'Platt Amendment' from Cuban political discourse and minds, replaced by a more indirect hegemony: without the legal framework for neocolonial governance, Cuba's dependence was henceforth determined by economic power and not military threat. That power was firmly enshrined in the new (1934) Reciprocity Treaty, which, substantially repeating its 1903 predecessor, determined Cuba's dependence and underdevelopment even more, at a time when many Latin American governments were backing state-led industrialization and diversification. More specifically, Cuba's economic future was cemented by the 1934 US sugar quota, determining annually the import levels and pricing for all sugar producers for the US market, which reduced the benefits to Cuba and the scope for Cuban governments and producers to plan. Meanwhile, the national bank still failed to materialize until 1950.

While the US military and legal power over the Cuban state had declined, US authority had also seemingly declined, because removing the military threat also ended the need to respect US coercive power, allowing Cuban governments and opposition parties to perceive some freedom to decide. On the one hand, US authority was still evident – in 1941 (as in 1917), Cuba's rapid entry into the Second World War directly and immediately followed the US example, while 1948 saw the supposedly nationalist *Auténtico* government quick to support the United States in the Cold War by repressing the PSP. Generally, however, US power and authority seemed to have lessened, creating a perceived space, perceptions which now shaped political action, especially as the 'Second Republic' belonged to a new generation, whose authority arose from participation in the 'heroic days' of 1930–3 and in the 1940 Constitution, which, by replacing the 1901 charter and decreeing radical measures, persuaded many that a new start had indeed been made.

However, the authority of the post-1934 state and system was rapidly corroded by a sense of disillusion (echoing the experience after 1902) with the state of Cuban political life. Batista's indirect populism did deliver some of what Cubans had demanded in 1933: stability, some economic 'Cubanization' (as sugar's global stagnation persuaded US interests to partly withdraw), some limited welfare and, most importantly, the 1940 Constitution. However, the failure to enact many of the Constitution's declared principles (especially under the *Auténticos*, who belied their manifestos by being neither radical nor nationalist), and the corrosive effects of a new endemic corruption (exemplified most vividly by *bonchismo* and the *Auténticos*' solution to that phenomenon) combined to undermine the authority of the 'generation of 1933'.

They also undermined a still-fragile state. Although some state building was attempted after 1934, with a national bank and some economic regulation (Dominguez 1978: 54–109), it still depended on the increasingly volatile sugar economy. Hence, Batista's unexpected March 1952 coup (largely to prevent the anti-corruption *Ortodoxos*' election) provoked a widespread collapse of public confidence, with widespread apathy and resignation among the main political actors. That was expressed in the population's surprisingly positive response to the students' immediate protests and open identification with Martí's memory and legacy, sharpened by the public celebrations of a highly questionable independence (1952) and of Martí's centenary (1953): apathy was otherwise absent, extending to the lack of any authority among rulers, the political system and the state itself. In that respect, the death of Chibás, the one politician who gave disillusioned Cubans a glimmer of hope, was symbolically important (Cairo 2010; Guerra 2018: 56–121).

Hence, the still-fragile Cuban state was surviving largely by default, given the lack of an alternative or direct threat. Moreover, Batista's ability to control it easily confirmed that fragility, and his ability from July 1953 to use it to unleash a random repression suggested that the state's authority no longer relied on what it delivered but on the power to coerce through key elements. In other words, the state – no longer based on direct and visible US control – was failing it its key aims of protecting and ensuring well-being and stability and providing an infrastructure for a cohesive society to function, overcoming the potentially divisive effects of inequalities. Inequality was one crucial area (along with corruption) where the opposition forces were able, eventually, to score points. Hence, power was now solely coercive, and the only option left to opposition was to challenge it with violence, claiming a historic authority to rebel. This perhaps explains the curious resonance created by the Moncada episode: what might otherwise have been witnessed with horror won a surprising level of admiration for its heroism, self-sacrifice and failure (Guerra 2018: 122–53).

All this meant that the system in 1956 (when the Sierra insurrection began) was not a system at all, but a highly fragile structure, where the state was in crisis, surviving largely through a challengeable coercion and lacking a clear basis for authority, the latter no longer found either in the 'generation of 1933' and its political mechanisms of populism and a rhetorical nationalism or in the old US link. Power was vested in the force of arms, to repress and to challenge.

One final consideration at this point, enabling us to better understand the complexities of the post-1959 processes, is to introduce the vexed question of the meaning of words, most specifically Cubans' often confusing use of the term 'revolution' (or 'the Revolution'). For we will see throughout this study that the terms have had a variety of meanings over the decades, usually reflecting the standpoint of those using them but often giving different meanings simultaneously. Hence, this book's trajectory will also trace the term's changing uses and meanings, hopefully throwing further light on the whole evolution of the process.

2

THE PROJECT TO CONSTRUCT A CUBAN NATION, 1959–61

Although it might seem strange to devote a whole chapter of this narrative to a three year period, those years saw the Revolution's transformation accelerated and radicalized more than anyone had expected, totally changing the process's direction, ideology and character. This period also saw significant changes almost every month, and sometimes many times within a month, in a bewildering maelstrom, constantly challenging all preconceptions.

This, therefore, brings us to the question of presenting the Revolution's trajectory through defined 'phases' or 'periods', the common practice in most studies of post-1959 Cuba, precisely because that approach enables people to simplify an always complex process. However logical this tendency, somewhat set by Carmelo Mesa-Lago's seminal study (1974: 1–9), and however useful as a teaching tool for those simplifying that complexity, this approach must be treated with caution. This is because the potential clumsiness of any 'simple' period or phase, always defined retrospectively in the light of subsequent developments, can never easily accommodate the complexity of any one period, let alone of the whole trajectory, with its inevitable simultaneous countervailing tendencies and within the equally inevitable mass of contradictions – inevitable because of Cuba's constant transformations, basic economic dependency and ongoing processes of debate and contestation. Nonetheless, because 'periodization', for all its dangers, does have some merits, making partly comprehensible the six decades of often confusing evolution, this history will not shy away from it but will depart significantly from the conventional approach in two key respects.

First, this book identifies the different periods (however chosen or defined) not as phases, perhaps suggesting some uncertainty among decision-makers, but rather as 'strategies', usually adopted after, and based upon, preceding debates, and usually reflecting conscious, if not always confident, policymaking. Secondly, therefore, it includes discussion of the idea of 'debate' (Kapcia 2008), whose existence and role are given a higher profile than normal in the literature. Consequently, the periodization proposed here includes each identified debate seen as a separate 'period'. Generally, where any debates are ever acknowledged in the conventional literature on the Revolution, they usually form (an often confusing) part of a supposedly longer phase. However, since the trajectory was rarely a case of 'zig-zagging', this study sees a closer relationship between periods through the specific relationship between 'debates' and the preceding and consequent 'strategies', based on an interweaving of the two categories.

Therefore, the first question arises about the definition and length of the first strategy of the whole process, an issue on which few scholars agree, their choice usually depending on an overriding interpretation of the Revolution's basic character. This study is no exception to that rule, for the basic premise of its interpretation – that the Revolution should be understood as a postponed, and therefore more radicalized, process of decolonization and nation building based on endogenous traditions and within a particular world context, both factors determining the character of the transformations and their ideological paths – suggests that the logical place to end the first phase is mid-1961, while recognizing that the following year saw many of the same processes and thinking of 1959–61, albeit changed partly by events, challenges and debates.

Hence, this chapter has a narrow chronological focus for several reasons. First, so many of the fundamental changes shaping the Revolution's processes of transformation began or took place during those years, a time of intense political debate and seminal mobilizations. Indeed, within this book's overall argument, this period is already unusual by combining both strategy *and* debate simultaneously. Some might justifiably argue that this character befits a process of deep social and political change, especially where the preceding insurrection had largely focused on overthrowing an authoritarian regime by stressing unity and consensus, that is, a lack of real debate.

Secondly, those years were the period to which on at least two occasions (in 1986–8 after 'Rectification' had been defined, and from the late 1990s, when the debate about the Revolution's historical character raged) the Cuban leadership looked back when assessing the need to identify the current strategy's substantial base in previous principles. Thirdly, this was the period which saw the historic breakdown of Cuba's long-standing and dependent relationship with the United States, creating a process of intense debate, visceral trauma and fundamental redefinition.

Before taking this discussion further, however, it is appropriate to elaborate on the question of 'debate': What exactly has this meant in Cuba since 1959? It is a valid question since it is widely assumed that post-1959 Cuba, as an authoritarian system, denies any meaningful debate. Hence what is meant by the term throughout this study is the leadership's periodic recourse to organized (and eventually ingrained) processes of discussion and consultation, usually responding to crises. Their nature varies enormously in scale, openness, levels of formality and depth, according to the relevant pressures; indeed, we often deduce their existence after the fact, by recognizing familiar signals. Most commonly, they have operated within the leadership and the successive ruling parties, seeking consensus between differing perspectives and ideological interpretations, initially over the Revolution's nature and ideology, but more recently over economic reform; these are often wider in scope and fierce. The debates' precise details are rarely known until their outcome is clear, but some have been more evident through publications.

Further down the structures, debates have varied considerably. Some (over systemic inefficiencies or (as in the late 1990s) over the Revolution's 'essence') have been reflected by the topics discussed in the media or in new books published; others have been visible and extensive; for example, following exhortations to discuss draft constitutions (1975–6, 2018–19) or reform policies, but these (usually been structured by the Mass Organizations) have increasingly been used as sounding boards or to legitimize key topics. Being organized institutionally, they have always operated within defined parameters (more than intra-party debates), but sometimes their feedback has influenced the detail of decisions.

Debate also raises the vexed issue of dissent and dissidence, long seen as central to interpretations of the post-1959 system. While many might understandably argue that a one-party communist state, historically associated with one leader, can never permit dissidence, this study will suggest that, since the scope of systemic debates has varied considerably over six decades (in terms of participation and account taking), the leeway for dissidence has also varied widely. As definitions of the Revolution's ideology and policies sharpened (1959–62), deep divisions and US hostility grew, creating a context (and possibly a pretext) for narrowing the parameters for open dissent from the process's chosen direction. As we will see, this initially meant right-wing and liberal opposition to radicalization and collaboration with the PSP and Soviet Union, which provoked (or justified?) detention (Húber Matos) or expulsion (Spanish clergy), and soon saw mass emigration as a means of siphoning off dissent (Camarioca in 1965). We will see all those responses used over the following decades, with varying degrees of severity, depending on the external pressures, yet we will also see periods of stress that do not produce those responses or manifested them less severely.

RETURNING TO THE EARLY REVOLUTION

When the first revolutionary government was formed within days in January 1959, its character and programme reflected the rebellion's ultimate breadth of support: while there were only a few M26J representatives in the government (under Manuel Urrutia, chosen as president because, as a judge, he had refused to sentence the *Granma* survivors in 1957), it was a coalition of social democratic and liberal politicians untainted by the old politics (Kapcia 2014: 67–8). That character was also seen in the government's first measures to address popular demands and urgent needs.

However, there was already a revolutionary programme envisaged by the rebel leadership. Despite differences between individuals and groups in the leading circles, some early reforms were predictable, as suggested in Fidel's 1953 defence speech (the M26J's first manifesto). Although one should always be cautious of a focus on Fidel, this expression of his ideas clearly merits examination: its proposed reforms (most visible in the defined 'revolutionary laws' after the rebels' victory) adhered closely to the stipulations and principles of the 1940 Constitution and were reflected substantially in the first 1959 measures.

The first law promised to restore the 1940 Constitution. This proved the very issue provoking criticism from the United States and Cuban liberals when competitive elections were not held, although the speech had noted that the post-victory 'revolutionary movement' had the right, as the 'circumstantial incarnation of [this] sovereignty, the only source of legitimate power' (Castro 1961: 55), to assume legislative, executive and judicial powers until such a time as 'the Cuban people' might change the Constitution. Indeed, the text was explicit that 'the Judicial Power . . .

would cease to exist' until 'its immediate and total reform' were complete (ibid. 55–6). Hence, the programme had always envisaged postponing elections.

The second 'revolutionary law' promised land reform, giving title 'to all tenant and subtenant farmers, lessees, sharecroppers and squatters who hold parcels of five *caballerías* of land or less', with appropriate indemnification of former owners on the basis of ten years' rental. The third law promised employees the right to 30 per cent of the profits of any large industrial, mercantile or mining enterprise (including sugar mills), agricultural enterprises being otherwise addressed in specific land-reform laws (ibid. 56). The fourth law addressed the rights of sugar planters (a broad term for the range of *colonos*) to a 55 per cent share of production and a minimum quota of 40,000 *arrobas* for all small tenant farmers with three years' rental (ibid. 56). Finally, the fifth law promised confiscation of all holdings and ill-gotten gains of those guilty of fraud 'during previous regimes', giving special courts the right of access to all corporations' records and using half of the proceeds to subsidize employees' retirement funds and half for 'hospitals, asylums and charitable organizations' (ibid. 56–9).

Beyond these five measures, others were outlined or suggested that were more revealing. These included a commitment to 'solidarity with the democratic peoples of this continent' (ibid. 59), and a promise to enact laws and 'fundamental measures' (the term *Leyes Fundamentales* (Basic Laws) was used subsequently for what were deemed amendments to the Constitution) on agrarian reforms (specifying cooperatives and the provision of resources, equipment, protection and guidance) and specific promises on the 'nationalization of the electric power trust and the telephone trust' with minimal or no compensation (ibid. 59–60). Referring to the Constitution's relevant clauses, a state commitment was promised ensuring full employment and 'a decent livelihood' (ibid. 65–6), the halving of all urban rents and increasing taxes on landlords, the replacement of shanty dwellings by 'modern apartment buildings' and a promise to give all urban families ownership of their own dwelling (ibid. 65–6). Finally, the speech addressed education, promising better salaries, sabbatical leave and free rural transport for teachers.

Therefore, although broad, the programme was detailed, suggesting that the subsequent description of 'a revolution without a blueprint' was inaccurate (Zeitlin 1970b: 117). Hence, within two days, a Ministry for the Recovery of Stolen Goods (Recuperación de Bienes Malversados) was established under a leading M26J member Faustino Pérez to tackle the running sore of corruption by depriving beneficiaries of their gains. More substantially, early moves saw the end of formal racial discrimination (decreeing universal access to all beaches and institutions) and the first measures against old social ills such as prostitution (retraining former prostitutes) and gambling (closing many casinos).

The government then launched the planned welfare programme, to enact the 1953–8 promises and immediately affect ordinary Cubans' lives. The most urgently needed reforms targeted income distribution, directly by lowering taxes and utility prices and raising wages, moving towards national guaranteed income levels, but it was the indirect redistribution measures that proved the most effective and enduring. These included the drive to reshape living conditions and housing security by successive measures in 1959–60 on urban reform: in March 1959, the 1953 promise to reduce urban rents by 50 per cent was enacted, immediately relieving the urban poor and increasing available income (Cantón Navarrao 2006: 24). A year later, the second urban reform abolished all rent, giving tenants (under certain circumstances) ownership of their hitherto rented properties (Cantón Navarrao 2006: 71). The result was to change radically ownership patterns, socially and racially: as wealthier and more conservative Cubans began to emigrate, their properties were redistributed to those most in need, many inevitably non-white. By 1970, Cuba boasted unusually high levels of owner occupation of housing. Eventually, a longer-term solution would emerge: the invitation to workers in overstaffed workplaces to volunteer for a construction *microbrigada* that, using prefabricated materials and specialist guidance, would build a series of three-storey housing blocks for the workplace employees to rent or eventually own, with modern facilities and welcome space. The result was that every city, town and large village saw thousands of such blocks built over the next two decades, which, despite their often plain and even deteriorating appearance, helped to rehouse those in overcrowded dwellings, contributing to social well-being.

Other early measures had similar profound effects. In 1962, as incomes rose and food production fell (partly driven by farmers' fears of expropriation), food shortages in many urban areas led to the introduction of a rationing system, introducing the ubiquitous *libreta*, ration book. While this reduced supplies for the middle class (further stimulating emigration), it benefited many of the poor, now guaranteed better nutrition, with access to more cheap food supplies via the *bodega* (rationed goods store). Equally, as the early health reforms (then largely affecting health education) included free medical provision, and as education was extended and delivered free of charge, the majority's hitherto inadequate incomes were effectively protected.

Rural Cuba, especially benefiting from those reforms, was deeply reshaped by the May 1959 agrarian reform, which, within months, attacked one of Cuba's most obvious social problems and examples of inequality, finally enacting one of the 1940 Constitution's most praised, but least enacted, stipulations. Before 1959, there had been little rebel consensus on the reform, partly reflecting differing political perspectives but also a degree of ignorance among urban middle-class activists. This was by no means new: 'land' had long been a vague, but much repeated, element in successive radical manifestos and nationalist proposals, mostly referring to small farmers, landless or tenant farmers, and the perceived evil of large (and especially foreign) *latifundios*. Hence, in January 1959, it took several weeks of intense and prolonged discussions within the revolutionary alliance (in camera in the little port of Tarará east of Havana) to agree on what was needed (Szulc 1986: 380; Kapcia 2014: 73–5). The emerging consensus was that land itself was not the fundamental issue (except for those already farming it without secure tenure) but, rather, employment and security; sugar's domination of the rural economic cycle was so total that what most rural labourers demanded was security of employment and payment.

Hence, that first reform (declared in a symbolically significant ceremony in the Sierra Maestra on 17 May 1959) focused on the minimum tenure entitlement (27 hectares) and a notional maximum (403 hectares), while allowing exceptions for efficient large landholdings. However, the reform also established the Instituto Nacional de Reforma Agraria (INRA, National Institute of Agrarian Reform) which effectively became 'the Revolution' in the countryside, setting in motion another long-term process which would totally reshape rural Cuba (O'Connor 1970: 90–134). For it was under INRA (with wide powers and authority from the very top, under Fidel's and Guevara's oversight) that a nationwide drive to transform rural life was launched, including the construction of housing, schools and infrastructure, and in 1961 supporting the Literacy Campaign. Meanwhile, four types of landholding were established as the norm: the residual large privately owned properties (tolerated for reasons of efficiency); state-owned large estates (known as *granjas del pueblo*, or people's farms), largely concentrated in the livestock sector; cooperatives of small farmers; and privately owned small farms (largely concentrated in tobacco and coffee).

The Literacy Campaign of 1961 was as seminal as the land reform and a classic example of the Revolution's early principles of mass involvement, rapid social transformation and inclusion and equity. Planned from the outset but preceded by detailed surveys of the scale, scope and location of the problem of illiteracy (recorded as 23.6 per cent in late 1960, with much higher rates in rural areas), it was eventually launched in June 1961, but after around over 100,000 mostly young and urban schoolchildren had been mobilized and trained (in empty hotels, including in the former tourist resort of Varadero), a total of 247,929 *alfabetizadores* (literacy workers) were sent out into the areas and houses of those identified as illiterate, many of them to live as individual teachers with their pupils until they could read and write, the latter proved by a letter of thanks to Fidel. Within six months, 667,484 had been made literate (the rate being eventually reduced by 1962 to less than 4 per cent) but the campaign's political and socializing effects proved lasting (Pérez Cruz 2001: 269; Fagen 1969; Smith 2016).

This was because the whole collective experience changed both the newly literate and those teaching them. The former became integrated better into the country's and the Revolution's social, political, economic and cultural processes, generating both a life-long sense of gratitude and a level of commitment to the process which had enabled that integration. This was helped by the openly politicized nature of the textbook used, *Venceremos* (We Will Overcome). For the latter, the experience opened their eyes to a poverty hitherto unknown and unimaginable for them but gave them also a sense of commitment and service to the larger project; again, this process was aided by the politicized nature of their manual *Alfabeticemos* (Let us Make Literate), and by the campaign's quasi-guerrilla tenor, structures and uniforms, including them all in a new battle against underdevelopment (Fagen 1969: 33–68). Furthermore, the campaign's success persuaded the Revolution's leaders of the power of commitment and mobilization, shaping their approach in the following years and the process's emerging ideology. Meanwhile, it confirmed that by 1961 the Revolution had a social policy of sorts; while longer-term ideas on educational structures and principles remained unclear or unagreed, some basic principles were being clarified and put into practice, especially the need for social integration, equality and rights to social welfare. The campaign also saw all of Cuba's schools and universities nationalized in mid-1961.

This fed logically into a parallel drive in the field of culture. The Movement had long argued for Cuba's need for what they called a culture of its own but precisely what that meant was never defined, nor did the many views within the revolutionary alliance agree on what a 'revolutionary culture' might mean. Yet it was clear that culture was neither incidental nor subordinate to the wider process but, rather, fundamental to the transformation of expectations, confidence, well-being and self-esteem on which a revolutionary 'consciousness' depended. Proof of culture's importance was soon given with two of the Revolution's first institutions: the cinema institute ICAIC was founded in March 1959 (given the task of creating a Cuban cinema, socializing Cubans in the Revolution and their own history) and in April the Casa de las Américas cultural centre and publishing house was created, designed to integrate Cuban and Latin American cultures.

Nonetheless, it took almost three years to get a measure of internal agreement on the desired definitions of culture within the Revolution. The 26 July Movement had no clear policy, tending to leave the issue to empirical decisions and to the imaginative work of their newspaper's weekly cultural supplement *Lunes de Revolución* (*Revolución* on Monday[1]). Those editing the supplement were largely the younger generation of intellectuals, artists and writers who, working abroad before 1959, had returned to be part of the Revolution, seeing an opportunity to open Cuba up culturally to the world; they therefore tended to define 'cultural revolution' in those terms, that is, bringing the best of world culture to everyone and educating them to appreciate it (Luis 2003). The PSP, however, were already much clearer, with a long and respected history of encouraging popular culture through local activity and their radio station Mil Diez, but also with residual admiration for earlier and contemporary Soviet culture, which implied a heavily politicized and didactic role. Some of the most influential intellectuals of the time (Mirta Aguirre, José Antonio Portuondo and Juan Marinello) followed that path. Meanwhile, ICAIC (although under a former PSP member, Alfredo Guevara and driven by the pre-1959 socialist group, Nuestro Tiempo) ploughed its own furrow, following Eisenstein's example but using Italian neo-realist cinema to build consciousness through education while defending the need for aesthetic quality (Hernández Otero 2002; Kapcia 2005: 104, 132).

As tensions rose, each side fearing the influence of the other or dismissing the other as either narrow or elitist, one incident (the effective banning of a television documentary *PM* made by *Lunes*) brought it to a head, forcing the leadership to clarify policy. That clarification was given by Fidel's speech on 30 June (called *Palabras a los Intelectuales*,

'Speech to Intellectuals'), after three weekly meetings of open and often bitter debate. The speech was famous for one, seemingly ambiguous, phrase defining the parameters of cultural expression as 'Inside the Revolution, everything (is allowed) . . . against the Revolution, nothing' (Castro Ruz 1980: 14); while many then and since took that to mean either 'inside' and 'outside' or 'for' and 'against', the crucial point of the dichotomy that was actually expressed was its asymmetry, that is, 'inside' and 'against', suggesting a more tolerant and even inclusive approach than many read into it, and only refusing to accept art that was explicitly against the Revolution (Kapcia 2005: 134; Kumaraswami 2009). When this whole episode was followed by the closure of *Lunes* (in November 1961) and the creation of the Unión Nacional de Escritores y Artistas de Cuba (UNEAC, National Union of Cuban Writers and Artists), seemingly modelled along Soviet lines and even run initially by a known communist, the poet Nicolás Guillén, fears of creeping Stalinism remained unassuaged.

However, one equally significant element of the speech has often been overlooked: the belief in democratizing culture through active participation, specifically the belief that everyone had the capacity to practice (and not just consume) some form or other of art, which put the onus on the Revolution, through *instructores de arte* (cultural teachers, sent out like *alfabetizadores* to take the cultural revolution to 'the people'), to discover which form that might be in every case and to train people accordingly.

The final area for reform focused on the question of independence, or 'national sovereignty', inevitable in any process of post-colonial nation building. At one level, this meant moving away from Cuba's close dependence on the United States, home and abroad, economically and politically. As already argued, once the Platt Amendment disappeared, US hegemony had been exercised particularly through economic dependence. The underlying implication there meant a triple-layered imperative for the rebels: breaking dependence on sugar (with Cuba more vulnerable than ever, given the global glut by the 1950s), on the US market and on US capital.

A new policy towards sugar was evidently the key to economic independence, but few knew how to achieve any change without a massive risk to income and viability. However, if Cuba were to catch up with other Latin American countries' post-1930 programmes of building a partial industrial base, through nationalization of resources and utilities and state-led investment programmes, that also carried enormous risks.

The greatest lay in the potential US response: with the Cold War already reducing the leeway enjoyed by earlier Latin American governments, the United States was unlikely to accept nationalization of US-owned land and enterprises. Moreover, without US tolerance of any reform, the sugar quota on which the whole economy had depended since 1934 was at risk, with wider implications. With the global sugar economy long dominated by consumers, poorer sugar-exporting economies always relied on a preferential but dependent relationship with one single developed market.

Given the dangers, but also the internal disagreements about sugar's role and any diversification (Movement radicals like Guevara preferring to escape sugar dependence and diversify rapidly, while more cautious PSP leaders advised gradualism and sugar's continuing use as Cuba's mainstay), no major decisions were taken for the first year or so. However, in February 1960, the die was cast when the Cuban leaders agreed with the visiting Soviet foreign minister Mikoyan to begin trade diversification through a small commercial exchange of Cuban sugar (425,000 tonnes) for Soviet oil (Cantón Navarro 2006: 59). At that point, US attitudes became crucial. Already cautious about the rebels' plans for greater national control, critical of the early public trials of *batistianos*, and then highly critical of the impact of the agrarian reform on US property, US policymakers needed little encouragement to oppose the exchange, especially as they worried about the PSP's role. Therefore, they responded by advising US oil companies in Cuba to refuse to refine the oil.

Meanwhile, the process of radicalization had already intensified internal tensions in Cuba, even beyond the differences within the governing alliance, differences which emerged more openly in July–October 1959 when one former rebel *comandante*, Húber Matos, was arrested for conspiring with others to oppose the Movement's collaboration with the PSP and for opposing Raúl's appointment as Defence Minister. Within a month of the first government being formed in 1959, the resignation of the liberal Miró Cardona had brought Fidel Castro the prime ministerial post; then in July, Urrutia resigned the presidency (principally over the close PSP links), only to be replaced by Osvaldo Dorticós, a radical Movement activist who had once been a PSP member, thereby seeming to confirm anti-communists' fears. By September, Gutiérrez Menoyo had led his guerrilla faction into armed opposition in the Sierra del Escambray, supported by small farmers and some Catholic clergy. In fact, local support for the rebellion proved remarkably enduring, based firmly in the inherent conservatism of more traditionally Catholic small and medium farmers, who feared both the advent of communism and the loss of their long-held farms. It was a particular characteristic of the Escambray and Trinidad areas which ensured the rebellion's survival until the mid-1960s, until a sustained FAR and militia-based campaign, coupled with the forced relocation of many of the farming communities based in more isolated places, finally overcame the resistance.

Mention of Catholicism enters a revealing dimension of the Revolution's evolution. While the initial popular welcome of the guerrilla victory included all of Cuba's churches, Catholic and Protestant, differences soon set in, often based on social class and colour, but also on the threat of the church's traditional ideological authority being challenged by a counter ideology. As the Catholic Church had long lacked the social presence and authority seen elsewhere in Latin America, largely because its social base was to some extent limited to the urban white (and often Spanish) elite and middle class, its loyalties lay with those classes, precisely the ones affected adversely by the Revolution. Its political orientation reflected that, reinforced by the long-standing conservatism and traditionalism of the global church, something reinforced by the advent of Soviet communism (with its overt atheism) and then the Cold War. Therefore, the church soon moved from an initial attitude of cautious welcome to one of open hostility (Kirk 1989: 65–109), which would result in the expulsion of hundreds of (mostly Spanish) clergy in 1961 and institutional pressure from PSP and some M26J activists to treat all religion as the 'opium of the people'. By the late 1960s, the church had retreated to a position of quasi-clandestine semi-isolation, in a self-imposed (but encouraged) internal exile, some of its clergy being harassed and even interned in UMAP camps. Meanwhile, some of the Protestant churches continued to be more tolerated by the authorities, given their firmer working class (and black) social base.

Meanwhile, internal divisions within the Confederación de Trabajadores de Cuba (CTC, Confederation of Cuban Workers) union confederation had developed, principally pitting radicals and PSP activists against more social democratic or liberal activists who feared the PSP's role in the organization. Hence, the external divisions between Havana and Washington were paralleled internally by those between the increasingly radical Movement and the more liberal erstwhile supporters of the rebellion.

On the external front, US opposition to the Soviet oil deliveries had immediately begun a chain reaction of tit-for-tat responses. The Cuban government responded by nationalizing the US-owned refineries, provoking a punitive reduction in Cuba's US sugar quota, which in turn sparked further nationalizations of US and Cuban enterprises, prompting the US government into eliminating the quota completely. By September, a limited US trade embargo had been imposed, leading the Soviet government to promise to buy any unsold Cuban sugar. Quite apart from any political advantages to Moscow, Soviet interest in Cuban sugar made economic sense. Soviet sugar demand always exceeded the Socialist Bloc sugar production, leaving a permanent shortfall of around five million tonnes annually. Hence, Cuban planners had found the one remaining large sugar market. Thenceforth, of course, the Cuban-Soviet economic relationship would become closer, albeit remaining relatively limited for over a decade. All of this, therefore, convinced the United States and many Cubans that Cuba was moving closer to Soviet communism, something which Vice President Richard Nixon had assumed back in April 1959 when meeting Fidel Castro during the latter's goodwill visit, sparking the decision to train a force of exiles against the Revolution.

Certainly, by mid-1960, as the Revolution radicalized divisively with the PSP clearly influencing some decisions, a large-scale exodus of political refugees was already starting, totalling 110,000 by the end of the year (Olson and Olson 1995: 55). This was potentially damaging, depriving Cuba of valuable expertise in the professional middle class, those whom the inevitably larger state bureaucracy would need to implement the reforms and subsidized systems. Therefore, to realize the desired rapid social and economic programme, the already weak Cuban state urgently needed to fill the gap. Better education would help but take time, and, once US sanctions began to bite, time was lacking. Moreover, recently acquired literacy did not mean advanced competence; training and patience were required to create a bureaucracy that was reliable administratively, morally and ideologically. At that stage, Soviet aid did not go beyond advisers, so such expertise could not come from the outside.

Hence, the immediate solution was the only one available without compromising the Revolution's aims, such compromise would almost certainly have come with the option of scaling back or delaying the pace of reform or the scope of a state capable of enacting the changes that all Cubans already saw as urgent and on which the Revolution's credibility relied. That was because active mass involvement had already begun to change expectations and public discourse, while grassroots union activity was generating a growing collective desire for empowerment.

Therefore, the solution was to mobilize, building on the leadership's own principles and growing awareness that the collective enthusiasm and involvement of January 1959 could be enhanced if collective expressions of 'belonging' to the new process (e.g. rallies and marches, alongside enlistment in collective tasks) were constantly maintained. In October 1959, a citizens' militia, the Milicias Nacionales Revolucionarias (MNR, National Revolutionary Militias) had been founded, partly to protect buildings against sabotage from counter-revolutionary armed groups but also to 'enlist' and arm ordinary Cubans to protect 'their' Revolution, producing a both collective and individual sense of commitment, determination and belonging, especially among those too young to have been involved in the insurrection, for whom this action constituted their Revolution (Rueda Jomarrón 2009; Manke 2014).

That proved to be the template for what would soon be called 'mass organizations': the politicized national organizations designed to mobilize and socialize specific groups of Cubans. The first was the most seminal: the neighbourhood Comités de Defensa de la Revolución (CDR, Committees for the Defence of the Revolution), created in September 1960. Their aim was simple: knowing that a US-backed exile-based invasion was probable, they were essentially neighbourhood watch bodies organized at street level to identify those likely to collaborate with such an invasion. They rapidly recruited many thousands of volunteers prepared to defend the Revolution's gains and future.

The second, the Federación de Mujeres Cubanas (FMC, Federation of Cuban Women)was soon equally important. Created and led by a former guerrilla (now Raúl Castro's wife) Vilma Espín, this was designed as the key mechanism for mobilizing women, thus bringing the social revolution to the population's majority, one of the sectors most urgently needing social change. The quality of its leadership and its highly committed grassroots activists soon gave the FMC an influential national presence that the CDRs lacked and its impact was immediate: bringing women greater access to the labour market (with training and with the freedom created by increased facilities such as creches and nurseries) and to abortion and divorce (both long legalized but still frowned upon), crucial in basic health education (Kirk 2017), and mobilizing them in the Revolution's defence.

In 1961, a third organization was created for small private farmers, the Asociación Nacional de Agricultores Pequeños (ANAP, National

Association of Small Farmers), ensuring that, although private farming was accepted as being more effective in some areas (especially coffee and tobacco, where scale, skills or terrain made centralization less efficient), those producers were included in the decision-making processes, and in access to vital facilities, credit, machinery and knowledge.

Two mass organizations already existed, the students' FEU and the CTC; both were more problematic, for different reasons. Since the 1920s, the FEU had been in the vanguard of radical dissidence against governments and US hegemony, but after 1959 the new government's aim of expanding higher education and changing the curriculum clashed with the innate conservatism of many middle-class students, who saw their prestigious universities (there then being only three, in Havana, Oriente and Las Villas) tainted by the influx of many less qualified entrants. Hence, the FEU became an early battleground between radicals and moderates or conservatives.

The CTC had a long but often chequered history. Founded in 1939 and led by Lázaro Peña (of the PSP's predecessor party) until 1948, it had been influential in winning workers' rights and social reform, but, after the Cold War began, communists were purged from the organization, which after 1952 became a fiefdom of Eusebio Mujal, an ardent but corrupt anti-communist, and a brutal supporter of Batista's machinery of repression. Hence, the CTC also became an early battleground for differing definitions of labour organization, between anti-communist 26 July activists and those willing to work in or alongside the PSP.

The point about these mass organizations was their political significance. Predating the creation of a single national party and enlisting hundreds of thousands of hitherto uninvolved Cubans in the tasks of, and support for, the whole process of transformation, they soon became valuable mechanisms in the Revolution's main initial thrust, in the early measures to spread and deepen a much-needed and much-demanded social revolution. They partly emerged by default, but, like the social revolution, their appearance was also logical, as was the social revolution itself.

On the one hand, any economic revolution (in whatever form) could not be achieved quickly, especially with US sanctions operating and (after 1961) needed increasingly to be compatible with Soviet interests. Meanwhile, the steady exodus of the pre-1959 elite and the lack of US investment removed the possibility of a strong and collaborative private sector, limiting the mixed-economy options. Equally, a political revolution, apart from the mass organizations and constant mobilization, would inevitably involve a slow process of constant negotiation, caution and conflict. Hence, the only dimension where revolution could begin immediately and be effected cheaply (using people as the key resource) was the social revolution, the process that aimed to improve daily lives of people in meaningful ways, in education, income distribution, access and popular involvement. Indeed, that prioritization probably proved seminal. The mass organizations, therefore, also fitted well within this prioritization. The CDR, in particular, after proving their worth in resisting the April 1961 invasion (see later), were soon widely seen as a crucial mechanism for all national and local processes of involvement and mobilization, for disseminating information, debating, educating, distributing goods and medicine and so on.

This discussion immediately raises one crucial issue about these, and indeed all, mass organizations at that stage, something which continued to shape their functioning thereafter: the fact that the three created in 1960–1 were seen from the outset as top-down structures for the leadership and Movement activists to inform, politicize and mobilize people at the grassroots – for defence and security (CDR), to achieve greater gender equality and tap into women's labour potential (FMC) and to regulate non-state agricultural activity (ANAP). In other words, they were never seen as democratically accountable to the grassroots, but as agencies for the involvement *of* the grassroots rather than bottom-up participation *by* them. Given the often volatile and contested past of the two existing organizations (CTC and FEU), the leadership always knew that both would have to be firmly directed from above, although the CTC's special nature (grouping and speaking for unions that had always been based on the idea (and a culture) of grassroots representation against those above) meant that such top-down directing needed to be treated sensitively. Thereafter, as we will see, the different mass organizations (soon to be christened formally with capital letters) would evolve with different levels of accountability, bottom-up communication and with either more or passive participation, but, at least until the Special Period, would always be headed by someone appointed from above, confirming the entities' purpose and centralized control.

Their existence was also crucial because, in the more overtly political sphere of the governing alliance, tensions were proving damaging and deep. Those tensions were rooted in several factors: generational differences between a predominantly young 26 July Movement and a much older PSP leadership; the PSP's questionable past alliance with Batista, coupled with their open criticism of the early Movement actions;

residual anti-communism within the Movement; fears of Stalinism emerging; and, above all, a growing sense at the grassroots that the PSP activists were infiltrating, and possibly seeking to take over, the Revolution.

Another tension, however, arose from differing interpretations of Marxism: the PSP's still largely accepted Soviet-led view of a Cuba which, lacking Marx's 'objective conditions' for an organic revolution towards socialism, could not yet be socialist was countered by those in the Movement (most obviously Che Guevara, already theorizing his version to argue that the 'subjective conditions' could replace that lack) who challenged this view, determined to move towards their version of socialism and eventually communism.

Those differences certainly helped delay the creation of the planned single unified party to lead the revolutionary nation building, a goal which both sides shared: the PSP read it as a necessary stage in any long-term transition from 'backwardness' to a progressive route to socialism (citing Lenin), while Movement members, albeit often admiring aspects of the early Soviet experience as a model for rapid transformation with equity, actually took their cue from Martí's PRC and Cuba's history of post-independence divisions, an experience subsequently shared by many other post-colonial processes. For the Movement, therefore, a single party was a quasi-corporatist mechanism for ensuring necessary unity and integration, especially as Cuba's 1902–52 experience of competitive democracy had been characterized by corruption and patronage. Any such single-party plan, however, would inevitably attract criticism from Washington, especially given the PSP's presence in the governing alliance, reminding older hands of Czechoslovakia's post-1945 experience of communist takeover.

By late 1960, however, such criticism came from several sides, as the US government-approved CIA-led plans for an invasion progressed. Finally, in January 1961 the path towards that invasion was cleared when the US government formally broke off relations with Cuba. By then, too, other measures were already defining things more clearly: in May 1960, all the independent private newspapers were closed (Ortega 1989), their presses being nationalized for other urgent needs and their role for informing being replaced by the two revolutionary newspapers – the Movement's *Revolución* and the PSP's *Noticias de Hoy*. By then, too, all of Cuba's major utilities were nationalized, including telephones, energy, transport and Cuba's only major airline Cubana. Finally, in October 1960, when the banks were taken over, almost 400 companies in all had been nationalized. The direction of travel could not be clearer, confirming the widening gulf between liberals and radicals, between Washington and Havana.

At one level this rapid unravelling was inevitable given the Cold War divisions and the residual McCarthyism in US political circles. However, it also had deeper roots in long-standing US designs on Cuba; these dated from 1823, with John Quincy Adams's indirect reference to Cuba as a 'ripe fruit' waiting to fall into American hands (Pérez 1983: 59), and from the 1823 Monroe Doctrine which partly reflected a US desire to keep Cuba free from British interests that might threaten the new state's vulnerable underbelly (Pérez 1988: 109). In the mid-nineteenth century three US presidents (Polk (1848), Pierce (1854) and Buchanan in 1857) had tried to buy Cuba from Spain, and the Cuban annexationist idea was briefly but ardently supported by US southern-states' interests. Even in the 1890s, a strong political lobby (led by Admiral Alfred Mahan) saw Cuba as a necessary US acquisition within a protective ring of 'buffer states' to ensure US security, an idea eventually defeated by the traditional US anti-colonial lobby who imposed limits on the post-1899 military occupation, indirectly generating the Platt Amendment. Hence, the breakdown partly came from a long-entrenched US view of Cuba which, misunderstanding Cubans' wishes and possibilities and manifested in different ways between 1901 and 1960, produced a countervailing nationalist resentment among many Cubans, which often coexisted (even within individuals) with the equally powerful admiration for US culture and a widespread sense of resignation to Cuba's historic need to live under the US shadow and benefit from US economic links.

Whatever the historic motives, in 1961 it all led inexorably to the Bay of Pigs, a debacle for the United States (although known in Cuba as the victory of Playa Girón) that became a watershed in so many ways. Militarily and politically the invasion was a clumsy strategy, undermined by poor planning and intelligence (based on émigrés' wishful predictions of overwhelming support), and finally by Kennedy's last-minute decision to withdraw air cover (Blight and Kornbluh 1998). On both military and political counts it was a decisive victory for the Cuban leadership, with both popular involvement (through the CDRs and militia) and good intelligence ensuring readiness, and also ensuring that any ordinary Cubans' collaboration with the invasion was minimal (Rueda Jomarrón 2009: 86–106); moreover, good military leadership trapped the invaders on or near the Playa Girón beach and ended the threat with air bombardment and dogged resistance, successfully capturing 1,202 of the original 1,316 invaders.

The political outcome was decisive too. US global embarrassment led to Operation Mongoose, the decade-long strategy of supporting sabotage by émigré organizations (Blight and Kornbluh 1998: 107–32) and to a determination to eliminate the dangerous Cuban 'example' by extending the embargo and isolating Cuba, duly confirmed by the Organization of American States' expulsion of Cuba in January 1962. It also led the Cuban-American political leadership and community towards a historic association with the Republican Party. Conversely, it persuaded the Soviet leadership to act on their undertaking to protect Cuba against any new invasion by siting nuclear missiles in Cuba, leading inexorably to the October 1962 Missile Crisis.

For the Cuban side, it confirmed much. The Revolution was publicly described (on 16 April at the funeral of those killed in the pre-invasion airfield bombings) as socialist, ending one politically mixed option for the Revolution (that of political pluralism and a mixed economy) and, ultimately, confirming a more militant and determinedly revolutionary option. By the time Fidel referred to 'making a socialist revolution' under the noses of 'the imperialists' (*Revolución* 1961: 13), 'socialism' already had a wide range of possible meanings in Cuba, depending on the speaker's preferences (for or against), although it generally implied a critique of untrammelled free-market capitalism while seeking a degree of state intervention (control, if not ownership, of key resources, utilities and public services) and a welfare programme. That broad perspective was shared by groups as diverse as the PSP, many *Auténticos* and *Ortodoxos* (Grau 1934); it had even been publicly shared by Batista in his 1938–44 CSD coalition. What socialism did *not* necessarily mean, however, was communism, especially one associated with the Soviet Union, but contemporary US political culture did not always distinguish between the two; the April 1961 'declaration' therefore justified US hostility.

THE EMERGING SYSTEM AND THE CHANGING MEANING OF 'REVOLUTION'

After two to three years of change, some things in Cuba were much clearer, such as the need to proceed without US protection, aid or trade, and the Revolution's widespread popularity, despite its weaknesses and problems. Only those increasingly numerous Cubans who felt obliged to leave dissented from that popularity, but they in turn were often resented by those remaining for having 'abandoned' the country at a time of national need (Kapcia 2018: 170); indeed, when those choosing to remain on the island ('within the Revolution') saw themselves close to realizing the long-held but historically frustrated goal of *Cuba Libre*, they saw those leaving as siding with a US government determined to halt, and even reverse, a process that they welcomed. However, while those remaining knew what they opposed and what changes they welcomed, few yet had a clear idea of the structures, systems and processes of participation, governance and communication (if any) which they might want, or which might evolve.

Most obviously, as already seen, the new mass organizations were growing in size and importance, and, through mobilization and scale, effectively constituted the emerging new state apparatus, to ensure well-being, social cohesion, protection, provision and citizen participation. Alongside them, the *milicias* also played their role in protection and participation. The role that all these bodies played was crucial, since large-scale emigration (of the very class that had hitherto provided the old state's administration, including its educational and social organization) had depleted the new state's stock of human capital which any rapid social transformation urgently needed. Meanwhile, the process of transformation constantly destabilized and weakened the already fragile state apparatus inherited in 1959 Revolution, with the constant mass mobilization of the first decade further undermining of any vestige of a strong and stable state.

The second obvious political reality of the new Cuba was that the authority and hegemony of the leading decision-making 'inner circle' had been at least partly clarified. While actual decision-making political power might not yet be fully clear, their political legitimacy and authority evidently were. Meanwhile, at the grassroots, actual power of governance and decision execution was still being hotly contested, although it seemed that the CDRs and the FMC at least were already rapidly building a pattern of active and influential involvement in shaping decisions, bringing their many members a valuable and political consciousness-forming experience of mass participation (Fagen 1969: 69–103).

This meant that unsurprisingly the shape of local governance was not yet clear. With the social structure in flux and economic patterns being constantly disrupted by the drive to revolutionize, and with the exodus of the middle class, no coherent and planned system of governance could have been expected to emerge quickly. Moreover, by 1961, the 26 July Movement's designs for a new Cuba had changed substantially, becoming increasingly radical and implying a continual process of rethinking all accepted strategies for a new Cuban economy, a new political structure, and, therefore, necessarily for a new state. The most controversial effect of this was that elections widely expected before 1959 (under the restored 1940 Constitution) persistently failed to materialize, giving both the alienated centrist and social democratic opposition and the United States a stick with which to beat the Cuban leadership.

As observed earlier, while some saw this failure as deliberate, holding on to power regardless of any PSP input, the Cuban leadership explained the delay by condemning the pre-1959 electoral democracy for its failure to address Cubans' social ills and economic dependence, and for its corrupt nature. Fidel's 1953 observation that elections might have to be postponed until all Cubans could at the very least read and write was based on that reading.

However, the reasons for delay went deeper than these contingent and short-term explanations. For Cuba's real problem in 1959 was the challenge and opportunity presented by the collapse of the fragile 1934–58 state. Challenge was posed by the fact that any system of political governance and participation needed the infrastructure for managing elections, governance and participation (which only a secure, stable and well-organized state could provide), and also for ensuring electoral fairness. In 1960–1, such a state did not yet exist and its character had not yet been determined. The other reality was that the human capital for constructing such a state did not exist either, given the unprepared capacity of Cubans (especially those new to literacy) to manage, or understand that.

Yet the absence of a state also created an opportunity, allowing the revolutionary state builders to design their own blueprint and create the basis for a new society to emerge, although the process of designing would be inevitably slow, given the internal debates within a range of different views of what the new Cuba should look like. This would imply necessary experimentation if it were to be constructed properly to ensure stability and security in the face of increased US hostility, the threat of invasion and subversion, a growing and often armed internal opposition (especially in the Escambray) and the material shortages which the new isolation would bring.

Indeed, to repeat an earlier observation, one of the most important features of the Revolution's state building stage during this cautious, but increasingly militant, period was that, in the absence of a clear and stable state to enact simultaneously the tasks of nation building and revolutionary transformation, the provision of the infrastructure to enable normal social life and ensure social cohesion, security and basic provision of supplies fell to the only forces capable of undertaking them, the mass organizations (hereafter capitalized, following their Cuban usage). Each one covered vital areas. When resources were inadequate or unusable, they tackled problems directly by large-scale mobilization; they helped organize the familiar periodic political rallies, but also voluntary labour, defence, local policing, provision of family facilities and (as with ANAP) the integration of defined sectors into the emerging national networks of production and management. Equally, the CDRs soon transcended their defence and vigilance roles, becoming local forums for communication at the lowest levels and incorporating Cubans into debates and garnering support for the changes.

Hence, by 1961, the evolving revolutionary state was based on their network. Consequently, although structures remained unclear, the patterns of power and authority were becoming clearer. Decision-making power evidently resided in the Rebel Army's leadership (the 'inner circle'), whose legitimacy was based on its popularity and historic role as the rebellion's vanguard, an authority enjoyed as the generation replacing the discredited 'generation of 1933', enabling it to wield real, longer-term, power at top and bottom. Meanwhile, between those two layers, the six provincial Rebel Army governors were equally crucial, while at base the army (all of whom continued to enjoy the same historical legitimacy) had already become Cuba's most efficient national organization for mobilizing; indeed, they were less 'the military' than what one writer insightfully called 'the civic soldier' (Domínguez 1978: 341–80), almost as 'the people in arms'. Certainly, the FAR's role in economic mobilization by the late 1960s suggested that Cuba was not 'militarized' in any conventional sense. The FAR were, for many, continuing their historic role rather than echoing patterns of military involvement elsewhere in Latin America (Azicri 1988: 198–200). Meanwhile, however, the M26J's organizational and numerical weakness meant that it always lacked numbers, or sufficiently capable members (beyond an unquestionable political commitment), to build the infrastructure for that power.

That was where the PSP came into play. At the base level (local *núcleos*), their organizational ability, discipline, commitment and political training enabled them to fill gaps left by their more popular, but inadequate, Movement comrades. However, although the PSP had once been more popular in elections and labour unions than many accounts immediately after 1959 argued, it never enjoyed the Movement's level of revolutionary nationalist authority, an authority earned more by its history of struggle against the odds, its reputation for clean politics and its clear identification with Cuba's heroic past than simply by the personal popularity of its leader.

The inevitable tensions between these two main political forces, let alone between each of them and the smaller DR, remained under the surface but sometimes more openly visible, given the disaggregated nature of political power, influence and participation as the new system was created empirically as much as deliberately, a pattern which allowed little 'fiefdoms' to exist and survive. Some of these small power bases were revealing. The freedom allowed to Alfredo Guevara's new ICAIC cinema institute was remarkable, not least that, despite his former PSP membership and continuing associations, he clearly did not share his political confrères' views on the nature of a revolutionary culture and held views much closer to those in the rebel leadership (Pogolotti 2006). Hence, no matter how restrictive the views of the necessary cultural policy might subsequently be under the remit of the new Consejo Nacional de Cultura (CNC, National Cultural Council), with former PSP activists Edith García Buchaca and Joaquín Ordoqui in positions of influence, ICAIC ploughed a very different furrow for the next two decades, even giving shelter to the young musicians whose *Nueva Trova* balladeering encountered resistance and disapproval in some quarters (Díaz 1994). Equally, Casa de las Américas, under Haydée Santamaría, showed an overt tendency to protect somewhat maverick writers and artists, who might otherwise have foundered in other areas of the cultural world. Furthermore, the internal battles over the new post-1960 Escuelas de Instrucción Revolucionaria (EIR, Revolutionary Training Schools), over the textbooks to be used there and the political line to be taught to newly trained *militantes* on the ground, revealed a depth of political differences of great significance for the future (Fagen 1969: 104–37).

Taking up the earlier discussion of the post-1959 system's matrix of power and authority and decision-making, in the light of the evidence given here of the vertical structures emerging soon after the victory as decisions were taken in both ad hoc and empirical ways by key individuals and groups (as befitted the process's dynamic nature), what horizontal processes of negotiation and consultation had emerged in those formative years? The answer is, perhaps inevitably, relatively few.

In great part, this can be attributed to the contingent, reactive and often urgent nature of decision-making in a revolutionary process where, as the US siege loomed increasingly, time and opportunity did not allow for coherent processes of negotiation to emerge. However, we have already seen the debates within the governing alliance, all of which suggested a growing need to negotiate at both leading and grassroots levels, at least within the defined groups.

Meanwhile, of course, as the Mass Organizations emerged it was inevitable that, as so much reliance for political socialization rested on their shoulders, they would cooperate at local level, although that varied. The CTC attention was always focused on the national decision-making and the local workplace and (given its federated structure via member unions, plus the traditional workplace culture of using such channels of upward communication) tended to have much more real grassroots involvement than some other Mass Organizations, while the upper reaches, under the PSP's Lázaro Peña (a veteran CTC leader of 1939–48) from 1961 to 1966, were inevitably more centrally run on a top-down basis. The FMC, meanwhile, tended to operate significantly at the national level, even more influentially and even autonomously than the CTC for the first few years (given Espín's profile and authority); however, the effectiveness of its local bodies (many run by either pre-1959 women's rights activists or ex-Movement members) meant that it tended to be strongest at the *barrio* and *municipio* levels (the latter structure still being the old, pre-1976, very variable municipality). The CDRs, however, were structured somewhat unevenly. While being unquestionably strongest at the most local (i.e. the street and block) level, given the numbers involved and the constant opportunity for activists to convene and run local meetings, nationally they were poorly represented in decision-making circles, compared to the FMC. Their national coordinator was appointed from above and was not included as a matter of principle in the upper reaches of decision-making, and they tended to have fewer national congresses than others. However, as national institutions, they ensured between them a high degree of communication and socialization at all three levels, a variation which made their cooperation more likely and more organic than if they had acted in competition. Hence, the best example of such cooperation (the 1961 Literacy Campaign) saw all three working together at each level, needing to communicate constantly if only to ensure comprehensive coverage as well as non-duplication. Hence, one could glimpse the start of the eventually more systematic horizontal processes of negotiation and consultation.

Finally, we are brought back to the meaning of 'the Revolution', with the leading question: What had the term meant during those early years of dramatic and rapid transformation and what did it mean as that period drew to something of a close? The answer takes us to the heart of the arguments about, and within, the process, since by the end of 1961 there were already at least two distinct meanings in the use of the term. The first was that soon implied by the increasingly common use of the eventually statutory term *el triunfo de la revolución* (the triumph of the Revolution): always referring to the rebels' victory in late 1958 and early 1959 and, with it, the end of the insurrection phase. In other words, that 'revolution' meant the act of overthrowing the Batista regime and with it the discredited *ancien régime* although few outside the leadership envisaged the scope of upheaval at the time of the victory. In that respect, therefore, 'the revolution' had clearly begun at the very least in early December 1956 (with the *Granma* landing and the start of the Sierra guerrilla campaign) but could justifiably be seen as starting on 26 July 1953 at the Moncada, since that episode's explicit purpose had been to generate a popular revolt through guerrilla warfare. That much was certainly true of the way that 'revolution' was understood by most non-Cubans at the time and since, who, when talking of subsequent events or issues, have mostly referred to the years after 1959 as 'after the revolution', rather than seeing the concept as referring to something continuing after the victory.

However, even that use (as 'insurrection') is problematic, assuming much about the rebellion's character and purpose. Was it always, or even gradually, seen as having a revolutionary purpose, that is, upheaval and the overthrow of a system, and not just of an individual dictator? Was it in any way a popular revolution, that is, with widespread active support? The answer to both is probably negative. Among the rebels, few thought until perhaps the late 1950s that what might result was a deep far-reaching transformation of the whole system; most who participated in it and supported it actively or passively saw it an opportunity to rid Cuba of a (by then) detested dictator, and perhaps in the process make a fresh start, without necessarily having clear ideas about what that might mean. After all, few had read *La Historia me Absolverá* sufficiently to know what the post-victory Cuba might entail but many had grasped its import.

That lack of clarity was further complicated by the fact that, from at least the 1930s, the term *revolución* had been used in Cuban political circles almost as a given. While Martí's use of the term *revolucionario* (as in his

PRC party) had been deliberate and meaningful, signalling an intention to end an empire and start a socially new *Cuba Libre* (Ibarra Cuesta 1980), the subsequent use of the adjective by the *Auténticos* had eventually been either naked opportunism (to benefit from the Martí association) or an automatic recourse to the language of the always rhetorically nationalist anti-government rebellion. Whatever the justification for the PRC-A's use of the terms *revolución* and *revolucionario*, as Llerena (1978) and Guerra (2018) have eloquently demonstrated, both soon became commonplace and standardized in political circles after 1902, used to refer to any armed rebellion, even by elite-based power seekers (as in the Liberal *revolución* of 1906 or 1917, the 1931 Unión Nacionalista rebellion against Machado under Carlos Mendieta), to some sort of implicit identification with some form of (often radical) nationalism – as in the 1952–3 MNR – or, very commonly, to the use of arms and clandestine activism by 'action groups'. The latter was true of the *bonches* who happily used *revolucionario* in their names (Movimiento Socialista Revolucionario, Acción Revolucionaria Guiteras and Unión Insurreccional Revolucionaria), although none were in any sense revolutionary, but also of other more ideologically driven groups such as the small clandestine Organización Celular Radical Revolucionaria. The 1933 upheaval was always called a revolution, even if it consisted of several contradictory strands, few of them aiming to overthrow anything other than the Platt Amendment and US dependency. Hence, to talk of the 26 July Movement's rebellion as by definition a 'revolution' was to be expected; certainly, the use of *Revolución* as the name of the Movement's newspaper from 1958 reflected this more than any clear-cut shared desire to produce a transformation of the kind that transpired.

As for the extent of popular involvement in the revolution, that too was unclear and debatable. While some have demonstrated skilfully the fundamental role of unions in shaping the rebellion's outcome (Cushion 2016), most histories record the role of the general strike of 1–3 January 1959 (securing Havana for the rebels), and while the Sierra Maestra peasantry certainly provided active logistical support for the guerrillas of 1956–8, most observers would probably agree that the rebellion's popularity was relatively inactive (though undoubtedly deep), undeveloped until late 1958 and widespread, but possibly superficial, in early 1959. Hence, the outcome was perhaps as much the result of political systemic collapse as the rebels' cohesion and military abilities.

What this all might mean, therefore, is that the meaning of *La Revolución* probably became clearer, and certainly more widespread, *after* rather than *before* 1959, a post hoc rationalization of what was already emerging and developing. Certainly, *el triunfo* would seem to suggest that what *began* on 1 January 1959, the accepted (if slightly inaccurate) date of the *triunfo*, that is, the start of a post-Batista Cuba with all that that eventually entailed, made what preceded that date part of *La Revolución*. Moreover, the symbolism of identifying the undefined change from one Cuba to another as 1 January (New Year's Day) would support that. After all, Batista actually fled on the night of 31 December, and the rebels did not take Havana until the night of 2/3 January, with Cantillo's attempted intervening coup met by the paralysing general strike.

Hence, the *triunfo* always referred as much to what followed as to what created the victory: 1 January was 'day one' of *La Revolución* coming to power and then (as time went by) starting the process of transforming Cuba into something different. Perhaps revealingly, the *rebeldes* of 1953–8 at some point became the *revolucionarios* of post-victory Cuba, and even the use of *rebelde* as an adjective for the new organizations did not last long, reflecting more the recent past than the implicit future. For example, echoing the continuing use of *Ejército Rebelde* (superseded within weeks by the wider tripartite *Fuerzas Armadas Revolucionarias*), the 26 July Movement's youth wing, the Asociación de Jóvenes Rebeldes (Association of Young Rebels) survived only until 1960, replaced by the Unión de Jóvenes Comunistas (Union of Communist Youth) after fusing with the PSP's JC.

However, whatever politically useful vagueness there might have been about *revolución* in early 1959, by September 1960, it was already representing something different. The creation of the CDRs assumed that 'the Revolution' was no longer a process of insurrection against a government but an entity with substance, something which could – and should – be defended. By late 1961, even that approach had developed. On the one hand, those who had already left or were about to leave Cuba (through political objections to the leftward drift towards socialism and possibly communism) clearly felt that the *revolución* that had, in their view, been betrayed by Fidel Castro (always personalizing the issue) or hijacked by a conspiracy of PSP and some leading rebels (usually identifying Raúl Castro and Guevara) was what had been supposed generally in 1956–8, rather than ever defined clearly. In other words, they had expected a 'revolution' in the then generally accepted sense of an armed and popular overthrow of a tyranny, with the prospect of some sort of ill-defined fresh start. Hence, for them, *La Revolución* had betrayed *La revolución*. On the other hand, however, Fidel's seemingly definitive statement of the Revolution's socialism in April 1961 indicated that, for him at least (and implicitly for those who accepted that definition without challenge), what had followed 1 January 1959 was indeed a deep process of revolution; indeed, far from being the date *after* which the Revolution's definition was socialist, his speech (and the key words 'What the imperialists cannot forgive us is that we are making a socialist revolution under their very noses') actually made clear that *by then*, the process was already socialist.

However, the arguments between Movement activists and PSP elements indicated that on the left not everyone shared that view, with Aníbal Escalante leading those in the PSP who felt that, according to 'scientific' Marxism, the *Revolución* could not by definition be socialist. While they accepted *la Revolución* as shorthand for a process that they welcomed as a progressive step and a stage in which they participated, they could not accept it as a revolution. Meanwhile, those emigrating saw the reverse: *la Revolución* was already tantamount to 'communism', and Castro's declaration of 'socialism' confirmed that.

3

DEBATE I

1962–5

The PSP–Movement tensions of 1960–2, together with a mounting economic crisis, led to Fidel's decision to launch a relatively public debate in 1962–3 to finally settle ongoing and potentially damaging arguments. Different ministries were already being run by different approaches, according to each minister's political provenance. The crisis itself was largely inevitable, caused more by structural factors than simply by incorrect decisions or policies. First, the costs of the prioritized broad-ranging social revolution were enormous, with huge subsidies and expenditure; secondly, the costs of the US embargo were rising, already leading to inefficiencies and expensive trade links. Meanwhile, the urgent need to staff the civil service with often poorly trained bureaucrats (replacing the departing expertise) meant inevitable inefficiencies; thus, action was needed.

However, that debate (in the pages of very specialist theoretical and economics journals, such as *Cuba Socialista* and in seminars, workshops and conferences) went beyond economics, going to the heart of the intense arguments about the Revolution's ideology. It lined up two camps. On the one hand, the 'radical' (and often nationalist) camp argued for rapid change from the traditional economy to a new socialist one. Its leading exponent was Guevara, whose Marxism had already been broadened and deepened by extensive reading, especially of the ideas of two of Latin America's the more maverick Marxists, the Peruvian José Carlos Mariátegui and the Argentine Aníbal Ponce, and of the writings of Antonio Gramsci, already translated into Spanish before the Anglophone world became aware of him. Guevara, however, also developed his interpretations through empirical observations of his Latin American and Cuban experiences (Lowy 1973).

Essentially, he argued several closely related propositions. First, challenging Soviet-influenced orthodoxy about Cuba's unreadiness for socialism or revolution, he argued that an underdeveloped country such as Cuba in the context of modern colonialism *could* experience a revolution and then enact a rapid transition to socialism. He based it on his notion of the 'subjective conditions' overcoming the lack of the 'scientifically' objective conditions, by which he meant firstly developing a heightened awareness (*conciencia*) among the key players and the population (leading him towards his emerging belief in the possibility of the desired 'New Cuban Man' (Guevara 1965; Beckford 1986)), and also a vanguard with high levels of commitment and awareness. On that basis, he argued, Cuba could leapfrog, or at least accelerate, the necessary socialist stage of historical development, moving rapidly towards communism.

While this position had other outcomes when applied to Latin America's readiness for armed revolution (covered in the next chapter), in this economic debate he advocated moving away from stimulating production through conventional material incentives (preferred by the PSP and Soviet Union), which he saw as perpetuating a capitalist mentality and preventing collectivism, towards a reliance on what he called moral incentives, that is, voluntarism and emulation, partly echoing the 1920s and 1930s arguments within Soviet Russia (Yaffe 2009). He also opposed the equally conventional wisdom about development based on growth, devolution and a mixed economy, as advocated by Lenin's 1921 New Economic Policy (NEP), and proposed an economy as centralized as possible and managed through what he called a budgetary system of finance, with the whole Cuban economy treated as a single enterprise. Finally, he argued vehemently against Cuba's historic dependence on sugar (echoing a long-held principle among many Cuban nationalists) and for rapid industrialization, initially within INRA (the agrarian reform institute) where he led its Industrial Department from May 1959 until February 1961 when it became the Ministry of Industry. Overall, his position characteristically mixed radical new Marxism with ideas espoused in the early Soviet revolution.

Against him (and others who shared his interpretation of Cuba's situation) were arrayed a greater number of more conventional pro-Soviet and social democratic politicians and economists. The former were inevitably ex-PSP members (notably Carlos Rafael Rodríguez) and those newly persuaded by Soviet orthodoxy, but they also included reformist Socialist Bloc economists influenced by Poland's Michał Kalecki and Oskar Lange and social democratic Keynesian economists. They all saw Cuba's future as depending on greater gradualism, believing that ambitions should not exceed what was possible; for them, socialism was a guiding principle rather than a stage to be superseded, since (especially for the PSP) Cuba's economy and society were still at least partly in the semi-feudal stage. The PSP especially believed (as with the NEP) that capitalism in Cuba needed to be accelerated before passing on to the socialist stage, and that any desire to achieve communism rapidly in Cuba was utopian, a view possibly shared by Raúl Castro although he kept his counsel.

Hence, the more orthodox followed the conventional 1960s wisdom about Cuba's development: using private finance wherever possible (if it could be retained, by ensuring that a middle-class and private enterprise remained in Cuba) and devolving and decentralizing economic activity and planning, without losing state control of the key sectors. Meanwhile, they argued pragmatically that, while the long-term aim should be to lessen sugar dependence, it remained Cuba's only viable short-term means of financing development, welfare and industrialization. This argument was reinforced by Soviet economic managers' view of the Cuban economy's usefulness, guaranteeing a continual supply of a much-needed five million tonnes of sugar. Hence, pragmatism coincided with conventional notions of 'comparative advantage'. Since, if Cuba was to be allowed into the Socialist Bloc's trading network, the Council for Mutual Economic Assistance (CMEA, or Comecon), which could only be envisaged with conventionally acceptable economic policies, the organization's guiding principles of internal and planned complementarity of members' economies would mean Cuba acquiring its necessary industrial goods from the Bloc's already industrialized or industrializing countries in exchange for Cuba's own specialist goods, especially sugar.

While this position made practical sense, it clearly clashed with the radicals' approaches and with nationalist notions of sovereignty; before long, the emerging ideas of dependency theory among unorthodox Marxists would suggest that what Moscow demanded of Cuba was little more than a socialist version of the old dependency, making it a quasi-imperialism. Moreover, when some argued that Cuba's continued dependence on the 'curse' of sugar was in Cuba's interests, denying

Cubans the industrialization necessary to overcome colonialism that Martí, Mella, Guiteras and others had advocated, many radicals linked this to the recently resented Soviet negligence (in the Missile Crisis) or even adverse influence in the recent Escalante affair (discussed later in the chapter).

Over almost three years, this debate raged, its complexity intensified by the reality that the different ministerial policies meant considerable institutional incoherence. However, the debate was already being shaped by the instincts (if not always clear ideas) of those actually taking decisions in the 'inner circles' of authority, if not power, because Guevara's position was often simply a 'Marxization' of the instincts largely shared by those who had fought in 1956–8. For them, the fact that a revolution had happened against all odds, that the Cubans had defeated a US-backed invasion (seen widely in Latin America, as well as in Cuba, as the United States' first military defeat in the region) and that rapid social changes had been effected through the force of popular mobilization (most notably the Literacy Campaign), all suggested that 'subjective conditions', or simple will and determination, had achieved much already.

Hence, the debate's outcome was already being decided. Meanwhile, a major step was being taken, reflecting the shift towards both more radical definitions and the logic and instincts of pragmatism. This was the October 1963 agrarian reform which formalized the empirical and shifting developments in land tenure since 1959. The four years since 1959 had seen the INRA deepen the reform's effects in many areas of social, as well as economic, development, but had also seen a steady drift of labour from the less reliable cooperatives to the security of steady wages on the *granjas del pueblo*, making a national decision over the coherence of the tenure system urgent and necessary (O'Connor 1970: 113–27). Therefore, momentum was already shifting towards the idea of greater collectivization, making the *granjas* the preferred system of all large-scale farming and leaving two kinds of agriculture as notable (and revealing) exceptions. One was the remaining private farms, accounting for around 30 per cent of farmland (O'Connor 1970: 130) and largely producing crops (coffee and tobacco) that, even to the most rigid planners, seemed best suited to small-scale individual farming, given either terrain (militating against economies of scale) or skills needed. The other referred to two kinds of cooperatives: either the most common credit and services cooperation of private farmers, pooling their energies and resources for greater efficiency, or what were called production cooperatives, largely limited to certain areas and crops. Overall, by 1963, the drift towards radical approaches was already taking shape, ideological priority coinciding with a clear pragmatic logic, a coincidence that could be seen in many areas, not least healthcare, whose nationalization in January 1963 was partly ideologically driven and partly a pragmatic move to ensure effective coverage.

Nonetheless, by 1965, the leadership's preferred direction amounted to a compromise, albeit favouring Guevara's ideas. What became known outside Cuba as 'the moral economy', evidently influenced by Guevara's notions of heavy centralization (leading later to the end of the urban private sector in the 1968 Revolutionary Offensive), moral incentives and labour-intensive human capital. However, the compromise came in the postponement of industrialization and the interim commitment to continue with sugar, as an immediate means of earning Soviet support and, by selling surpluses on the world market, invaluable hard currency. This would soon lead (after 1966) to a commitment to the famous strategy to harvest a record ten million metric tonnes by 1970, the perceived tipping point to settle Soviet debts and invest in industrialization and diversification.

However, what did these economic debates and decisions reflect below the surface? The debates had only settled the policy and ideological arguments; underneath, the tensions bubbled away. On the internal antagonism, Movement members' underlying resentments and the PSP members' dismissive attitude continued, aggravated by what was seen as a serious PSP threat to the Revolution. It arose from the pattern of the processes of politicization after 1960, as the PSP and Movement leaderships concurred on the need for a single overarching party as a mechanism for debating policy, communicating decisions and opinions and for mobilizing activists. The latter element meant the use of PSP cadres as the grassroots manpower for that process, causing resentment among rank-and-file Movement activists. While the PSP may have seen this as a logical and necessary step to control, following Marxist-Leninist theory (of democratic centralism and the political vanguard) and Socialist Bloc practice during the stage of building socialism, or as building alliances before any move towards socialism, Movement people saw it as desirable and practical, as something of a 'war coalition' (while US hostility and émigré activism threatened internal stability and unity), but also as following Martí's successful example.

As talks about this fusion (also intended to include the DR) continued, cooperation between activists at lower levels also developed.

However, these levels saw as much tension as the leadership talks, with the Movement still divided ideologically between radicals, reformists, socialists and even some liberals, and largely lacking organization, cohesion and numbers, as well as ideological confidence and certainty, the opposite of the PSP's cohesion, discipline and loyal obedience. The result was that, as grassroots fusion was developed empirically, the PSP cadres tended to dominate local discussions and ad hoc organization, and, following the PSP view that the Revolution was not socialist, they operated as though they alone possessed ideological certainty. Even the EIR, created in 1960 to train grassroots activists, were dominated by PSP members and under the direction of Lionel Soto of the PSP nationally, given their more confident ideological grounding, although Soto was a long-standing friend of Fidel. The three key texts used were a revealing mix: Blas Roca's very orthodox PSP manual *Fundamentos del Socialismo*, Fidel Castro's 1953 *La Historia me Absolverá* and Movement-based training manual of the MNR militias.

These tensions worsened in 1961 as the planned united-front Organizaciones Revolucionarias Integradas (ORI, Integrated Revolutionary Organizations) was established, and especially after the widely respected and experienced Escalante was given the key task of constructing ORI at all levels. The tensions finally surfaced in a public scandal in March 1962. The catalyst was Movement leaders' anger when, on 13 March at the already annual ceremony to commemorate the 1957 death of the DRE's Echeverría, the PSP representative leading the ceremony neglected to mention Echeverría's Catholicism, which everyone knew had shaped his political commitment. Days later, this anger was amplified to include Escalante's creation of the ORI's twenty-five-member National Directorate: fourteen from the Movement, ten from the PSP and only one from the DR. What followed was Fidel's public criticism of Escalante (and, implicitly, the PSP) for partisan politics and, implicitly, for using ORI as a vehicle to appropriate a revolutionary process which the PSP had once opposed and to which they had pragmatically adapted in time, while refusing to recognize its socialist character.

The outcome was clear enough. The PSP was promptly relegated within the rebel alliance (although the reshaped Directorate was only marginally changed), remaining in that position for years, forced to accept the Movement leadership's ideological interpretations unquestioningly, biding its time. The whole process was, thereafter, firmly in the Movement's hands, and the post-ORI single party always planned, the Partido Unido de la Revolución Socialista (PURS, United Party of the Socialist Revolution), was now accelerated. Established in 1962, its leadership bodies (the National Directorate and relevant councils) were Movement-dominated, while the party's name constituted a clear reprimand to the PSP (and Moscow) – not the United Revolutionary Socialist Party (i.e. aiming for socialist revolution) but explicitly the party *of the socialist revolution*, against the PSP's arguments about what was theoretically impossible.

The underlying tensions between Cuba and the Soviet Union, although never as bad in those years as the PSP–Movement tensions, were hardly warm once it became clear that Moscow not only supported Escalante's reading of Cuba and perhaps even approved his attempt at influencing the Revolution's path but also considered Cuba inappropriate for Comecon membership, refused in 1962. What really brought out those tensions very publicly was the Cuban Missile Crisis of October 1962, which was the logical outcome of both the close links of 1960–1 and the fears (of a new and stronger invasion) aroused by Playa Girón. After the victory, the Soviet leader Krushchev responded to Fidel's request for active support against any future attempt by offering to place Soviet nuclear missiles on Cuba, believing (after the June 1961 Vienna summit) that Kennedy was a weak leader.

The result of that decision is well known. Once the missiles' presence was identified by US spy planes, thirteen days of threat and brinkmanship followed, neither side wanting the seemingly inevitable nuclear hostilities nor wishing to back down. As the world breathed a sigh of relief with the news that the Soviet ships en route to Cuba had turned around on reaching the US naval quarantine, and as the US and Soviet leadership, via third parties and roundabout face-saving postures, found a form of words to step back from the brink (in the so-called secret protocol), Fidel's anger was palpable. Not only had Moscow proved unwilling to realize its promises to defend Cuba and then negotiated over the Cubans' heads (reminding Cubans of the US-Spanish Treaty of Paris in 1899) but those negotiations had also failed to include the US embargo in their bargaining for an agreement (Brenner 1992). Although Fidel's rhetoric seemed to suggest that he was prepared to accept all-out confrontation, ending the embargo and the US occupation of Guantánamo Bay was what he really sought as a minimum (Bain 2019: 117–18). Hence, although that same protocol had guaranteed Cuba's security from potential US invasion (soon creating unexpected opportunities abroad), Moscow's neglect seemed to confirm Soviet high-handedness, if not quasi-colonialism. Given Cuba's new sense of isolation, that was significant.

That isolation followed the January 1961 rupture of US–Cuban relations. In January 1962, it was confirmed when the Organization of American States (OAS) voted overwhelmingly to expel Cuba, given a perceived incompatibility between communism and the OAS Charter, and most member countries (except Canada and Mexico) agreed to join the embargo. Thereafter, Cuba's isolation seemed complete: already surrounded by hostile neighbours, only two still willing to trade, Cuba now also seemed part-abandoned by the Soviet Union. Isolation became siege, intensifying a long pervasive siege mentality, already created by the growing exodus from early 1960.

That exodus was still mostly on political grounds, fearing the Revolution's radicalization, but also often driven by falling living standards, as communism, isolation and the embargo ate into the economy, and as rationing was introduced in March 1962, a move which, perhaps inevitably, lowered living standards for the middle class while raising those for the majority. Soon, calling themselves exiles, echoing the historic posture of anti-Nazi governments-in-exile in the Second World War (Kapcia 2018), the émigrés were already creating in the United States a cohesive political community which, after the Bay of Pigs fiasco, would shape US policy irrevocably, confirming the isolation.

That emigration meantime flowed steadily, until one flashpoint was reached in October 1965 at the north port of Camarioca. There, 5,000 people were allowed to leave to defuse the situation, leading to a rapid US–Cuban agreement to operate a US-run weekly 'airlift' of emigrants to the United States which lasted until 1973 (Olson and Olson 1995: 60–1). Then, in 1966, the US Congress approved the controversial Cuban Adjustment Act that gave Cuban refugees unique migrant rights in the United States, whereby any migrant (legal or illegal) who reached the US mainland would automatically be entitled to temporary residency rights and, if approved, could therefore qualify for citizenship after a year and a day. It was controversial because it was unique to Cuban immigrants, suggesting that it was designed to increase a brain drain from Cuba, discrediting the Cuban system.

Curiously, however, the siege mentality did not, as many feared, translate into a narrow approach to cultural policy, as Fidel's *Palabras* and its crucial dichotomy of *dentro* and *contra* played out with remarkable accuracy, generating less of outright censorship and Stalinist socialist realism and continuing with more of the relatively open debates of 1959–61, in film (with ICAIC arguing openly with more narrow-minded PSP cultural experts), in literature and in art and music, where the focus was often on quality, quantity and spreading the benefits of the new culture. Interestingly, that emphasis on quality did not preclude a slowly growing admiration for Soviet cultural production (Loss 2103; Story 2019).

THE EMERGING REVOLUTIONARY STATE AND THE MEANING OF 'THE REVOLUTION'

With the debates and tensions largely settled or at least calmed by 1965, how had the experience of intense change, energetic but fragile consolidation and ever-deepening revolution shaped political power, political authority and the emerging state? The simple answer is that, although those years had seen the first highly contested steps towards the desired single party, and although the internal battles had established the Movement's primacy, instincts and aims within the rebel alliance and in access to decision-making power, wider political power was still contested, not least locally. Moreover, stubborn resistance to a radical definition of 'revolution' by some farmers in the Sierra del Escambray (backing a long counter-revolutionary guerrilla struggle) suggested that rural power was not yet a foregone conclusion, needing coercion and mobilization to effect stability and control (Suárez Amador 2014).

Nonetheless, there was little doubt that political authority and historic legitimacy rested with the Movement's 'inner circle' of Rebel Army veterans, and especially the three leaders, each earning respect for different qualities but collectively ensuring that leadership (as opposed to the Revolution's direction) was rarely contested. Anyone who contemplated challenging that leadership recognized that they could not compete with those leaders' authority. Therefore, in ways that would become characteristic, that authority meant that, although decisions might be taken at different levels by people outside the 'inner circle', no one contemplated contradicting the leaders' known preferences. In other words, authority was already a clear element in the Revolution's patterns of power. Hence, the Great Debate had not been as abstruse as it seemed, settling the question of authority, from which all power now stemmed. Therefore, whatever its name and form, PURS represented this primacy, its national directorate clearly in Movement hands and its leading decision-making circles dominated by the Rebel Army veterans. Meanwhile, on the ground, local PURS branches (*núcleos*) were equally in the hands of Movement veterans although a steady politicization had already begun to shape most Movement activists' understanding of 'socialism'.

As for the power of political governance and representation, that was still very much under debate, a disagreement partly determined by ideological differences, between ex-PSP and Movement veterans but also between radicals and more centrist reformers outside the PSP, and even between radicals whose ideas led them to argue for different models of governance. Hence, the outcome of these debates was always contested. As one solution was found and experimented with, alternative solutions were immediately brought forward as problems emerged with the first solution. Therefore, there was already an essential culture of experimentation and a pattern of empirical, and not simply (or even ever) theoretical, process (Collins 2017). In terms of grassroots governance, the first local bodies created, the Juntas de Coordinación, Ejecución e Inspección (JUCEI, Coordinating, Executive and Inspection Boards), reflected the time's urgent priorities rather than addressing any theoretical debates about democratic representation. The JUCEI had one simple purpose: to administer locally in the most effective and inclusive way, reflected in their somewhat managerial and bureaucratic title. Other priorities prevented any settling of the question of local political participatory power, especially the need for an effective low-level state structure.

Given that, the following few years would see a pattern emerge that would characterize the Revolution's whole trajectory. Any period of intense debate would invariably be followed by a period of greater confidence and certainty, while the debate's provisional outcome was put into practical effect, with policies, strategies and institutions that reflected that.

At this point, it is also pertinent to mention the Fuerzas Armadas Revolucionarias (FAR, Revolutionary Armed Forces), the new three-service structure created in 1959 out of the Rebel Army and some reliable elements of the pre-1959 army, navy and air force: because, after April 1961, the FAR continued to enjoy the Rebel Army's historical legitimacy (Pérez 1976). Moreover, the introduction of conscription in 1963 institutionalized the FAR as Cuba's most effective, disciplined and most popularly credible mechanism for mobilizing and enacting decisions. Whatever the structures of the state, governance or representation, it remained a basic element of any state or political structure. Indeed, 1963 also saw the start of FAR's sustained politicization, a process that would make the FAR one of the ruling party's firmest bases (Domínguez 1978: 364).

Returning, finally, to the continuing thread of the changing meanings of the term 'revolution', we can see that, within that context, by 1965, one could see the concept being defined by the leadership following the April 1961 cue: a socialist process of nation building. In October 1965, an insistence on the process's socialist character and on its rapid march towards communism was seen explicitly when the PURS Congress transformed itself into the Cuban Communist Party (PCC), making a clear ideological point about its character and purpose to both the Soviet Union and the former PSP leaders. Thereafter, said the Cuban leaders, their Revolution would be communist and explicitly so.

4

THE MAVERICK REVOLUTION AND 'CUBAN COMMUNISM', 1965-70

Given that the official debate of 1962–5 focused on economic policy and development models, it is apposite to begin this chapter with that focus, if only because the debate had a clear and seminal ideological dimension and, moreover, effectively launched what would eventually (outside Cuba) be called the 'moral economy', that is, the role within the new development model (agreed after the debate) played by the 'moral', rather than material, incentives. As already seen, that strategy largely followed Guevara's ideas (although, in 1965, he left Cuba permanently to lead a wider Third World revolution), especially on *conciencia*, voluntarism and a faith in a highly centralized economy.

However, alongside this 'Guevarist' approach, the compromise ending the debate upheld the opposing camp's belief in Cuba's continuing need to rely on sugar, which, for the short term at least, remained the mainstay of the economy, especially as the Soviet Union needed both Cuba's sugar and Cuba's survival, to protect the Soviet prestige in the Third World. Hence, since the Socialist Bloc–Cuba exchange had steadily begun to develop beyond the original oil-for-sugar swap, sugar exports already meant a trickle in of much-needed machinery and manufactured goods imports, and a small flow of technical and educational aid and healthcare modernization, given Cuba's emigration-generated personnel deficit. While Moscow continued to resist Havana's requests for Comecon membership (given Cuba's seemingly even more chaotic, unorthodox and inefficient economic model), those Bloc imports compensated a little. However, while that refusal freed Cuba from greater dependence on primary-based specialization (under Comecon's principles of socialist comparative advantage), it also constrained diversification plans and any expansion of production. Moreover, the 1970 *zafra* (sugar harvest) was now well established as the catalyst for any new diversification and industrialization strategies, to be achieved by *conciencia* and organization.

The *conciencia* question inevitably raises other issues, not least the Great Debate's ideological dimension, since this new period of more intense radicalization saw the Cuban leadership embark on a broader ideological challenge to Moscow's (and the PSP's) interpretation of communism in several adjacent areas. While the literature on this period generally tends to associate this new heterodoxy with Guevara's influence (Mesa-Lago refers to 'Sino-Guevarism': 1974: 8), we have to remember that the new policy actually coincided with Guevara's absence from Cuba, leading to his eventual death in Bolivia in October 1967; hence, any direct influence would be unusual without his presence to drive it forward. Therefore, rather than simply following his ideas, the new strategy also saw those ideas coincide with (and articulate in Marxist terms) the thinking of others in the leadership who were increasingly driven by a nationalist-oriented desire to both accelerate Cuba's development and challenge what they saw as a potentially quasi-colonialist Soviet desire to force Cuba into a role that suited 'the other' superpower. Moreover, with debates settled for now, PSP influence had diminished considerably without the political space to pursue their own definitions and policies or resist the more radical definitions of 'the Revolution'.

Ideologically, this meant a radical redefinition of communism, rejecting the Soviet and pro-Soviet communist parties' orthodoxy. That radicalism lay in three aspects. First, as we have seen repeatedly, the Cuban leaders rejected the notion that communism (seen since Marx and Engels in 1848 as the highest stage of historical evolution) could only come when socialism had been perfected or at least reached its logical conclusions, and, following that logic, also rejected the credo that socialism could only occur anywhere once capitalism had been fully developed, collapsing under the weight of its own contradictions. Finally, they rejected the resulting conclusion that socialism (and therefore, logically, also communism) could not occur in an undeveloped economy such as Cuba's, since, according to that orthodoxy, Cuba and the rest of Latin America were still partly in the feudal stage of historical evolution, making its post-1958 economy not fully capitalist. Therefore, since Moscow believed that Cuba's revolution could not be socialist, Cuba's impatient and uncompromising leaders – buoyed by their successful defiance of US hostility and regional hegemony and by their initial successes in revolutionizing Cuban society – were bound to reject that notion as a demeaning form of ideological colonialism.

This, therefore, made the Cuban leaders' response to the Soviet interpretation defiant and proud: taking Guevara's belief in the power of 'subjective conditions' but also taking their cue from Lenin's own redefinition of the possibility of revolution in a seemingly backward Russia (based on his notion that imperialism – which Marx could not have fully foreseen – had distorted the otherwise 'objective' expectation of a transition from capitalism, making Russia more than ready for socialist revolution), Cuba's leaders argued that the newer variants of imperialism seen in pre-1959 Cuba also made socialism more than possible in Cuba. Equally, they argued that a socialist revolution there could rapidly transcend that stage, moving towards a communist society despite 'underdevelopment', precisely because of that dependency. Indeed, that interpretation was reinforced by the emerging notions of dependency theory, which argued (especially through Andre Gunder Frank) that, because Spain in the 1500s had not been feudal but proto-capitalist, Latin America's evolution had been capitalist (with only apparent remnants of feudalism), enhanced and modernized by British and then US neo-colonialism in the nineteenth century (Frank 1967).

The Cubans' claim, however, not only was heretical in theory but also constituted an open challenge to the Soviet Union's primacy in the Socialist Bloc, Moscow having begun to argue that only one genuinely communist society (the Soviet Union) existed in the world, making other related societies socialist at best or 'people's democracies' on the road to socialism, meaning that their governing parties tended to follow the 'united front' principle, their names usually including adjectives other than 'communist'. Hence, the Cuban leadership's naming of the new party was an implicit challenge to Moscow.

Meanwhile, an even more blatant challenge to Soviet policy was already under way in the developing world when the Cuban leaders began to enact a foreign policy based on their unorthodox Marxism. Even from 1959, individual Cuban leaders (with other leaders' tolerance) were supporting rebel expeditions to neighbouring states to support a similar revolution there (Abreu Cardet 2009; Brown 2017: 47–72); now, from 1961, Cuba's foreign policy beyond US–Cuban relations (formally constrained by the 1962 agreement) and Cuban-Soviet relations (slowly shaped by commercial exchange) became focused on the idea and the practice of armed revolution. This meant that not only could, and should,

Cuba be a communist society but it was also a revolutionary's duty to challenge (US) imperialism and not settle for the comfortable 'peaceful coexistence' which Moscow had agreed.

Hence, a policy of sustained support for Cuban-style guerrilla groups (all stimulated by Guevara's famous 1960 *Guerrilla Warfare: A Method* and by the resulting notion of *foquismo*), the new theory that the leading role in the progression towards revolution (hitherto claimed by the communist parties) should be played by free-standing and mobile guerrilla groups (*focos*), spearheading a violent popular struggle, meant that the Cuban Interior Ministry housed a secret Liberation Department, run by the head of specialist intelligence Manuel Piñeiro, to train, advise, arm, supply and fund such groups all over the continent, challenging both authoritarian and democratic governments equally, challenging the United States head on and also challenging the Soviet Union side actively with 'the people in arms'. However, this was not simply the 'pure' ideology (or idealism) that it seemed. The 1962 US undertaking not to invade Cuba meant that the Cuban leaders had nothing to lose by such a challenge (other than Soviet anger, which was anyway limited by Moscow's need to continue supporting Cuba) and, if any one rebellion emerged successfully, Havana had much to gain by breaching the siege. Hence, Guevara's decision to leave Cuba in April 1965 to spearhead such a strategy in person fitted perfectly within that challenge, stimulated most recently by the speed with which the US government dispatched troops to the nearby Dominican Republic (explicitly to prevent 'a second Cuba', given the unrest there), leading Guevara to proclaim the aim of creating 'two, three, many Vietnams' all over the continent to drag the United States into a series of unwinnable wars (Guevara 1977: 598).

In January 1966, the Cuban heresy then saw the Tricontinental Conference of anti-colonial movements and parties from across the Third World, hosted in Havana but at Moscow's behest, in the hope that the Third World could be attracted towards Moscow and away from the Chinese overtures. However, the Cuban leaders, seeking to exploit the Sino-Soviet split (despite frustration at Beijing's unwillingness to support Cuba more substantially), had other ideas. The event was soon taken over by the Cuban 'line' of outright opposition to US imperialism through revolution. The Organization of Latin American Solidarity (OLAS), which the event spawned in 1967, defiantly displayed its slogan 'The duty of the revolutionary is to make the revolution', in explicit challenge to the Soviet and communist parties' line of waiting for the conditions to emerge. By 1968, therefore, this heresy was at its peak, when a public disagreement with the Venezuelan Communist Party, which criticized Cuba's involvement in the Venezuelan left's political direction and actions, demonstrated openly how far Havana and Moscow had drifted apart. Moreover, when Fidel openly accepted the justice of the Soviet-led invasion of Czechoslovakia in August, it was not the olive branch to Moscow which many then and since interpreted it as (Karol 1970: 509–10), usually reading it as a 'pay-off' for Soviet aid to bail Cuba out of the impending economic crisis, but instead a logical statement of Cuba's global posture, seeing the Czech reforms and decision to leave the Warsaw Pact as dangerously breaching the global front against imperialism. Indeed, he also expressed the hope that Moscow would do the same for Cuba if needed, a double-edged criticism of the Soviet failure to support Cuba fully in October 1962 (Bain 2019: 117–8). In March 1968, a new 'Escalante affair' surfaced when Fidel revealed publicly the existence of a treasonous 'micro-faction' (led by Escalante after returning from Czechoslovakia in 1966), which had been plotting against the Cuban leadership to change Cuban policies across the board, at home and abroad. Without specifying it, Fidel implied a conspiracy with Moscow's approval or knowledge to end the Cuban leadership's deep ideological heresy and bring Cuba more firmly into a Soviet fold.

In this sense, the fusion of (rather than tension between) ideology and pragmatism was also reflected in the 'moral economy' and the drive towards mass mobilization and 'voluntarism'. Just as the Mass Organizations had stood in for the state in the early years of the transformation, so too did voluntarism now respond not only to Guevara's notions of *conciencia* but also to the practical shortage of skilled manpower in an economy weakened continually by the emigration of the anti-Revolution middle class. Equally, the principle of moral incentives was underpinned by the practical reality that any salary increases implied by material incentives would create inflationary pressures in an economy where demand would fast outstrip the severely limited supply, given the effects of Cuba's isolation from both much of the Western world and the still limited possibilities offered by Comecon. That whole philosophy culminated eventually in the March 1968 'Revolutionary Offensive', which took state control even further by nationalizing around 55,000 small urban, mostly self-employed businesses. Since the 1963 agrarian reform had left around 30 per cent of agriculture in private (if regulated) hands, after 1968 that was all that remained of the old Cuban private sector.

Hence, the conventional classification of this phase of the revolution as 'idealist' or 'Sino-Guevarist' needs to be nuanced somewhat; while

Guevara's influence before he left Cuba in 1965 was considerable (whatever the sensationalist allegations at the time and since, there is little evidence of any split with Fidel Castro having caused that decision to depart), as the rebel leader best versed in Marxism, there was also a coincidence between what he formulated and articulated better than anyone and the spirit which drove most of that vanguard – of uncompromising defiance, nationalist determination to find and defend their own definitions of everything and challenge the former neocolonial master. Hence, it was as much the vanguard's instinctive and principled rejection of imperialism and, more importantly, colonialism of the mind and culture, which shaped Cuba's growing identification with the Third World as any slavish adherence to Guevara's ideas. Indeed, as early as 1959 and often thanks to the dynamism of Foreign Minister Raúl Roa, the leadership had sought alliances with anti-colonial rebel movements in Africa (most openly with the Algerian NLF and the Angolan MPLA) and then with newly decolonizing governments in Africa and Asia, as part of a new and independent Cuban foreign policy. That commitment saw Cuba join the Non-Aligned Movement in 1962 and obviously informed the Tricontinental Conference.

It is also pertinent to observe that, whatever apparent similarities there might have been between 1960s Cuba and communist China, there is little evidence that the latter was ever a significant model for the former. Guevara and others admired what they knew of China and his emphasis on the peasantry's revolutionary potential took heart from Maoism, but relations with Beijing were never close or without tension. That probably reflected Chinese suspicions about Cuban-Soviet relations and also Cuban reluctance to allow growing disenchantment with Moscow to seriously threaten Soviet willingness to support despite everything (Bain 2017).

That same 'Third-Worldism' now also found its expression in the Revolution's evolving cultural policy, which moved towards a desire to create both an authentically 'Cuban' culture and a militantly committed one, and which therefore demanded such commitment from Cuba's artists and writers. This meant that what was often feared and described as Soviet-style Stalinism in the cultural world was actually the influence of the ex-guerrillas (rather than the pre-1959 PSP) in their defiant rejection of a cultural colonialism. The Havana Cultural Congress of January 1968 expressed that position clearly, with its focus on the role of the intellectual in the Third World; the overall lack of any conventional drift or pressure towards the feared 'socialist realism' in culture also reflected that posture, since it was militancy and a non-adherence to the mores and models of Western cultural poles which was desired, and not Soviet-style representations of heroic workers although the attraction of Soviet models continued to pervade many areas (Loss 2013). Those same fears, however, arose from the 1967 centralization of publishing in one single national body, the Instituto del Libro, seen by some Cuban writers and many outside observers as a step towards monolithic control of content or form. What it really reflected, however, was a drive for efficiency and for the best means of spreading active literacy across the island (Kumaraswami and Kapcia 2012: 95–8). However, in 1968, two UNEAC prizes were awarded by an international jury to controversial books: in poetry, Heberto Padilla's *Fuera del Juego* (Out of the Game) and a play by Antón Arrufat, *Los Siete contra Tebas* (Seven against Thebes), about a society under siege. UNEAC acted on its promise to publish both, but added prologue disclaimers objecting to the books' questionable political tenor. When the decision was made to dispense with prize juries selected from non-Cuban intellectuals, it raised the old 1961 fears of a creeping Stalinism in cultural policy.

At this stage, and given these seemingly pertinent issues, it is worth reflecting on, and developing more deeply, the surprising significance that culture seems constantly to have had within the Revolution, in terms of focus, expenditure and profile, the latter even including the surprising degree of autonomy and political authority enjoyed by the prominent actors within the cultural apparatus. While there is extensive literature on the importance of culture in different regimes, ranging from the common 'bread and circuses' approach (of culture – widely defined – distracting 'the people' from rebelling by entertaining them) to the alleged power of an imposed culture to shape the (passive) population's brains and responses (largely extending the notion of totalitarianism), the Cuban case is interesting because there has been no consistent and unbroken 'official' approach to, or policy for, culture within 'the Revolution', despite the fact (as already observed) that the 26 July Movement before 1959 always advocated the need for a (never-defined) 'Cuban culture' (Kumaraswami and Kapcia 2012). In other words, if culture was such a significant element of all plans, why was there no consistent policy on what it was, why it was important or how it should be channelled?

As this study has already recounted, one of the most fundamental explanations is the political and ideological breadth of the revolutionary alliance, most explicitly in the early years but still evident during the following decades, which would at least partly explain the lack of consensus on policy. However, the underlying issue of precisely *why* culture was (and long has been) seen as crucial is not easily fitted into that explanation. To discover possibly deeper explanations for that, we must look at the historical experience of both pre-1959 and post-1959 Cuba to uncover some continuities and some ruptures.

Mention of 'continuities' immediately brings us to the historically important case of Martí and, beyond him, the role that culture played in the emergence of a shared sense of a Cuban identity in the nineteenth century even at a time when the political forces to act on that identity were inadequate. Taking the latter issue first, one possible approach is to reflect on the many experiences (not least in the well-recorded cases of European nationalism) of colonized societies where, several decades before a political manifestation of nationalism emerged as a consensual force for change, a nascent cultural nationalism could be seen emerging through the attempts of the society's composers, poets or visual artists to incorporate elements of the society's popular (or usually folk) culture into their work, which was otherwise generally following the norms and the canon established outside that society in well-developed centres of cultural leadership. One might observe that what those exponents were essentially doing by that incorporation process was suggesting that, even if there was as yet no consensus about the notion that the colonizing power might be at least part of colony's historical 'problem' (the prerequisite of any forceful challenge to that power), as opposed to the colonialists' justification of that power being 'the solution' to the 'problem' of the colonized, it was possible that, in some respects at least, the colonized might not entirely be a 'problem'. Hence, building a sense of pride in some aspects of the colonized people's own culture became part of those artists' wider mission. Examples of that abound: the work of Chopin, Smetana, Sibelius, Dvořak and Matejko, for example, are some of the best known from Europe, but one might equally bring in other examples from the Americas – in Argentina, the epic poem *Martín Fierro* and Sarmiento's *Facundo*; in Mexico, José Joaquín Fernández de Lizardi's *El periquillo sarniento* (often seen as Latin America's first novel) and the *costumbrista* artist Ramón Torres Méndez; in Venezuela, Andrés Bello's dictionary and even in the United States, Longfellow's stylized representations in *The Song of Hiawatha* (Franco 1967). In other words, those artists were in a sense precursors and pioneers of a wider and deeper sense of pride (and resentment and anger) which would emerge in political form in due course, as the structural circumstances encouraged and eventually allowed space for that. Hence, culture has long constituted a powerful force for, and expression of, an emerging sense of difference and identity, and therefore of belonging, partly based on familiarity (of folk tunes learned in childhood, or whatever), but also based on the power of the imagination, to develop the ability to imagine in a shared way a different reality: once imagined, that reality had a greater chance of being realized, perhaps.

That, in turn, brings us to a key aspect of any ideology – the latter broadly defined as a shared 'world view' that explains the 'world' as it has been, as it is and as it should be; a view that mixes beliefs, values, codes and ideas into a shared definition and a drive to action (Kapcia 2000: 12–19). If that definition has any value, then it stands to reason that culture, which addresses and expresses what Cubans would call the *imaginario* (the imaginary) must play a vital role in shaping and developing that shared view, not least the imagination and what it imagines, with a greater persuasive power on emotions than any written ideas. Imagination can allow the individual to conceive of things autonomously and dynamically, while written ideas can by definition often be more static and limited. Hence, the power of the *imaginario* was already being felt and expressed in Cuba before any clear and shared and strong sense of separatism emerged unchallenged. The contribution of Cuban composers such as José Mauri Estévez, Gonzalo Roig, Alejandro García Caturla and Ernesto Lecuona, who increasingly brought African-origin rhythms and instruments into their work long before intellectual and political elites had accepted the black contribution to a Cuban identity, is an outstanding example (Carpentier 2004).

Hence, culture was already central to any emerging consensus for change before 1959. That was where Martí's importance came into the picture, for his unquestioned position in the popular collective Cuban *imaginario* after his death, which saw a direct relationship between the acknowledged leading poet (widely respected outside Cuba for his pioneering poetry), the influential and eloquent chronicler (using his writing to persuade), and the heroic exponent and then leader of the successful independence movement, privileged the creative mixture of culture, identity and politics which throughout the twentieth century shaped the emergence of both radical approaches to political change and the many currents of nationalism. Hence, the Movement's acknowledgement of the importance of culture already reflected a felt reality.

Given this, it was perhaps inevitable that culture should go on to figure prominently in all the evolving plans of the Revolution, however the latter were defined. When we add to that the growing importance attributed by many rebels (not least Guevara and Fidel) to *conciencia* and subjective conditions in shaping and radicalizing the population's support for the process, then that prominence becomes even more significant. Culture, in other words, mattered fundamentally (Kumaraswami 2015). Indeed, that was precisely why it became the focus of so much attention, not least to cultural democratization, the 'other' message of Fidel's 1961 *Palabras* (when stressing the need to develop all Cubans' artistic and creative talents), and the motive behind another characteristic educational campaign of this period: what was called the *piratería* (pirating) of books.

In 1964, after Fidel had discussed with activists in Havana University's Politics Department what textbooks they recommended for the vastly increased numbers of students resulting from massification, 'missionaries' were dispatched to Europe armed with cash to purchase single copies of those books which were then brought back, translated, printed and distributed free of charge to the students as *Ediciones Revolucionarias* (revolutionary editions) of the original text, deliberately flouting international copyright laws as an anti-colonial statement. Shortly afterwards, a similar approach was adopted for works of literature, the best of world literature being brought back to Cuba, translated and reprinted (often on cheap newspaper materials), to be sold cheaply to the newly literate population, thus ensuring that they too shared in the benefits of 'good' literature (Kumaraswami and Kapcia 2012: 83–5).

THE STATE AND THE MEANING OF 'THE REVOLUTION'

By the end of the 1960s, therefore, Cuba had changed substantially in so many ways, the rebel leadership shaping a new nation according to both the original project but also in response to the constraints and opportunities of the Cold War, developing a distinctly sui generis version of both 'revolution' and 'socialism'. As a result of the earlier battles and the whole emphasis on constant, if not Trotsky's 'permanent', revolution and of the continuing processes of transformation, the structures of governance and representation remained in a still inchoate state. Governance, if anything, took second place to the need to mobilize, which was, in itself, often deemed a form of 'revolutionary' governance, using voluntarism and the famous and often repeated concept of 'direct democracy', which usually referred to rhetorical exchanges in the Plaza de la Revolución between Fidel and the listening crowd (Bengelsdorf 1994: 79–89).

However, local experiments continued apace, JUCEI being replaced in 1966 by the equally experimental Poder Local (Local Power), until it too fell out of favour for its perceived inadequacy. Nonetheless, that latter experiment did offer one element that would become characteristic of all subsequent forms of local governance: the regular requirement for all elected representatives to be publicly accountable to constituents via the *rendición de cuentas* (literally 'rendering of accounts').

By 1968, government, governance and power at national level were all clearly in the hands of the former guerrillas, which in turn helped shape the tenor and principles of this period. However, 'the party' was less dynamic as a power structure than it would later become – or than seemingly similar Socialist Bloc communist parties were – with the 'inner circle' still dominating the PCC's ruling councils and Movement activists still in the ascendancy locally. However, the lack of a PCC congress in 1970 (as scheduled by its own constitution) indicated that internal debates were only temporarily settled, and that the leadership did not feel the need to be accountable to a nationally structured party to drive forward its version of Revolution. Hence, in the vacuum, the Mass Organizations continued to fill gaps, providing human capital and labour for the many mobilizations, and enlisting ordinary Cubans in the revolutionary process, although the CTC continued to be problematic and to exercise little national power or influence. That latter reality arose less from the pre-1959 CTC's problematic history (as in 1959–62) than from the problem familiar to the Socialist Bloc: uncertainty about the precise role of a workers' union in a self-defined 'workers' state'. Hence, the CTC was now seen by the leadership more as a force for mobilization (including for labour) than for protecting workers although locally the latter often functioned extremely well (Fuller 1992; Zeitlin 1970a; Ludlam 2018). That top-down purpose was, of course, reinforced by Peña's position in the CTC leadership after 1961.

Who or what, therefore, enjoyed authority or wielded power? And what did the still-emerging state look like? Precisely because the second half of the 1960s, despite the apparent consolidation suggested by the PCC's creation, saw more and not less instability and transformation, the state structures still remained embryonic at best, the defensive and security apparatus notwithstanding. The notoriety in the period 1965–8 of the camps called *Unidades Militares de Ayuda a la Producción* (UMAP, Military Units for Aiding Production) being used increasingly for forced 're-education' of supposedly problematic Cubans, such as juvenile delinquents or 'drop-outs', homosexuals and, supposedly, uncooperative religious leaders, suggested that in that respect a defender or coercive state was certainly stronger than in the early years. These developments indicated that the state's purpose of ensuring 'defence' could, and perhaps might inevitably, be extended to include the need for 'internal defence', to be used against opposition deemed a threat to the state's other declared purposes. Indeed, the strength and effectiveness of the emerging organs of law and order (notably the National Revolutionary Police (PNR) and the security Dirección General de Inteligencia (known as G2), built by Camilo Cienfuegos in 1959 and Ramiro Valdés from 1961, above all) indicated the evolving state's priority given to defence.

Overall, however, this period was one of state stasis, with little progress towards a consolidated infrastructure that might suggest stability but also stagnation and the long-feared bureaucratic inertia. Instead, what seemed to be happening in many people's eyes was an explosion of bureaucratization (Bengelsdorf 1994: 92–8). For the bureaucracy had indeed grown, as was always necessary to ensure some sort of functioning network of provision, but also as was inevitable to enact and then ensure centralization and nationalization. However, this was when 'bureaucracy' became a dirty word, as seen in the 1966 public campaign against it. Yet what was often seen as the inefficiencies or petty controlling and blocking carried out by low-level bureaucrats was often the result of the inability of a hastily trained and politically willing workforce to cope with the contradictory pressures of a steadily multiplying set of ministries, Mass Organizations and committees for everything (designed invariably to ensure the correct decision-making). Equally, of course, those same bureaucrats could be 'time servers', using their little island of power in the system to give them authority and a degree of leeway and space.

Hence, while it could be said that the state at that time did more or less perform its functions of ensuring defence, security, stability, well-being, governance and participation, it never did so with any real efficiency (apart from coercion – though even that could be random – and protection against natural disasters), but did so with some often impressive (political) effectiveness.

As for decision-making power, that was clearly held by the ex-guerrilla inner circle, with a handful of activists from the *Llano* and more trusted PSP leaders. They largely held power by default, but more importantly because of their historic authority and (gradually) their ability to persuade enough Cubans of their determination to both protect and provide. It was as much an affirmation of faith and loyalty as a recognition of their effectiveness.

The only real difference between this period and the preceding one was that the PCC now existed with some degree of formal authority at least at two levels: the national leadership and central committee (essentially the same as the old inner circle) and the grassroots *núcleos*, now mostly free of PSP cadre domination. There were still local and national dissenters, as the 'micro-faction' affair demonstrated (confirming Escalante's ability to find and coordinate like-minded activists in the PCC's middle and upper reaches), and the grassroots tensions still emerged where the PSP had once been strong. However, for the most part, power and authority were uncontested.

As for the emerging matrix, vertical as well as horizontal, the latter were still more inchoate and in a process of formation than the former, if only because the vertical structures were still the most vital for decision-making but also for the debates (and battles) over definitions, policies and even power. With the PCC still unclear in its structures and vertical chains of communication, its lowest layers tended to vary in the extent of local power and authority, depending on personality, local history and accidents of membership. That, therefore, left the Mass Organizations still in a potentially more influential position at the lower levels because they could claim to be more representative than the PCC, reflecting better the grassroots ideas and complaints. Although the CTC and FMC enjoyed national authority (not least through their leaders, the PSP's Peña and Espín), the CDRs, lacking such a profile nationally, put their efforts by default more into local processes than national ones. Hence, there was still a high level of cooperation between these bodies, and occasionally with the local PCC and UJC *núcleos*, but it still tended to be contingent and not yet systematic.

Returning therefore to this study's continual thread, by late 1969 what did 'revolution' or 'the Revolution' now mean? The answer lay in the public proclamation on 10 October 1968 of '100 years of revolution', commemorating the first rebellion for independence in October 1868, making it clear that the post-1959 revolution was not just radically socialist but also firmly embedded in a Cuban heritage, the natural and necessary culmination of the two previous 'real' revolutions for national independence, that is the birth of a long-overdue 'Cuban nation': the 1868–78 rebellion and Martí's 1895 rebellion. Hence, 'the Revolution' now had explicit roots in Cuban national history, organically related to the present, as well as an implicit future in communism, seen as the only possible means to achieve true equality and Cuban independence. Ironically, therefore, when the New Left in the global North extolled the Cuban Revolution during the 1968 'student revolt', for offering an attractively maverick version of socialism or communism, the Revolution itself was being redefined domestically as an essentially patriotic manifestation of socialism, with a specifically Cuban communism seen as the culmination of a history of struggles for independence, sovereignty and identity, against different imperialisms.

5

DEBATE II

1970–5

While it was the 1970 *zafra*'s spectacular failure (spectacular because so much had publicly been staked on it) which, according to most the literature on that period, stimulated the rethink that led to the 1970s' 'institutionalization', in many respects that failure was simply the last straw. Failure and internal stresses had long been evident, in growing absenteeism in the workforce (partly through disillusion and ennui, and partly because moral incentives did not encourage commitment or productivity), in many young Cubans' tendency to 'drop out' (forcing a clampdown on 'anti-social' behaviour and wilful unemployment, expressed in the 1971 *Ley contra Vagancia*, Law against Idling), and in talk of delinquency (Barreto 1984) and in a growing economic inefficiency. The Revolutionary Offensive, intended to accelerate the drive towards the 1970 goal, counter-productively guaranteed that the goal would not be reached, the measure's clumsiness leading to breakdowns in the systems of supply and production (Azicri 1988: 134). Hence, it was really a combination of processes, problems and pressures which led to the rethink. The 1970 failure was the most prominent (encouraging Fidel's public admission of blame and offer to resign), but others included the growing economic crisis, the lack of consumer goods arising from the limited Cuban–Soviet link, popular exhaustion at continuing austerity and Soviet pressure (whether through the ex-PSP contingent or the emerging class of pro-Soviet or Soviet-trained 'technocrats') to conform more to Socialist Bloc precepts and abandon heterodoxy. Finally, of course, the 1962–5 debates had only ever been temporarily and conditionally settled; since success had not come, debate was bound to resurface.

Finally, the die was cast in 1972 when Comecon at last allowed Cuba into the club; since the previous refusal had been based on Cuba's unacceptable economic policies, we can assume that certain guarantees had been given by Havana to enable that rethink. Whatever the case, the moment had probably come for reassessment, which as ever meant yet another internal debate. This time, however, the debate was less visible, strictly limited to largely within the PCC's upper reaches and the inner circle of power, which meant that few Cubans participated and even fewer knew of the debate's existence. . That invisibility may also have reflected a reality that part of the debate was already settled above the PCC's head once Comecon changed tack.

Another perhaps revealing area of unproblematic change was in foreign policy, where three things happened (Domínguez 1989b). First, Cuba's relations with the United States entered a less hostile phase, Washington being now prepared to tolerate Latin American countries' recognition of, and trade with, Cuba. Secondly, the Cuban leadership became publicly less critical of the Soviet Union's lack of support for Third World revolution; in 1973, Fidel shocked the Non-Aligned Movement (NAM) summit in Algiers by supporting the Soviet Union's claims to be an ally to the Third World, while Cuba shifted its Middle East policy into a closer alignment with Moscow's, breaking relations with Israel. Finally, the old insurrectionary policy in Latin America, encouraging armed struggle, was seemingly quietly shelved, better relations with governments in the region now being sought.

The latter shift, however, suggested that these changes were not necessarily attributable to either Soviet pressure or any victory by the more orthodox elements in internal debates. For that old policy had actually begun to change in 1968 when Cuba recognized the political advantages and possibilities of Peru's military-led 'revolution' under Velasco Alvarado, alienating one sector of the previously pro-Cuba Peruvian Communist Party (*Bandera Roja*), which thereafter rejected the Cuban model for a Maoist one, eventually becoming the notorious Sendero Luminoso.

The reason for that shift was simple. The Peruvian regime (coming from a more socially aware and inclusive nationalist perspective, as the latest example of what is often termed 'the reformist military', based on a radical developmentalism in the new military school) was willing to challenge Washington and recognize Cuba's government. While that new attitude was paralleled by similar contemporary shifts in other 'new style' military regimes in the region (Bolivia, Ecuador and Panama), it also reflected a wider shift in Latin American politics, towards a more defiant attitude to the United States, as seen in Frei's Christian Democrat government in Chile from 1964, whose decision to allow trade with Cuba led to recognition in 1969, and Andrés Pérez's 1974-elected Acción Democrática government in Venezuela in the wake of the OPEC oil crisis. These and other moves reflected the new US mood, now tolerant of Latin American trading with Cuba. Once Jimmy Carter was elected the US president in 1976, he sought to mend fences with Latin America, resulting in a partial first-stage low-level recognition of the Cuban government, setting up the permanent interest-sections notionally under the auspices of third-party embassies in separate buildings. Therefore, Cuba's policy had to change anyway, with the embargo being slowly breached and with Havana having more to gain from constructive dialogue than outright hostility.

Moreover, by 1972–3 it was clear that the old insurrectionary policy had largely failed, as the many guerrilla attempts to repeat the Cuban example had ended not only in Guevara's death but also mostly in collapse or defeat, or, as with Nicaragua's Sandinistas, a fundamental change of strategy from rural to urban struggle, eventually bearing fruit in July 1979. Furthermore, 1970–3 saw Allende's Unidad Popular coalition elected in Chile, which was widely seen as the most promising example of the 'peaceful road to socialism' long advocated by Moscow and the region's communists. Their success in being elected and then, despite US sanctions and pressure and a deteriorating economy, their increasingly electoral popularity in 1973 suggested that 'armed struggle' should generally give way to electoral politics. Ultimately, of course, September 1973 saw Allende overthrown and killed by the US-backed military, leading Fidel to declare that it confirmed that only with arms could a revolution be made (Castro 1973). Nonetheless, the Latin American political scene was by then more promising, offering Cuba more likely outlets for trade and normal relations than the guerrilla option.

It thus seemed by 1974 that the 1960s' maverick radicalism and defiant resistance were well and truly over. However, even if all debates (however limited) seemed to be over, with everything seemingly moving relentlessly towards a widely assumed 'Sovietization', the reality was otherwise. First, the delay in holding the PCC's scheduled five-yearly congress (due in 1970) indicated that arguments were still raging since the purpose of all such congresses was to legitimize decisions agreed in preceding internal debates. Secondly, it actually took over five years after the 1970 *zafra* crisis for some of the more convincing indicators of shift to emerge, the eventual congress (1975) being accompanied by a new economic strategy, the Sistema de Dirección y Planificación de la Economía (SDPE, System for Economic Management and Planning) and in, 1976, the apparently Soviet-style pyramid electoral structure of governance and (indirect) representation, Órganos de Poder Popular (OPP, Organs of People's Power).

There was also one further area where the outcomes of debate seemed to suggest one direction (greater 'Stalinization'), whereas closer examination suggests that they represented something quite different. This was the always different world of culture, which reflected a fundamental truth: that, while defined 'phases' often made some sense for interpreting political or economic patterns, any perceived cultural phases often did not correspond. Certainly, this 1970–5 period of debate in other areas seemed unparalleled in culture, where the preceding 'Third-Worldist' militancy (expressed loudly in the weekly youth cultural magazine *Caimán Barbudo*) was ended suddenly by the notorious *caso Padilla* (Padilla affair) of 1968–71, generating in turn the grim *quinquenio gris* (literally 'grey five years'). This period was launched by the Congress on Education and Culture of April 1971, an event that was scheduled to deal solely with education, but to which 'culture' was added at the last minute in an angry response to the outcome of the latest stage in the cultural authorities' battles with Padilla.

When he was briefly detained and then 'invited' to deliver a public *autocrítica* (self-criticism) to UNEAC members, an open protest letter was written by formerly pro-Revolution European or Europe-based intellectuals, accusing the Cuban government of Stalinist practices. The renamed congress then adopted a strident tone, explicitly condemning both the protest and also the un-revolutionary and 'indecent' behaviour of homosexuals. The resulting widespread view in the foreign media that saw a 'Sovietization' of Cuban cultural policy (Franco 2002) was enhanced when the CNC, under the ex-guerrilla Luis Pavón from May 1971, launched what became a five-year period of *parametración* (imposition of parameters), with greater restrictions placed on artistic expression in some, but not all, areas of culture, but most evidently in theatre and literature and on selected artists and writers (Gallardo Saborido 2009). Several were marginalized and denied the possibility of publication, performance or exhibition (Kumaraswami and Kapcia 2012: 107-15). Furthermore, the 1971 Casa de las Américas prize was awarded to Cuban literature's main, if not only, exemplar of the feared 'socialist realism', Manuel Cofiño López's *La última mujer y el próximo combate* (The Last Woman and the Next Battle). What would later be termed the *quinquenio gris* indeed seemed to herald what many had feared in 1961.

Inevitably, however, the whole issue was much more complex than the immediate reaction and subsequent terminology suggested. For, as we have seen, the pressure on Padilla had begun in 1968. In retrospect, what seems to have happened was that both authors fell foul not so much of 'Stalinism' (of which there was little or no evidence in the cultural apparatus, PSP people having long ceased to exercise any authority) as of the militant 'Third-Worldism', led not by the political authorities (though Fidel did become embroiled personally in the affair) but by the politicized cultural authorities.

In other words, Padilla and Arrufat were deemed guilty not of the familiar Soviet 'sin' of 'decadent bourgeois' tendencies, but, rather, of a cultural mimetism, of slavishly following the cultural models set by Western Europe's traditional colonialist Meccas rather than being guided by the priorities of revolutionary Cuba. In Padilla's case, his 1960s experience as correspondent for *Prensa Latina*, the Cuban press agency, had allowed him to travel across Eastern Europe, witnessing a very different version of socialism from Cuba's and meeting artists and writers on the edge of political acceptability. Both he and Arrufat also belonged to what many politically introverted radicals had begun to see as a 'tainted' generation, afflicted with what Guevara in 1965 had famously described as their 'original sin' as pre-Revolutionary bourgeois intellectuals (Guevara 1965): while developing their art before 1959, they had lived and worked abroad and looked to foreign models for inspiration. Indeed, most of those marginalized in 1971–6 also belonged to that generation.

There was, moreover, a further dimension to it all: Pavón's own role. From May 1971, he had begun to use his relative autonomy within the CNC to exercise his own power, following his own criteria, based less on Stalinism than his guerrilla background, evidently sharing with other ex-*combatientes* a distaste for others' unconventional or 'socially irresponsible' behaviour. Such attitudes had created the notorious misuse of the UMAP camps, outlawed wilful idleness and condemned long hair in young males. Hence, the clampdown on homosexuals in culture (a significant number of those marginalized after 1971 were known to be homosexual) arose from a mixture of a military mindset and a narrow-minded determination to develop a distinctly 'Cuban' culture, not aping the culturally colonizing poles of world culture. In fact, just as the UMAP were closed after UNEAC representations (led by the ex-PSP Guillén) to the Cuban leadership (Kumaraswami and Kapcia 2012: 26), UNEAC helped end the *quinquenio* by supporting successful individual legal challenges to marginalized writers' loss of rights (ibid.: 120-1). Moreover, Pavón's remit was limited to the CNC and those genres under its control; cinema remained defiantly outside those restrictions, as did Casa de las Américas where some of the marginalized were given 'refuge' in employment.

Therefore, however much this cultural *parametración* seemed to reflect a wider 'Sovietization', it actually represented the apogee or nadir of the preceding patterns of militant Third-Worldism and a defiant strand of often narrow cultural nationalism, confirming once again that the evolution of policies for culture did not fit easily into wider patterns of thinking or policy. Hence, while debate might continue elsewhere, the only debate in culture in those years of transition and uncertainty was the coexistence of (but never really a dialogue between) different ways of thinking about the kind of culture Cuba should have.

Beyond culture, however, (as already seen) there was indeed a sustained debate, which directly affected, and largely delayed and even halted, the processes of consolidating the structures of political power, governance and representation. The debate effectively delayed both experiments (the usual prelude to decisions about local structures) and crucial decisions for most of this five-year interim period. Hence, no replacement was yet found for Poder Local although experiments would take place in Matanzas in June 1974 for the OPP electoral and representation system which emerged in 1976. Within the PCC, meanwhile, the limited debates only really ended around 1973 when preparations at last began for the long-delayed congress in 1975.

While those debates were often essentially ideological (about principles and definitions), they also reflected the unresolved internal tensions over access to power and authority. That was clear in 1972 in the one area where we can see decisions taken that did substantially affect the Revolution's subsequent direction: the economy. For the decision to allow Comecon membership was partly taken to cement the authority inside the decision-making circles of the ex-PSP elements and the Soviet-trained economic 'technocrats', who had opposed the ex-guerrillas' preference for an uncomfortably heterodox approach to Cuba's future economy. Once Cuba was linked to Comecon's trade structures, it was inevitable that the resulting material benefits (consumer goods, investment and reliable markets) would shift Cuban opinion at all levels towards one line of argument and one group of decision-makers, especially as the authority of the heterodox (including Fidel) had been weakened by the 1968–70 crisis and shortages. Moreover, as the preparations proceeded for the PCC congress, the prospect of a more solid structure of ideological power or authority threatened to bypass that historic authority; by 1974, tensions seemed less an issue of factions or a struggle for control than a shift in the balance and bases of authority, the result of a slow consolidation process.

This period's dialectical nature, with deep and fierce disagreement over Cuba's future path, made it a time when the definition of 'the Revolution' was never openly debated, but when ongoing debate continued under the surface between the same poles as in the 1960s: a radical 'Cubanist' and revolutionary definition of a popular process of deep change and nation building (which some continued to argue was necessary despite the 1970 failure, attributable in their view to a conjuncture of several processes, events and pressures) against a definition aiming for a more gradualist, static, stable and stabilizing, and therefore more materialist, system of protection, support, involvement and governance. One indication of the subterranean debate was the strange survival of an evident *guerrillerismo* in the formal discourse at a time when it might have been expected to disappear (Clayfield 2019).

6

INSTITUTIONALIZATION, CONSOLIDATION AND GREATER ORTHODOXY, 1975–85

With those post-1970 debates largely settled (although, of course, such debates in the Cuban system have never been 'finally' settled), 1975–7 saw new patterns of thinking, policy and political structure. Usually given the term 'institutionalization', the decade until 'Rectification' came in 1984–6 meant a period of consolidation, slowing down the 1960s sometimes frenetic pace of change and finally building more solid and more permanent institutions. In retrospect, that shift might well have come anyway after 1970, since ordinary Cubans could not withstand much longer the pressures and disruptions of constant frenetic mobilization, with most Cubans craving some sort of material satisfaction as well as ideological comfort or certainty. In other words, over a decade of a revolution which 'fed the soul' but never fully fed 'the body' to allow comfort and recreation had left many hankering after the reverse: feeding the body and leaving the soul to take care of itself or to rely on material satisfaction (Kapcia, 2009).

'Institutionalization', however, had always been feared by some of the more radical rebel leaders as possibly opening the door to future Escalantes, using stronger and more permanent structures as sites for exercising their individual and group power. Indeed, the decade did see some rehabilitation of those proposing gradualism in the early 1960s, often now rising to positions of influence in quieter times. Equally, the Soviet leadership had clearly hoped to influence the debates' outcome, less by threat or ultimatum (accepting Soviet advice or risking chaos) than by setting in motion the internal Comecon-driven pressures for more orthodox thinking. By 1975, Comecon membership was already making a difference to the availability of material goods, and a new generation of those professionally trained in Socialist Bloc higher education was making its voice heard in lower and middle levels of many structures.

Since economic pressures were the strongest, it is logical to start there in explaining the new phase's character and direction. Essentially, what began in 1975 was a rejection of most, if not all, of the principles and approaches of the 1960s so-called moral economy. Instead of the earlier model's rigid centralization, the new economy (probably approved by Raúl, but directed by Humberto Pérez, a more orthodox guerrilla-turned-technocrat, and overseen by Carlos Rafael Rodríguez) would become more devolved, like the Socialist Bloc's 'decentralized market socialism', with a slightly more consumerist approach based on Comecon's product exchange mechanisms. These were already generating increased imports of the manufactured goods which were hitherto out of Cuba's reach; by 1980, Hungary and Poland accounted for around half of that new trade (Díaz Vázquez 1985: 27). Hence, with more goods available to Cubans, the previous restrictions on material incentives were abandoned, along with the principles of *conciencia*, which meant that wage differentials could now be applied, allowing for personal ambition to result in extra income.

Because the old system had so clearly failed to achieve productivity (Mesa-Lago 1974: 38–40), this easing of pressure was accompanied by an unprecedented opening to the global economy beyond Comecon. Although Western Europe and Canada had traded with Cuba throughout the 1960s despite US pressure, that trade was often more symbolic than economically significant, given Cuba's lack of credit or hard currency to buy imports (Hennessy and Lambie 1993; Roy 2009). Now, however, the Cuban government sought commercial loans on the global markets. Where trade did matter more was with Latin America, now much more open for business with Cuba with US approval after 1971. By the late 1970s, many Latin American governments had started to trade normally, allowing some US companies' Latin American subsidiaries to export to Cuba.

As a result of the new economic ordinance, trade and material benefits, the Cuban economy improved markedly, as did most Cubans' living standards. While this eventually created tensions, which led to the reshaping of policy in 1984–6, it gave substance to the now more visible achievement of greater social equality, as material wherewithal confirmed that equality was not just about legality and attitudes. This coincided with the steady replacement of lost expertise in healthcare through a costly training process, enabling a visible improvement in health standards beyond the early benefits of health education and prevention. In another curious twist, however, the long-standing principle of linking higher education to guaranteed employment now shifted policy away from the early 'massification' towards a more Soviet-style specialization, with greater selectivity that made university entry commensurate with available employment. Socially, therefore, the early 1980s saw a mixed picture: evident improvement for most (making that period seem later to be something of a 'golden age'), alongside growing doubts about principles possibly abandoned.

'Institutionalization' was much more accurate in politics, where consolidation meant building firm and permanent institutions, ending the 1960s somewhat makeshift and disruptive mobilization-based involvement. There were several dimensions to this. The first (and most noticeable) was the PCC. For its first decade, it had led a somewhat hollow existence, operating effectively at the top, where the *Buró Político* and Central Committee acted to channel the views and influence of the former Movement activists, while local *núcleos* acted as sounding boards for the upper layers (rather than active feedback mechanisms) and as vehicles for mobilizing the committed. Without the necessary five-year party congress in 1970–4, no moves were made to change this until it became clear that a consensus of sorts (even if only temporary, as ever) was emerging. Hence, in December 1975, the first congress finally took place, with membership of the higher structures elected for the next five years. One result was that grassroots membership was vastly increased, rising from 50,000 in 1965, through 101,000 in 1970 and then 203,000 in 1975, finally reaching 443,000 in 1981 (Domínguez 1978: 321; Azicri 1988: 79), making for a larger, and thus theoretically, more responsive and accountable structure.

The PCC's ruling structures also expanded to extend membership of the *Buró Político* and Central Committee beyond the ex-guerrillas to include ex-PSP activists (now welcomed back into the fold at all levels, with a new authority from having been 'proved right' in the 1960s' debates and with Soviet backing) and increasingly numerous younger Socialist Bloc-trained Cubans. There was also a new Secretariat as an adjunct to the *Buró*, probably aimed at devolving some of Fidel's decision-making power to more notionally reliable leaders and soon becoming a *Buró* executive committee, taking decisions without reference to the 'parent' body (Gonzalez 1976). Another accompanying feature was the growth of several permanent and well-staffed Central Committee departments, to research, discuss and ideologically recommend issues to the Committee. As these were increasingly run by committee or *Buró* members, they soon enjoyed semi-autonomous authority and power, as sites for the long-feared *apparatchiks*. Indeed, Cuba's ruling structure of political power and ideological authority gradually began to resemble those of the Socialist Bloc, with the same terminology, rules and categories. Once again, therefore, institutionalization would prove double edged.

What followed, arising from the congress's decisions, was the Revolution's first Constitution in 1976. Until then, the 1940 Constitution (on the basis of which the rebellion had been fought) had remained formally in place, with a series of *Leyes Fundamentales* (seen legally as amendments) updating legislation in accordance with the ever-changing new reality and growing radicalization. Now, after seventeen years of this ad hoc approach to constitutionality, a new charter was drafted, approved by referendum and then enacted. Like many constitutions, it was essentially retrospective, legitimizing the changes realized since January 1959 and, on that basis, laying down the rules of future political behaviour and rights. As well as codifying the post-1959 ordinance, echoing the Bloc patterns in its explicit debt to Marxism–Leninism with the PCC taking a 'leading role' (although the Cuban term was *rector* or occasionally *dirigente*, both possibly also meaning 'guiding'), and confirming the one-party state, it also established the rules for an electoral system at last, the OPP, or Organs of People's Power.

Again, this seemed to echo the Soviet pyramid structure of representation. At the lowest (municipal) level, delegates were directly elected by their constituents from a list of acceptable candidates (one per district) drawn up by a commission which formally excluded the PCC. Thereafter, the higher assemblies (provincial and national) were elected by municipal delegates rather than grassroots constituents, making both assemblies indirectly elected. Moreover, the crucial National Assembly would meet only twice a year for two weeks at a time, with one clear function: to ratify, rather than debate and decide. The only obvious difference from the Bloc models was the process of a six-monthly *rendición de cuentas* at every level, with delegates obliged to defend their record in each assembly to an audience of their electors. This mechanism had been tried in earlier experiments of local representation and seemed to Cuba's leaders and local activists to ensure a desirable degree of accountability, so it soon constituted a distinctly Cuban element to an otherwise seemingly imported model.

Therefore, the 1970s seemed to have ushered in what many saw as 'Sovietization' – of ideas, models, people, principles and even power and privilege. Even the formerly rebel-oriented FAR had been restructured in late 1973 along Soviet lines (Domínguez 1978: 352–3). Certainly, it all seemed far away from the Revolution familiar to Cubans and the outside world in the 1960s. As if to confirm that, and in keeping with the strictures of the 1971 Congress on Education and Culture, many of those associated with Guevara's thinking – not least in *Pensamiento Crítico* in 1967–71 (Artaraz 2009) – found themselves marginalized and ostracized, unable to publish or work in their specialist areas of expertise; even Guevara's writings ceased to be easily available in bookshops, found only in libraries and personal collections. Indeed, the only memory of Che was in the huge poster in the *Plaza de la Revolución* and the annual commemoration of his death, plus the ritual morning assembly chant of schoolchildren about seeking to 'be like Che'. He was too symbolically important and too well loved by most Cubans to be ignored and made into a 'non-person', and many PCC members at all levels still deeply admired him, his example and his ideas, but those who had once fiercely opposed his perspectives and unorthodox readings of Marxism certainly did not want his memory to be more than a symbolic presence.

Abroad, too, the new Cuba tailored its approach to the United States, closer to Soviet policy, although, as with foreign policy generally from 1970, also responding to regional and hemisphere changes: for Carter's election in 1976 heralded a significant (if brief) shift in US attitudes. Since even the Nixon Administration had reputedly considered changing policy towards Cuba, the fact that it now changed substantially in a US political culture chastened and even penitent after Vietnam and Watergate should have been no surprise. Whatever the cause, US–Cuban relations did suddenly improve, culminating in the 1977 agreement to move in stages towards eventual full recognition. The first step was establishing 'interests sections' in the two capitals, formally under third-party embassies' authority. This immediately generated the first influx of (mostly second-generation) Cuban-Americans, allowed by both sides to visit their Cuban relatives.

That episode, however, had unforeseen effects. The arrival of so many materially comfortable relatives, contrasting with ordinary Cubans' conditions, generated a flood of asylum seekers to occupy Peru's embassy in April 1980, resulting in an unprecedented disorder which led Fidel to announce a Camarioca-style exodus at the port of Mariel. The result was that around 121,000 Cubans left in a few weeks, excoriated by the media and politicians but bringing considerable poor publicity to the Cuban system and, slowly, generating a rethink on attitudes towards emigration, seeing them less as political refugees than as economic migrants (Port 2012). Once again it seemed the systemic recourse to siphoning off a very broadly defined dissidence was being used rather than driving all opposition underground or into detention.

The detente, however, soon ended with Reagan's election (1980) halting any planned escalation of mutual recognition for over three decades; the Reagan administration from January 1981 heralded a renewed and extended isolation as part of his drive to reheat the Cold War and 'roll back communism', targeting Cuba as the alleged source of all Central America's problems of unrest and rebellion. That threat was sufficient to revive the militias in Cuba in February 1981, now called Milicias de Tropas Territoriales (MTT, or Territorial Army Reserve), against any real hostility (Rueda Jomarrón 2009: 135–76).

The new hard line also, in turn, meant a closer alliance between the US Republican Party and the parallel 'historic' generation' of Cuban-American émigrés, who now became a forceful political lobby in the US Congress and a powerful leadership in Florida, which, given that state's growing electoral significance, gave that leadership unprecedented and enduring influence on US–Cuban policy. That was when Radio Martí and TV Martí began to operate with US funding, and when the embargo was again tightened, May 1982 seeing new restrictions for US travellers to Cuba.

Reaganism also resulted in two examples of the isolation strategy, each attempting to end Cuba's external links and restrict Cuban influence and trade. The first was sustained opposition to Nicaragua's Sandinista revolution, the sole example of a Cuba-backed guerrilla movement surviving the late 1960s reversals, adapting and succeeding in July 1979; there, Reaganism meant economic sanctions, a credit squeeze and active (if eventually illegal) support for the *contra* rebels. The second was the October 1983 invasion of Grenada: Cuban involvement there had amounted to advice on social reform and political structures, and aid to expand Grenada's airport for long-haul tourist flights, but that was sufficient to bring sanctions and finally an armed expedition of 8,000 troops, which brought the only example of Cuban troops and militia (guarding the airport) fighting US troops, with twenty-five Cuban deaths. In 1989, George Bush would follow the same principle in Panama; by removing Noriega (officially for his drug threat to US security), he cut off a valuable outlet for Cuban trade and finance links to the outside world.

Washington's clampdown now, therefore, produced a revived 'siege mentality' in Cuba and a renewed defensiveness, whose severity was perhaps best exemplified by the 1987 *Ley de Peligrosidad* (law against dangerousness) which recognized, as a crime against social peace and national security, the amorphous definition of 'anti-social' behaviour, used henceforth against juvenile delinquents, openly protesting dissidents and any others deemed counter-revolutionary in the broadest sense. Curiously, however, this new siege mentality did not extend into the cultural world, where, as we have seen, the new ministry had ended the *quinquenio gris* and opened up more opportunities and scope. Beyond culture, however, tensions continued for a while, until the mid-1980s, when relations with the Catholic Church improved enough to bring the start of an understanding to tolerate a degree of dissent based within the Church's remit, suggesting that the 'siege mentality' was not necessarily universally applied or on the scale of previous periods of 'siege'.

This may well have responded to a new reality that Cuba's isolation was less than before. In addition to Socialist Bloc relationships (now bearing fruit economically and materially) and better Latin American relations, the mid-1970s had launched a new dimension to Cuban foreign policy, in what was called 'internationalism'. Building on the old strategy of constructing alliances against Washington by any means (trade, pragmatism or affinity with would-be revolutions) and benefiting from two decades of training a new generation of specialist professionals, this policy took the earlier practice of sending volunteers in medicine (Feinsilver 1993; Kirk 2015) to help with natural disasters and expanded it spectacularly, eventually reaching over forty developing countries.

It began with the decision in October 1975 to respond positively to the cry for help from newly independent Angola's MPLA government, against the combined threat from US-backed, China-backed and South Africa-backed UNITA and FNLA factions of the former anti-Portuguese struggle. Cuba promptly sent thousands of Cuban volunteer troops to shore up the MPLA defences. This was widely seen as Cuba acting as the Soviet Union's proxy army (since it involved Soviet weaponry and Soviet air transport), but it eventually emerged that the decision had been taken in Havana, the Cuban leadership seeing both a need (for anti-colonial solidarity) and an opportunity to distinguish Cuba from both the United States and the Soviet Union. Hence, rather than Cuba being a satellite proxy, it was Havana which acted, then obliging Moscow to provide the infrastructure for the involvement (Gleijeses 2002: 246–72).

The result changed the course of African history. Not only did that involvement see over 200,000 Cuban troops defeat the rebellions, but in March 1988 at Cuito Cuanavale the South African army was defeated, preventing its conquest of Angola and forcing its withdrawal, which eventually led to the unravelling of apartheid and the emergence of Mandela's new South Africa. Meanwhile those troops were accompanied by several more thousands of volunteer medical personnel, agronomists, technicians, teachers and cultural activists, all contributing to the MPLA's urgent nation-building tasks. The whole involvement put Cuba on the world map very differently: instead of leading anti-imperialist insurrection, Cuba was now widely seen as the defender of the developing world, gaining allies and admiration inside the NAM (leading to Fidel's election as NAM head from 1979) and inside the developing world's Group of 77. The Angolan involvement was soon followed (1977–8) by a less easily understood but successful defensive involvement in Ethiopia, with 17,000 troops defeating Somalian incursions. It all then launched the wider strategy, whereby non-military volunteers were routinely sent to support nation-building experiences in needy countries, and medical and infrastructural aid to disaster-hit countries.

That experience brought many varied benefits to Cuba. It gained valuable allies and global recognition and respect, helping Cuba's annual post-1992 campaign in the UN General Assembly against the US embargo (each supportive vote further confirming the embargo's international illegality). It gave thousands of young professionally trained Cubans an unprecedented opportunity to travel and acquire hard currency, while developing a new or renewed commitment to the Cuba's values. Many young volunteers now saw more positively the contrast between Cuba's social provision and the dire poverty which they encountered. It also helped engender a significant shift in thinking on race. While the 1960s had seen that concerns about the potential divisiveness of any Black Power emphasis on colour (plus a residual racism in some quarters) had led to an institutional downplaying of the question of race, Angola opened a new chapter in the collective self-definition of a Cuban identity, with Cuba's African roots being extolled rather than painted out (Peters 2012). Generally, internationalism brought much national pride and confidence to Cubans, making the renewed 'siege' more bearable, soon to prove an invaluable resource. Whatever domestic concerns may have arisen over Angola among ordinary Cubans (ranging from irrational fears of dengue and AIDS to sadness at the loss of life resulting from combat), most Cubans continued to take heart from Cuba once again punching above its weight internationally.

Confidence also returned in another crucial area: culture. While the supposed 1970s 'Sovietization' brought fears of monolithic structures, it was actually post-1976 institutionalization (with the new, seemingly Soviet-style, Ministry of Culture under Armando Hart) that ended the *quinquenio*. This confirmed that the periodic cultural restrictions of the 1960s or 1971–76 had resulted not so much from a monolith but from the opposite. The disaggregated chaos of cultural institutions had created discrete, and often autonomous, 'fiefdoms' for individuals or groups to exercise greater power (e.g. ICAIC or Casa de las Américas) or greater repression (as in the CNC) (Kumaraswami and Kapcia 2012: 94–5). Hence, one single ministerial structure for all cultural activity, especially under the flexible Hart (an ex-Movement leader and the imaginative 1960s Minister of Education), meant a greater institutional capacity for some accountability (for decision-making and policy formation) and fewer spaces for hidden repression. Hence, although it took some years for the *quinquenio*'s agonies, tensions and antagonisms to disappear from the bureaucratic structures (leading some to talk of a *decenio*, rather than *quinquenio*), the reality from 1976 was a new atmosphere of openness and opportunity.

That contradiction (between an expected hard line and the reality of openness) highlighted the more complex reality of 1970s and 1980s Cuban culture. Certainly, in non-Cuban studies of the Cuban cultural world, expectation often drove observers to continue perceiving restriction (Franco 2002), suggesting that it was often the observers, rather than Cuban culture, that were in a 'time-warp'.

Inside Cuba, the old debates were still under the surface, occasionally emerging more visibly. The 1977 creation of the Centre for Martí Studies showed this clearly; in the late 1960s and early 1970s, the more orthodox side of the debates, often unsure about how precisely to interpret ideologically (within the teleological sweep of 'scientific' history) Cuba's non-socialist *héroe nacional*, tended to pigeonhole him as a 'progressive bourgeois intellectual' rather than as the hero of past struggles for a Cuban nation. Meanwhile, the more 'Cubanist' side was clear that Martí was (as Fidel had claimed repeatedly in 1953) the Revolution's *autor intelectual* (Castro 1961), making their *Revolución* as much *martiano* as Marxist. Hence, a prestigious research and cultural centre devoted to Martí spoke volumes for his centrality, worth studying in depth and placing firmly on a pedestal.

There were other indications of the continuing 'nation-focused' discourse. The whole 'internationalism' strategy, for example, was partly a visible manifestation of national pride, although one should not rule out the idea of it extending onto a global stage the post-1920 quasi-nationalist and continentalist anti-imperialism that had so radically transformed many nationalisms in Latin America. Meanwhile, the seemingly orthodox political structures contained such indications: besides the survival of the *rendiciones* within the new electoral system, the CDRs' survival and continued use (for mobilization, communication and dissemination) long after 1961 suggested that the more characteristically ad hoc phenomena of the 'heroic' days were still valued. The PCC may have become more institutionalized (the 1980 congress happened as scheduled with few startling developments), but the Mass Organizations continued in their extra-party political importance.

THE STATE AND THE MEANING OF 'THE REVOLUTION'

This, therefore, brings us to the they key question of the structures of power and governance at the end of this period: What did the Cuba of 1985–6 look like in terms of who exercised what power and in what form? Superficially, it looked little different from 1970–5, with the guerrilla generation evidently still numerically dominating the upper structures of politics and with so many of the old structures still in place. However, after a decade of a larger and more orthodox PCC and the People's Power electoral and representation system of national, provincial and local governance, it operated differently and certainly felt different.

To take the PCC first, its rapid growth had brought in new blood, especially at the grassroots, but by 1985 it had begun to display long-feared features of the Eastern European ruling parties. Increased size now also meant a slower-moving, and perhaps less responsive, structure. While the 1980 second national congress suggested that institutional accountability and continuity did matter at least theoretically (something that Raúl, among the leaders, always valued within a correctly run and fully operating PCC), the sense within the party ranks was that the body was becoming more bureaucratic, more monolithic, with limited space for debate and uncomfortably closer to the Socialist Bloc models. Certainly, the rehabilitation of former PSP activists at the top and the grassroots suggested a possible revival of the pro-Soviet ideological narrow-mindedness characterizing one side of the early debates. Thus, although the upper reaches still showed a strong Movement presence, their influence was partly weakened by the strength of more orthodox members. Moreover, besides the appearance of a feared 'bureaucracy', PCC institutionalization and growth (suggesting less rigid entry restrictions), alongside greater access to material goods, now meant that for the first time at the lowest levels PCC membership could be seen as a vehicle for personal advancement for the ambitious and for petty corruption, nepotism, patronage and privilege. It did not go unnoticed: when private farmers' markets were opened in 1980 (at the behest of economic modernizers), only to be closed in 1982 after engendering a resented inequality, with richer farmers charging consumers inflated prices, it reflected some of the more nefarious opportunities which structural reform had allowed (Wierzbicki 2005: 28).

Meanwhile, the People's Power system was proving much more effective at lower-level representation than either the CDRs or previous experiments. However, by the mid-1980s, it was clear that the simultaneous reconfiguration of the new *municipios* across fourteen new provinces (from November 1976) had created an evident structural gap. While the CDRs continued to involve people at the very lowest (street or block) level, albeit still more about mobilizing and informing them than effectively feeding upwards their complaints or opinions, and while the national and provincial assemblies provided something of a representative forum at two higher levels, there was no element in the new structures to deal with the intermediate *barrio* level, where most Cubans operated and with which most identified. Moreover, with only 169 *municipios*, all ranging in size between 50,000 and 100,000 inhabitants, many Cubans (especially in rural areas) found the municipal assembly distant, despite the (at least theoretical) possibility of genuine feedback through the *rendición* process. The latter mechanism, in fact, varied widely in its effectiveness over time and according to specific local circumstances. At times (noted especially during the Special Period), *rendiciones* could prove more than simply cosmetic, resulting in extensive replacement of unsatisfactory *delegados*, but more often those assemblies operated more as opportunities to question and perhaps express dissatisfaction than to effect real changes. Moreover, their scope for genuine effectiveness was limited structurally by the openly (and always open air) public nature of all discussion, which some participants could easily see as intimidating, given that others present would know their views and perhaps categorize them as politically suspect: curiously, the more public (and transparent) the context for criticism, the more restrictive it might be.

There were also question marks over the National Assembly's credibility: with its few short meetings, it was never a forum for ongoing and constant debate, seeming sometimes to be more a rubber-stamping legitimation of decisions, taken most typically in the PCC's *Buró Político*. Furthermore, the pre-selection of a list of acceptable candidates (exactly matching the number of seats available in each assembly) was often seen as too limited a choice; although the PCC was legally prohibited from institutional involvement in the selection process (apart from the probably crucial electoral commission) and the initial nominations of municipal candidates came from voters in a given 'ward' (*circunscripción*), usually involving local Mass Organizations, the reality was that PCC membership was always a badge of acceptability, leading to a greater likelihood that candidates would either already be PCC members or, on election, be invited to join. Finally, the Assembly's credibility was challenged by the indirect nature of its election, unlike the municipal *delegados*.

In this context, therefore, the Mass Organizations had a role that was even more crucial than in the late 1960s and early 1970s, remaining by definition more open to all and therefore potentially more inclusive than the officially selective PCC. Hence, they involved ordinary Cubans more effectively, more actively and more continually than the electoral structures. However, they too showed signs of becoming more institutionalized, reflecting the tenor and principles now governing politics; that meant that their leaderships were still usually appointed from above, usually from key PCC members, and their purpose was still essentially to mobilize and include people rather than give people the crucial decision-making roles. Thus, the once most effective CDRs became more of a local vehicle for mobilization and dissemination (though no less necessary or effective for that) than a forum of debate and discussion, and their weaker national structure (with fewer national congresses and no de facto representation on higher decision-making bodies) left them little opportunity and few channels for feeding upwards local members' views.

The CTC, however, now came into its own in new ways: as material incentives created wage differentials, workers had more local bargaining power than before, allowing unions to operate as channels for workers' complaints and having mechanisms for defending workers in disciplinary hearings and for channelling their complaints against management.

Nationally, meanwhile, the CTC became an effective player in the emerging national system of negotiation (Ludlam 2018).

One final element in the changing picture was totally new. In the mid-1980s, a new political group appeared on the national stage although few were yet aware of its existence. This was what was called the *Grupo de Apoyo* (formally the Coordination and Support Group), effectively a 'kitchen cabinet' or 'think tank' composed of twenty young Cubans, nominated by the UJC and the FEU (prominent membership of the latter normally leading to UJC membership) and then selected by Fidel himself as suitable for training for future leadership roles. Fidel saw it as partly a means of escaping the restrictions imposed by the PCC, since the Grupo remained accountable to him alone, but he also recognized that, with the guerrilla generation ageing (being already in their 40s and 50s), it was important to prepare a cohort of younger reliable activists to replace them.

What all this meant for the structures and patterns of power and authority and for the shaping of the state was significant. Taking the state first, it was clear by 1985 that, however fluid and contested the new revolutionary Cuban state might have been for the first decade and a half, a well-structured and consolidated state had at last arrived, bringing greater stability, more efficient distribution of goods and services, and if not greater efficiency at least more visible lines of command, accountability and decision-making. Precisely because this new set of structures now existed also meant that political decision-making power had the capacity to be both institutionalized, rather than be ad hoc or personal, and more impersonal and potentially bureaucratic. A much larger and more extensive state apparatus meant that every corner of Cuba now had at least theoretical access to the benefits of the state (and thus of 'the Revolution'), and a set of structures theoretically allowing consultation and participation to be more institutional than ad hoc.

Hence, those previously dominating decision-making in the inner circles of political power and authority now had their wings clipped, while those who operated better within more stable structures were, in turn, more empowered. In simple terms, that meant less actual decision-making power for the ex-guerrillas and Movement activists but more day-to-day, and even longer-term, power for the former PSP elements. However, that impression was only the simple interpretation: whatever truth that may have reflected, the situation was actually more complex and fluid than a stereotypical picture of factions and tensions. As already observed, alongside the old PSP were the new generations of both Socialist Bloc-trained academics, state-enterprise executives, and middle and upper PCC *funcionarios* and opportunistic entrants to the lower-level PCC structures, who simply saw the new infrastructure as spaces for developing their niche, with a degree of local decision-making and, more often and more importantly, decision-executing power. Hence, power was actually now more widely spread, and thus potentially more diffuse, although any tendency towards a multiplicity of 'fiefdoms' was likely to be offset in some areas by the survival of the usual processes of negotiation and consultation, which acted as correctives to this potential.

For, while decision-making power might now be more in the hands of those advocating institutionalization, decision-influencing power was now more likely to be enhanced by a more internally accountable PCC, more structurally significant Mass Organizations, and, above all, by the new power and powers of the municipal assemblies and their delegates. Indeed, while the 1960s' *por la libre* ('anything goes' or freewheeling) Revolution might have been exciting, heroic and dynamic, accountability had been limited at best and even relegated in the constant battles and mobilization. Now, however, although the more institutionalized structures might threaten a greater inertia and create more interim power to 'jobsworth' office-holders, the PCC and electoral structures at least now offered clear channels for upward and downward communication and negotiation, even if the reality could often prove more frustrating.

However, these developments had inevitable implications for the horizontal processes of negotiation, which, until 1970, had tended to remain somewhat contingent on local variations and accidents of personality and local character. If the PCC was now much more systematically structured than at any time since PURS's creation in 1962, with clear evidence of new internal power bases and decision-enacting power at intermediate and local levels, that was clearly going to affect the so far ad hoc capacity of the Mass Organizations to reflect local people and their input to any discussion and questioning of decision-making. Equally, with People's Power enjoying a more structured and systematic character than either JUCEI or *Poder Local*, and with clear local authority to decide, interpret and enact decisions, the provincial and municipal assemblies and their executive bodies were the clearest example yet, alongside the equivalent PCC structures, of authority and power below the national level being much more systematic than hitherto.

However, while those developments might often mean that the provincial or local PCC and People's Power layers now enjoyed more direct power and authority than any of the Mass Organizations' relevant structures and layers, the People's Power processes did give the Organizations a much clearer role, not least in the nomination and selection process of local candidates for *delegados*. That, in turn, gave them formal and recognizable power in, and input into, the relevant assemblies, formalizing in new ways their local, provincial and even national authority and access to the power of decision-making. Hence, by definition, as the whole network of structures and processes became more complex after 1976, all the Mass Organizations had to be systematically consulted and involved in local execution of higher decisions, as well as in feedback up through the relevant vertical structures. Once again, the seemingly monolithic structures now operating often turned out to imply more, rather than less, negotiation and consultation than when those structures were more dynamic. One caveat here, of course, is that the pervasive presence of the PCC (now more significant) ensured that such negotiation and consultation mostly remained within clear or implicit parameters.

Moreover, for all that the traditional leadership and long-standing political activists might have seen their power trimmed, their historic authority still far outstripped any enjoyed by the newer influx of decision-makers, whose authority depended ultimately on their ability to deliver the stability, material benefits and accountability that they promised and officially espoused. Hence, when two of those benefits seemed open to question by the mid-1980s, their always more contingent authority was threatened and could not compete with the so-called old guard. Furthermore, as one visible effect of the processes of institutionalization was a publicly criticized and popularly resented degree of corruption, privilege and self-serving opportunism at middle and lower levels, the ex-rebels' historic authority was further enhanced by the clear evidence of their freedom from those 'sins'. Therefore, when it came to the debates of the mid-1980s, the authority still largely wielded within the party hierarchy by the 'old guard' played out in their favour, in ways that might not have been expected back in 1968, enabling them to press ahead with a 'rectification' which few ordinary Cubans understood in detail but which most already felt was necessary to reverse some of the adverse effects of the successes of 1975–82.

What then did all this mean for the shifting and multiple definitions of 'the Revolution' by the mid-1980s? The preceding decade had probably enhanced its definition as a 'system', the infrastructure of procedural and institutional participation, material well-being and stable security, that is, to some extent the emerging state. Hence, 'the Revolution' now mostly meant a stable static and safe structure which, formally following the principles of equality and well-being, had delivered and could go on delivering. In a sense, the promise of the nation-building project of 1959–61 seemed to have been realized, and the need for the hectic fast-changing and mobilizing Revolution of the first decade had seemingly passed. The 'body' was being satisfied, and the 'soul' more symbolically remembered. Did this then mean that the Revolution as a process of change was dead and finished? Had the 'Cuban Revolution' ended finally? Some certainly thought so, but others had different ideas.

7

DEBATE III

1985–9

By the middle of the 1980s, therefore, the old internal battles and differing definitions of 'revolution', 'The Revolution' and 'socialism' were not just simmering below the surface (with the *cubanista* radicals, in discrete pockets of the system, clinging doggedly to visible traces of their readings of Cuban history and of the Revolution's essential meaning) but were beginning to come to the surface itself, as doubts emerged about some aspects of institutionalization. Therefore, some sort of reckoning, perhaps yet another debate, was due just as in 1962 and 1970.

But what exactly was the crisis behind this new round of debate in Cuba's perpetual cycle? The reality was that it was complex and not necessarily visible, quite unlike the early 1960s crises (with the massive disruption wrought by rapid transformation and sudden isolation, and with the relatively public nature of the open discussion) or the 1969–70 crisis of confidence, active support and effectiveness. In fact, there were at least three parallel, but not necessarily related, developments, which together called into question many of the assumptions of the preceding decade.

The first was one of the most basic, affecting Cuba's ability to survive and sustain the comfortable economic evolution widely enjoyed since 1972: the growing, but not yet fully evident, crisis within Comecon itself, with potentially serious implications for a newly Comecon-dependent Cuba. This crisis had long been brewing within the somewhat ossified Soviet-determined (and Soviet-benefiting) structures and processes: it chiefly affected the productivity of both the carefully constructed and rigid trade mechanisms of many Comecon countries' own industrial and service-sector operations, both often depending on massive state subsidies and now becoming increasingly unsustainable and expensive. It also affected consumer purchasing power everywhere, in turn affecting production and income. For Cuba, Comecon membership had clearly become a life raft, much more so than any alleged direct Soviet support or subsidies; Cuba's post-1972 opening to so many markets hungry for Cuban agricultural goods, together with those same economies' ability to exchange (mostly manufactured) goods to a product-hungry Cuban market, had allowed the Cuban economy to grow and partly diversify impressively, something long sought by the rebel leadership. For the Socialist Bloc economies, however, the costs of Comecon's operation were spiralling uncontrollably, breeding frustration at the system's outdated regulation of what and how much each country could produce and trade internally, preventing development into new areas, investment in greater productivity and any incentive to move into new products or challenge competitor countries within the organization. Hence, by the mid-1980s, the organization's credibility was being questioned, as was already seen spectacularly in Poland with its widespread discontent (expressed through Solidarity) and Jaruzelski's martial law from 1981.

Cuba's leaders, increasingly aware of this, prepared to seek ways out of the looming dilemma. Hence, a reassessment began, officially so in 1986 with the convening of the delayed 1985 PCC congress; that event formalized the 'Rectification' process which partly addressed ways of coping with Comecon's imminent breakdown. Interestingly, it was within the FAR, under Raúl Castro's pragmatic direction, that attention was now paid to an urgent economic streamlining, even adopting administrative models from Western (including Japanese) systems (Domínguez 1989a).

The deep structural and institutional crisis was, however, deepened for Cuba after 1985, when Mikhail Gorbachev became the Soviet leader, creating a second, and more immediately threatening, challenge for the Cuban leadership and system. First, Gorbachev made it clear to all concerned (including Cuba's leaders) that Comecon was unsustainable, spelling the imminent end of its benefits for Cuba. Instead, he advocated a Bloc move towards a more free-market and less state-controlled economy than hitherto imaginable, a freedom to which the still embargo-strapped Cuba had no access, blocked from international credit or investment. Secondly, Gorbachev's determination to end the Cold War at any cost had serious implications for Cuba: admitting the Soviet defeat in the military and economic race with the United States, he acted increasingly on US terms set by a Reagan Administration determined to end any 'Cuba problem'. Hence, the message for Havana was clear: long-lasting and often vital Soviet economic, political, social and even military support was doomed, implying an imminent end to real or implicit subsidies (e.g. in the historically low prices for Soviet oil and high prices for Cuban sugar), with commercial relations thereafter on a commercial, and not solidarity, basis. It also meant an inevitable Soviet refusal to undertake the usual periodic rescheduling of Cuba's ongoing Soviet debts when falling due in 1989–91. Hence, if Comecon's crisis was already serious enough for Cuba, Gorbachev struck at the heart of Cuba's recently enhanced economic security and social well-being, and perhaps therefore at the system's steadily improving popularity.

More worryingly, Gorbachev's surrender to the US terms suggested that the long-standing guarantees for Cuba's wider security and military protection were no longer valid. While few believed that the Pentagon would agree to military action against Cuba (long since ruled out by US military strategists as costly and politically dangerous), renewed US hostility aroused deep-seated fears in Havana. Even the October 1962 guarantee of Cuba's security from invasion seemed threatened.

The third crisis had little directly to do with these challenges, although it too came from Gorbachev: his insistence on reform of the Soviet Union, through his twin policies of glasnost (openness) and perestroika (restructuring). Besides threatening the survival of the Soviet system (in Fidel's publicly expressed view) and of the Socialist Bloc, those policies also threatened the Cuban system. For they soon proved attractive to some younger Cubans, even within UJC ranks, who had long questioned and become frustrated by the perceived sterility, authoritarianism, hierarchies and power-concentration of the evolving Cuban structures of power. To them, the news from Moscow were welcome, even literally so as Soviet magazines became unprecedentedly popular among young Cubans, forcing the authorities in 1989 to restrict their dissemination (*Washington Post* 1989).

This challenge was, however, related to the final crisis which also unravelled – albeit one that, in many respects, suggested the opposite of the usual interpretation of what followed – namely that the post-1986 strategy of 'Rectification of Past Errors and Negative Tendencies' was simply a conservative resistance to Gorbachev's policies of reform, openness and acceptance of the free market. For it transpired that reform was also now being considered by many in the ex-guerrilla 'pole' of the leadership. However, this was not reform towards neoliberal and pluralist models (seemingly favoured by Gorbachev); instead, those reformers saw Cuba's ills in the emerging Eastern European-style *nomenklatura*, in a PCC and state bureaucracy using power for its own purposes and benefits, creating a distance between party and people, with the long-feared emergence of privilege and corruption. These 'sins' were, of course, exactly what many ex-rebels had feared about 'institutionalization', but their criticisms resonated more widely; indeed, the criticisms levelled by the pro-Gorbachev young were being echoed by their more radical leaders and the older generation although the solutions suggested by the two generations differed substantially.

Hence, when the 1986 congress declared 'Rectification' (the 'Past Errors' referring to the ideas behind some aspects of 'institutionalization', and the 'Negative Tendencies' to excessively pro-Soviet models), it meant a victory for the radical reformers, for disagreements had been fierce. The congress, due in 1985, was postponed until February 1986, but then, after opening, it was suddenly suspended, sending delegates back to their bases to discuss it all further, until it was reconvened in December 1986. What finally emerged was the new strategy, responding to the several crises and challenges. On the one hand, it accelerated the economic streamlining needed with the Comecon crisis and Gorbachev's warnings; on the other hand, it also partly meant returning to the principles and ideas of the 1960s.

One prime example of this return to type and earlier ideas was the visible resurrection of the ideas and example of Che Guevara. As already noted, his ideas (as opposed to his image and myth) had been marginalized in 1975–86; now his ideas on the economy were given new attention, and articles and books began to be published on him and his thinking (Tablada 1987; Martínez Heredia 1988: 31; Abreu Cardet 1989; Ariet 1992; Alvarez Batista 1994). Furthermore, many of those formerly associated with that thinking, especially those marginalized former *Pensamiento Crítico* people, were now restored to positions of ideological authority and influence, their work being published at last. Significantly, it was the PCC Central Committee-based research Centre for Studies of the Americas (CEA) that became their new base, encouraged to take up the old ideas and examine their contemporary relevance.

What, however, did 'a return to the 1960s' really mean? And was 'Rectification' to be defined as a clear-cut 'phase' or 'period' or, rather, as a 'debate'? The answer to the first question essentially comes with the answer to the second: 'Rectification' was not yet a defined direction for the process to follow, largely because it would soon be overtaken by the even deeper crisis that beset Cuba in 1989–91. Hence, it was only ever a still unsettled argument about Cuba's desired future direction: the nature and sequence of those 1985–86 congress postponements indicated that, although the 1960s radicals held the upper hand sufficiently to exercise internal hegemony, there was still resistance, perhaps counting on Moscow's support.

Hence, the 'return' which was being advocated was not simply turning back Cuba's historical clock, or a conservative or nostalgic reaction to Gorbachevian 'modernization'. It was essentially a battle for the Revolution's 'soul'. One side was composed of the 'radicals' who (rooted originally in radical definitions of an essentially nationalist perspective) had always seen 'the Revolution' as a route to the long overdue nation building, based on Cuban precepts and principles and Cuban interpretations of socialism. They now took up the standard of Guevara and his allies in 'the Great Debate', arguing against a slavish following of Soviet models and then seeing the post-1975 institutionalization as leading to a less ideologically committed and more materialistically motivated population, a more corrupt and less responsive PCC, and viewing the Soviet link as necessary but to be treated with caution.

Against them were ranged two forces. First, there were the familiar 'orthodox' elements, largely associated with or members of the old PSP, who had advocated a slow and mixed transition towards a socialism to which some believed an underdeveloped Cuba could and should not aspire. Secondly, as already seen, they were now supported by a younger generation who, while not sharing young people's admiration of glasnost and perestroika, had been trained and educated in the Soviet Union and Socialist Bloc, returning with deep admiration of the Soviet social and technical successes, to which they believed Cuba should aim.

Essentially, therefore, the new debate simply continued the old ones. However, by the mid-1980s, the radicals' hand had been strengthened by what they saw both in the Bloc (a degeneration of the socialist dream into corruption, privilege and stagnation) and even potentially in Cuba, where ideological commitment ('the soul') had been downplayed, giving priority to material aspirations, where egalitarianism had been subordinated to divisive differentials, and where the front line against imperialism (now manifested in a newly rampant Reaganism) had been weakened by inadequate commitment from the Soviet Union (within the Third World) and potentially from many Cubans, but also from a slavish application of external models which diluted Cubans' determination to create a genuinely radical and different nation.

THE STATE AND THE MEANING OF 'THE REVOLUTION'

Broadly speaking, during this period of intense and often destabilizing debate, the apparatus and infrastructure of the emerging state remained largely intact, enabling the system to survive the initial shocks of the coming years. However, power and authority had clearly shifted: at the top, they were again in the hands of the 'historic generation', within the PCC and, increasingly importantly, within the government, which would also help decision-making in the coming years, when quick thinking and responses and flexibility would be needed, rather than proceeding slowly through somewhat inert vertical structures. Moreover, since crisis already loomed, those leaders' traditional authority grew still more, as many Cubans looked to the traditional leaders to steer Cuba out of the crisis, guarding the popular unity that all desired.

At lower levels, the authority of municipal delegates and assemblies had grown steadily, as ordinary Cubans saw the results of their governance and as participation continued to contribute to the lower-level debates. While the CDRs might have lost much of their authority as decision-contributing bodies and decision-debating forums, the Mass Organizations generally (especially the FMC, CTC and ANAP) seemed to have grown in authority nationally and locally, not least by the effectiveness of their internal communications and negotiations and their ability for local grassroots pressures to result in local decisions on provision or facilities, something at which, as already observed, the lower levels of the CTC especially excelled. Hence, power and authority were once again being rethought at all levels, something which the coming years would take still further.

In 1985, therefore, 'the Revolution' was again being defined in different, and even opposing, ways: either as seen in 1959–61 and then enacted in the following years, that is, the radical and rapid transformation to build an equal nation, or the materially focused and institutionally structured and stable 'system' after 1975 – either as process or as system.

8

CRISIS AND THE SPECIAL PERIOD, AND DEBATES IV AND V, 1989–2005

However, those debates around Rectification were soon overtaken in 1989 when the once seemingly impregnable Socialist Bloc began to fragment spectacularly and then disintegrate, most visibly and symbolically in the dismantling of the Berlin Wall. When that was followed in June 1990 by Comecon's rapid disbandment, the warning signs for Cuba became more ominous, although (as already seen) Cuban economic policymakers had already been preparing for a crisis of some sort. Finally, 1991 saw the most startling event: the sudden implosion of the Soviet Union itself. Although Fidel may have warned Gorbachev of that possibility, the collapse was so rapid and complete that it was a traumatic shock for most Cubans, signalling the worst-case scenario imagined in the preceding years.

It meant, firstly, the disappearance overnight of all of Cuba's post-1962 guarantees of military protection; only two years after the first Bush administration, knowing that Moscow would not challenge it, had sent troops into Panama in 'Operation Just Cause' (on the grounds of the security threat from drug trafficking), this vulnerability raised immediate fears of a possible invasion. Indeed, the July 1989 decision to try and execute the high-ranking General Arnaldo Ochoa, for using his department (tasked to find ways of evading the embargo) to allow Colombian traffickers to tranship drugs through Cuban airspace, may well have reflected the concern that drugs might become a pretext for an unrestrained US military action in Cuba. After all, the 1962 US undertaking had been agreed with a Soviet Union that no longer existed.

Secondly, the collapse of both Comecon and the Soviet Union suddenly deprived Cuba of twenty-one major trading partners: six

Eastern European economies and fifteen ex-Soviet republics, none now needing to trade with Cuba and all seeking US support and investment. The Bloc's disappearance affected at least 80 per cent of Cuba's trade, conjuring up an immediate future of grim economic collapse.

Finally, the series of hitherto unthinkable events suddenly removed all hope for many Cubans after more than a decade of steady economic and social development had generated a high degree of relative tolerance of the governing system. It immediately raised the question: Would Cuba now become the 'next domino' to fall? That became even more pertinent when this 'Armageddon' scenario was followed by the US Congress's passing of the 1992 Torricelli Bill (Cuban Democracy Act), which aimed to capitalize on Cuba's plight and the absence of any superpower deterrent by tightening the economic embargo, perhaps fatally. Ironically, while Washington simultaneously responded to the Soviet collapse by mending fences with Vietnam rather than seeking to destroy that country's system, the US step proved that Cuba still deserved a special focus. With the Cuban economy already in a downward spiral by late 1992, there now seemed no way out: by 1994 official figures indicated that the economy had shrunk by some 38 per cent in five years, with production falling to some 60 per cent of its previous levels (Brundenius 1994).

The statistics tell a story of imminent total collapse, deep and probably terminal crisis and desperate shortages for all Cubans. Lacking the necessary protected preferential market for sugar, and thus lacking export income to finance survival (let alone growth), Cuba was thrust into a deep financial crisis. Without Soviet support, the government had to find external capital or loans from somewhere, while US influence precluded the usual sources for struggling economies, that is, IMF, World Bank or Inter-American Development Bank. Moreover, why would any commercial lender risk lending to a seemingly doomed Cuban economy? Export collapse also meant a commensurate fall in imports: of manufactured goods (all now necessarily bought with scarce hard currency), of food (with the Cuban diet so long structurally geared to staples impossible to grow in tropical Cuba) and, most damagingly of all, of oil, whose supply fell by some 90 per cent in a matter of months (Wierzbicki 2005: 31).

Without that oil, energy generation fell drastically, leading to years of long debilitating and demoralizing power cuts for all Cuban homes and workplaces, seriously affecting normal life and normal work. All transportation was severely hit, seriously reducing the provision of buses, trains and goods lorries, affecting travel to and from work and therefore also workplaces' labour supply, and the supply systems for goods and food. The emergency purchase of thousands of Chinese bicycles eased things for some, but only for relatively short journeys. Meanwhile, many workplaces were forced to move staff onto short-time working to save energy, even laying off workers, creating an unprecedentedly tolerated unemployment, although those thus unemployed were guaranteed payment equal to 60 per cent of their previous salary. Meanwhile frequent long power cuts made normal life impossible (disabled fans and air conditioners creating hot-house conditions in homes, and powerless refrigerators affecting the quality and quantity of food), television and radio broadcasting was reduced to a minimum, leaving families without familiar recreation or channels for news and information.

How then did the Cuban leadership respond? The first response came on 1 August 1990, a year before the Soviet collapse but after Comecon's disappearance: Fidel declared what was euphemistically (but not inaccurately) called 'the Special Period in Peacetime', effectively locking Cuba into an appropriate 'war economy'. For the Revolution was indeed now beginning a fight for survival, with talk of an even starker 'Zero Option' of all-out resistance to a total collapse of all structures sustaining Cuba's society, economy and political system. The 'Special Period' decreed the scale and detail of the austerity programme to allow the most basic elements of everyone's daily existence and trade to survive. These included those swingeing cuts in electricity and oil usage and in employment and transportation. The only nationwide measures to counteract this drastic austerity were the increase in, and greater distribution of, the old rationing system and the politically crucial guarantees to protect high (though somewhat reduced) levels of expenditure on the 'crown jewels' of the welfare state: healthcare and education. While this gave a valuable message of a determination to protect the Revolution's most cherished *logros* (achievements), the rationing system and the *libreta* (ration book) was what saved things on the ground, keeping faith in the system and guaranteeing basic provisions, as in the 1960s, but without those years' hope.

Meanwhile, the Torricelli Act deepened the gloom, making 1992–4 the nadir of the crisis. This was reflected in the explosion of illegal emigration, via hijacked boats and makeshift rafts (*balsas*); by summer 1994, that outflow was such that in early August 1994, when the Cuban navy rammed and sank a hijacked ferry in Havana harbour leading to several deaths, popular anger exploded into violent protest in Old and Central Havana. The protests led to Fidel's arrival, personally talking to the protesters, and then to a repeat of the 1980 Mariel solution of allowing an exodus of *balseros* (rafters) from the beaches east of Havana, but this time on their own crafts rather than being collected (Martínez Milagros 1996), eventually totalling some 35,000 people in two months, which then shifted US policy significantly. In 1980, the US Coastguard had embarrassingly turned away *marielitos* rather than risk Florida being overwhelmed by thousands of migrants needing vetting and processing; now, however, a migration accord was agreed with Havana in September 1994 whereby those *balseros* rescued at sea by the Coastguard would be returned to Cuba, with guarantees about their legal status afterwards. These were duly called 'wet-foot' migrants, while any Cuban able to reach US dry land (thereafter 'dry-foot' migrants) were eligible for the usual treatment under the Cuban Adjustment Act (Olson and Olson 1995: 111–122).

DEBATE IV: HOW TO SAVE 'THE REVOLUTION'?

By that stage, however, there were glimpses of hope after three years of intense soul-searching at all levels, with the reforms addressing the immediate economic crisis. As in previous crises, the system now displayed its familiar recourse to debate; however, this time the usual post-debate consolidation (of any agreed strategy) was curtailed by the urgency of decisions. Moreover, for the first time, one debate followed a previous one ('Rectification') rather than an agreed consolidation. Nonetheless, the process was familiar, although discussions were severely limited by transport shortages and the daily demands of survival, and also by falls in PCC membership (reflecting either disillusion, the end of personal advancement, or the universal focus on family survival rather than collective strategy): at all levels of the system and in all structures, they addressed one simple but urgent imperative – 'save the Revolution' quickly, before demoralization and discontent took a toll. Indeed, crisis had already brought open dissidence to the surface, emboldened by a belief that the system was in its death throes and that (as in Eastern Europe in the late 1980s) the US government would support opposition. The latter expectations proved correct: after 1992, the US Interests Section in Havana began to support dissident groups with funds, materials and space. However, recognizing the reasons for dissent and its potential to destabilize, the authorities decided to desist from outright large-scale suppression, focusing instead on the economic crisis as a priority.

By 1991, the debate had reached some firm, but not universally welcome, conclusions, helped by Rectification's initial attempts at economic streamlining. Perhaps because the discussions had been more restricted than any since 1970–5 (i.e. entirely inside the PCC, with some involvement of specialist economists, many likely to be PCC members anyway, but with some more marginal reform-minded economists making their views known more publicly, often outside Cuba), unusually rapid consensus was reached. The 1991 PCC congress materialized on time in October, despite the controversial reforms proposed: the scale and gravity of the crisis had obliged everyone (even those seeing the reforms as anathema) to recognize that they had no choice but to accept the hitherto unacceptable. The congress, therefore, agreed an emergency programme that few could have predicted some five years earlier.

The most effective change was the 'decriminalization' of the US dollar, allowing and encouraging emigrant remittances to Cuban families and also giving the cash-strapped government access to some valuable hard currency to purchase on the world market. The second change was to resurrect tourism as an alternative to sugar as Cuba's mainstay: the traditionally high levels of sugar production (between four and seven million metric tonnes annually), sustained by Comecon oil and fertilizers, could not be sustained, since production was collapsing to below two million tonnes (lacking oil, inputs and workers, and after decades of inefficient mills) and Cuba now lacked alternative markets to replace the former reliable demand. In 2002–4, 71 of Cuba's 156 sugar mills would be permanently closed.

Hence, tourism was the short-term answer: it had to be interim, according to many economists, given its tendency towards imbalances in small economies, implying dependence on imported manufactures and food (to provide acceptable levels of comfort for demanding customers). Although Cuba, the Caribbean's largest island, might have considerable potential for exploiting its natural resources this way, tourism had been neglected since the early 1960s when moralistic mores and an increasing anti-capitalism in Cuban thinking had closed the Havana's hotspots, the destination for those seeking sun, alcohol and sex. Only in the 1980s had some efforts gone into making Cuba a cheap (state-subsidized) Caribbean destination for the less discerning, possibly more politically sympathetic and less wealthy tourists, usually in tours organized by communist or leftist parties. Thus, Cuba's limited hotel stock, the ageing and somewhat forbidding 1970s concrete edifices, had to be replaced by more impressive tourist-friendly facilities.

However, investment could not come from a state still focused on ensuring survival; instead it had to come via one of the reforms under 'Rectification', namely joint ventures between the Cuban state and foreign investors, in the form of tourism enterprises, with the foreign investor limited to a maximum 49 per cent stake in the enterprise and to labour chosen by the Cuban state and paid in Cuban pesos. The result was increased hotel construction in Havana, Varadero (east of Matanzas, with its own airport for direct international flights, especially from Canada) and, slowly in the many keys off the northern coast, where tourist enclaves began to be developed with Canadian, Spanish and Brazilian enterprises. Tourists began to arrive steadily, numbers rising from around 80,000 in 1988 to a million (1997), 1.7 million (2000) and over 4.5 million in 2018 (ONEI 2019). With tourist arrivals came other opportunities adjacent to the new economy, in employment in and around hotels, in transport, in hard-currency tips and in other services.

Paramount in the latter were the new *paladares* (private restaurants). For another reform agreed in 1991 was the resurrection of urban self-employment, defined as economic activity by *cuenta propia* (on one's own account), which was banned in 1968, but was now allowed for a limited range of activities: the *paladares* being the most visible and successful, although the 200,000 *cuentapropistas* created within a couple of years had declined to about 100,000 by the end of the decade, reflecting either a lack of realism or investment or an excess of bureaucracy, regulation and taxation. The latter (taxation) was a novelty, for explicit direct taxation had not existed from the early 1960s, since low wages and the 'social wage' of free education and healthcare and heavily subsidized food, transport, communications and many other items, de facto meant that wages were taxed invisibly; now, however, the new entrepreneurs trading legally in hard currency were taxed, ensuring that the state acquired some of that currency.

If some in the PCC looked askance at, or even opposed, the resurrection of what was feared could become a new 'petty bourgeoisie', a Trojan horse for a return to capitalism, the other tourist-oriented service was even less acceptable: *jineterismo* (a neologism from *jinete*, literally 'rider, or horseman') which included street-based hustling, tourist-focused black-market activity and outright prostitution. The latter once proudly banished in the Revolution's first days but now a source of embarrassment, threatening to turn Cuba once again into the *prostíbulo* (whorehouse) of the Caribbean, a destination for sex tourism (Daigle 2015). Both hustling and prostitution, however, were temporarily tolerated, since they guaranteed access to much-needed hard currency especially for those lacking such access via remittances. Since around 85 per cent of emigrants were white, it was their (white) relatives in Cuba who most immediately benefited from remittances, often already possessing vehicles for private taxis or owner-occupied dwellings for bed-and-breakfast *casas particulares*. However, that left many in the non-white population, by then probably constituting around 60 per cent of the total but receiving only around 15 per cent of remittances (Morales 2013) deprived of that invaluable means of personal survival, unless they engaged in illegal activity. Indeed, to many Cubans' shame, it soon seemed that non-whites were disproportionately represented in the profile of *jineteros*, for precisely that reason.

One of the principles behind *cuenta propia*, that individual incentives might help boost production, also contributed to another 1993 reform: the break-up of state farms into a new form of cooperative, the Unidad Básica de Producción Campesina (UBPC, Basic Unit for Peasant Production). Their aim was to give former farmworkers an incentive to produce for the private market (since all cooperatives – by then occupying an estimated 80 per cent of Cuba's agricultural units – were also now allowed to sell directly to the public in new *agromercados* (farmers' markets) for any produce exceeding their commitment to the Acopio state purchasing agency) but it also aimed to create a new small-farmer class whose new land ownership would make them a bulwark against any attempts (by Cuban-Americans) to reclaim land lost in the 1960s, since any former estates would now be owned by many individuals determined to resist such a claim.

One final area of significant change was the cultural world, one of the areas of social life that was especially badly hit by the austerity and shortages, suddenly bereft of the often substantial funding and facilities that characterized the previous decade. Now, simply, the state could no longer provide either on anything like the same scale, leading to a rapid decline in output, morale and opportunity, to which some writers, film-makers, visual artists and musicians responded appropriately, their work often manifesting demoralization, disillusion or a degree of dissent (Fernandes 2006; Hernandez-Reguant 2009; Whitfield and Birkenmaier 2011). The cultural authorities' response was to allow cultural producers, unprecedentedly, to earn hard currency abroad, either by travelling and working abroad temporarily or by sending their materials abroad. This step was taken partly because the government could no longer guarantee the hitherto remarkably high levels investment in culture and sport and partly because the high profile of Cuba's best-known painters, writers, musicians and sportsmen and sportswomen would give Cuba bad publicity if they were seen to be unable to create. Hence, many of the best-known musicians (for which Cuba was now becoming world-famous) thereafter worked extensively abroad, returning to Cuba periodically to bring back hard currency (a proportion of which, under the new rules, they were expected to pay to the government) – the Buena Vista Social Club were the most visible and best-known example. Even writers began to benefit from the opportunities to publish in Spain, although Spanish publishers often sought works which most responded to and reflected the European and North American reading public's growing taste for Cuban writing, emphasizing the exotic, the erotic and the dissident (Kumaraswami and Kapcia 2012: 136; Whitfield 2008).

However, the dollar's sudden legalization, which these changes implied, presented two major problems for the Cuban leadership. The first was that those new dollars were often entering Cuba but, precisely because the dollar was freely exchangeable outside Cuba, not benefiting the state by being held by Cubans. The second was, therefore, that the inflow was never adequate nor equally distributed, leading to a divisive and corrosive dual economy, in which those with hard currency had more opportunities and options within a better-provided dollar-based economy, while those lacking it had to survive in a peso economy where goods were scarcer and where the peso was always falling in value. The solution would soon become a characteristic of the whole economy: the creation of a dollar-equivalent *peso convertible*, which worked internally as a dollar, therefore compensating domestically for the relative shortage. For over a decade that was the function of the *peso convertible* (or CUC, as it was known). However, as the post-2000 Bush Administration restricted the flow of remittances (most clearly in 2004), the Cuban government's response was to make the dollar no longer legal tender inside Cuba, replacing it entirely by the CUC to ensure that the government became the repository of all inflowing dollars (Cubans receiving remittances or hard-currency earnings obliged to exchange them for CUC, at a commission), enabling it to settle debts and purchase goods abroad.

That mechanism, however, did not solve the dual currency's other effect: the drift of labour from the state sector to the perceived opportunities in the hard-currency economy. As tourism boomed and hard-currency opportunities grew, more and more Cubans who depended on Cuban peso earnings within a challenged peso economy left their state employment (often in hospitals or schools), choosing instead to earn their living on the edges of the tourist-oriented economy, often as taxi drivers, hotel workers, *jineteros* or other suppliers of services and goods. While this enabled many ordinary Cubans to cope successfully with the scarcities, it also created a crisis for the sectors which they left, depleting the workforce in the two areas on which the Revolution's traditional claim to international prestige had been based – healthcare and education. Moreover, as more Cubans (especially in Havana) gained access to CUC, that currency's growing purchasing power meant a parallel decline in the already fragile purchasing power of the peso (known as the *moneda nacional*, or national currency); it even ate into the basic *libreta* provisions, as the CUC's power increasingly attracted illegal and black-market trading in goods siphoned off from the state's stocks reserved for the subsidized peso market. Thus the initial collapse in the peso's value in 1993–95, which traded legally in the newly created *cajas de cambio* (exchange kiosks), known as *Cadecas*, at 130 to the dollar, having been officially worth the equivalent of the dollar but informally seven pesos to the dollar (Wierzbicki 2005: 35) in the late 1980s, took years to regain its value and only with government pressure to strengthen the supply of peso-oriented goods.

This much-publicized dual economy or dual currency afflicted all Cubans apart from those with remittances or those able to act illegally, who flourished in the mid-1990s, as the economy struggled and as hard currency's availability was slow to improve: that was when Cuba's long-trumpeted freedom from crime (thanks to the CDRs' vigilance and the levels of equality achieved) and from prostitution began to be seriously undermined, especially as the authorities initially seemed unwilling to clamp down on either infringement of the traditional values. Only in 1996, when there were more police stationed and active in tourist-frequented areas of Havana and tourist resorts, often then excluding Cubans from tourist hotels, did the hitherto embarrassingly visible prevalence of sex workers (male and female) begin to decline somewhat.

This, therefore, brings us to the political and social implications of the damaging sequence of crisis and reform. On the one hand, the economy had clearly been 'saved' by 1995: that year registered the first measures of growth since 1989, a pattern to be repeated annually henceforth, although not reaching the 1989 levels until 2004, given the depth of the collapse and the terminal effects of some aspects of the whole crisis, especially in traditional sectors such as sugar, agriculture and industrial production for the domestic market. However, on the other hand, the social effects of that same sequence – crisis and reform – were visible and a serious concern to many, not least activists within the PCC and Mass Organizations. Those most worried by the social effects also included Cuba's churches, whose leaders and clergy began to lament and seek to address the first signs of a growing inequality and poverty (the latter often addressed through charitable shipments through the churches' international links), but also began to discuss with the Cuban leadership how to work together to lessen those effects and defend the values of the old system. In particular, both the PCC and the churches, including the once hostile and marginalized Catholic Church hierarchy, were concerned about the possibility of a more individualistic and possibly selfish mentality undermining any sense of community and solidarity, both previously shaping many Cubans' daily and weekly lives and attitudes. Both feared a serious decline in social stability and a rapid process of social disintegration.

Therefore, totally unlike Poland in the 1980s (when the deepening crisis of the Polish economy saw the Catholic Church lead the opposition to communism, supporting and protecting Solidarity), the Cuban Catholic hierarchy reacted by cooperating with the PCC and state, expressing their shared concerns publicly and starting a crucial process whereby the authorities were more tolerant of dissident groups which operated through the church organizations than of those who preferred to work with the US Interests Section and US-based émigrés, who felt the full force of the system's punishment. That step proved decisive in both partially (but not officially) legitimizing the church-linked dissidents by conceding them a degree of space through magazines – *Espacio Laico* and *Palabra Nueva* – that largely avoided censorship by agreeing to restrict their criticism to 'within' the system, while delegitimizing those US-linked dissidents whose open support of the embargo (at a time of shared national crisis) made them both formally lawbreaking and informally seen as treasonous. It would also prove crucial in the coming years: recognizing that new dialogue and spirit of cooperation, in 1992 the PCC rules changed, allowing *creyentes* (believers) to become members and thus overturning decades of formal or implicit atheism and the imported assumptions of the Socialist Bloc communist parties. It was in effect an opening of sorts, to increase the scope of Fidel's 1961 concept of *dentro*.

One area where church and state shared a common view was in their valuation of the family unit. While the churches' perhaps more predictable view was that the family unit was natural and morally sound, that a communist state equally extolled the virtues of the family seemed curious to many outsiders. However, the Cuban education system and laws had long formally valued the family as the basic social unit of Cuban society, as witnessed in the country's educational materials and the laws and customs which, while allowing divorce, also privileged marriages and newly-wed couples (Smith 2016). Indeed, the 1975 Family Code, while principally targeting persistent *machista* male attitudes, clearly upheld the family's basic role, although slightly differently from the churches. While the latter largely extolled the traditional nuclear family, eschewing divorce, the government recognized the multilayered and multi-polar families (created by easy divorce and easy remarriage over the decades) as the base unit of society's complex networks of protection, guidance, mutual help and social cohesion. Indeed, Cubans' survival during the Special Period was not solely attributable to the state (through provision of goods and guarantees) or to relatives' remittances but also to the enhanced role and strength of that much-extended Cuban family, wherein one member's access to scarce resources might extend to offspring, parents, siblings and more distant relatives, as well as enabling migration from the countryside and provinces seeking hard currency-related jobs. Hence, while many passing media observers attributed that survival to a new individualism in Cuban society, it was really a more collectivist, if somewhat traditional, context which ensured continuity and access (Andaya 2014).

However, beyond that base unit, another pattern soon emerged, created at the lowest level in the immediate aftermath of the onset of scarcity and crisis: once the leadership sent the clear message (passed down through the PCC and Mass Organizations' structures) that it could no longer sustain spending sufficiently to guarantee the familiar structures of governance and decision-making, distribution or even mobilization (now in serious decline, threatening the usual channels of communication and active solidarity), committed local activists began collaborating at *barrio* level (the only one possible in the circumstances) to ensure that basic channels, structures, forums and arenas for discussion and decision-making were maintained and even improved. This process was, in fact, nothing totally new, since the usual processes of assessment and debate in the late 1980s (part of 'Rectification') had begun to recognize that the post-1976 People's Power system, by reducing the number but increasing the size of the 169 *municipios*, had created a distance between ordinary citizens and the municipal layer of formal representation and governance, while simultaneously weakening the CDRs' functions. The result had been the familiarly experimental creation of intermediate *consejos populares* (People's Councils) in some places. Seen as purely administrative bodies and composed of relevant municipal assembly delegates and local representatives of Mass Organizations and other relevant bodies or associations, they operated at the neglected *barrio* level to ensure distribution of goods and services. It was, therefore, to these entities that the local activists now turned in their task of maintaining structures and rebuilding the damaged state from at the grassroots (Collins 2017). Hence, in 1990–2, the government formalized this process by spreading the *consejos* nationwide, as an official layer of governance, with every *municipio* now consisting of anything between ten and thirty *consejos*. Meanwhile, the concept of *lo local* (the local) was also redefined, the same pattern of thinking also leading to a new, or increased, emphasis on small communities within the *barrio*, in a partly ad hoc process of creating small *comunidades*, *consejos comunitarios* and even a so-called *cultura comunitaria*.

Therefore, despite its parlous condition and the scale of the crisis, the Cuban state survived the crisis, bruised and battered but possibly in better condition than in 1988, given its new local relevance and focus, despite the government's much-reduced ability to coerce, as illustrated most clearly in the FAR's rapid and drastic reduction. Hence, with a weakened military capacity and with transport and communication difficulties affecting the usual forms of vigilance (police and CDRs), it was difficult to attribute the system's survival to coercion alone. In fact, in 1994, the FAR leadership (possibly including Raúl himself as minister) seemingly stressed opposition to being used against ordinary Cubans, given their prime duty of defending Cuba against external threat (Klepak 2005: 57).

Those drastic cuts in personnel also had another dimension. The FAR's ethos and training had long made it one of Cuba's key institutions (respected for its efficiency, success and loyalty), with the PCC especially strong within its ranks; therefore, the loss of half of that loyal, ideologically committed base was a political problem, just when the beleaguered system needed every bit of active support. The solution in December 1993 was the creation of a new mass organization (although never attaining that formal status), the Asociación de Combatientes de la Revolución Cubana (ACRC, Association of ex-Combatants of the Cuban Revolution). Under one of the most widely respected ex-guerrillas, Juan Almeida, this was a military veterans' body for both ex-M26J members and newly demobilized soldiers, giving them a formal vehicle for united participation in the political decision-making and consultation. A few years later, the PCC allowed neighbourhood *núcleos* to be formed (outside the usual workplace), thus also allowing retired soldiers to remain members.

These base-level changes were also accompanied by a parallel reform, equally effective in achieving a credibility beyond gesture politics: amendments to reform the Constitution in July 1992. As already observed, the post-1976 National Assembly principles of indirect election and two short annual sessions had long weakened the Assembly's credibility in terms of decision-making and any real or effective debate. Therefore, an amendment now allowed half of the Assembly *diputados* to be elected directly, copying the *municipios'* principles of selection, candidature and *rendición*; the rest of the *diputados* would still be elected by municipal *delegados*. While this still left the Assembly a less than fully directly elected chamber, it did restore some credibility, witnessed in increased turnout in the 1993 elections, compared to the recent years' evidence of a steady and worrying decline (Kapcia 1995).

Moreover, the Assembly also now gained further credibility through two moves. First, its new president was Ricardo Alarcón, a stalwart of the early radicalization of student politics in 1959–62 and then Cuba's long-serving and respected UN ambassador, frequently negotiating with the US government. His appointment thus indicated the Assembly's new importance. Secondly, the problem of a two-session parliament was addressed by making the intervening Standing Commissions more numerous, more permanent and more engaged in actual discussion and decision recommendation between sessions. While these commissions still lacked the power that they would later achieve under Raúl, they now offered the prospect of an alternative pole of political activity to the seemingly less credible PCC, whose membership was still based on selection via the (now somewhat less relevant) workplaces, and whose membership was still weaker than before.

A further constitutional amendment changed the charter's preamble, adding to the statutory reference to Marxism–Leninism (as the basis of the Cuban state) the concept of *martianismo* as the Revolution's guiding principle, formalizing the statement implicit in the 1977 Centro de Estudios Martianos. Thus, when Fidel Castro reportedly observed wryly in 1991 that the Soviet collapse at least allowed Cuba to make its own mistakes, he might equally have said that Cubans were now free to rescue *their* 'Revolution' from the Cold War straitjacket and return it to *martianismo* and *la nación*.

Indeed, that was already clear in the first days of the crisis when the public discourse changed from stressing communism to calls for unity to save the *Patria*. The universal emphasis was now on the need for solidarity and a common effort to the national cause, appealing to patriotism to save 'the Revolution', a concept which had discursively long become synonymous with the *Patria*. The discourse now focused on episodes and myths of Cuban history: Antonio Maceo's 1878 determination (at Mangos de Baraguá) to reject the rebel leaders' surrender after a decade of rebellion, a gesture now extolled with billboards declaring *un eterno Baraguá* (permanent resistance). Playa Girón was now frequently used as the reminder of victory to stimulate collective pride and determination. Meanwhile, the narratives of past heroes were hailed and repeated. If anyone had previously doubted the Revolution's roots in both a revolutionary and a popular nationalism, that was now absolutely clear. Although there was more than a hint of desperation in those appeals, they nonetheless struck a chord, persuading enough Cubans to keep the faith and to at least passively accept a continuation of the system in some form, while wishing for rapid economic improvement. The year 1994 was also the moment when official encouragement was given to stress Cuba's history of national struggle, witnessed in the creation of the Bayamo-based *Casa de la Nacionalidad* (to research Cuba's national past) and the annual *Fiesta de la Cubanía* (Festival of Cuban-ness) on 10 October, commemorating Céspedes' declaration of rebellion.

That depth of tolerance or passive support was certainly needed. Despite signs of economic recovery in 1995, 1996 saw the US embargo again tightened, when President Clinton reluctantly signed off a measure which he had previously opposed. The bill which, proposed by the Republicans Jesse Helms and Dan Burton to extend the effects and scope of the Cuba Democracy Act, had been overwhelmingly passed in the Senate in 1995 was not accepted by the Democrat-dominated House. Now, Clinton's hand was forced by a crisis in February 1996 when the Cuban air force shot down (in Cuban airspace) two private planes which, piloted by Cuban-Americans, belonged to a sustained operation by the Florida-based organization *Hermanos al Rescate* (Brothers to the Rescue) to rescue Cuban *balseros* in the Florida Straits to prevent them becoming 'wet-foot' refugees. This incident was driven by the organization's determination (against repeated US and Cuban warnings) to breach Cuban airspace to provoke Cuban retaliation which might end any prospect of improved relations with Cuba, which the 1994 agreement and the Clinton Administration's softer line had recently suggested. The strategy worked: the pilots' deaths (both being US citizens) sparked a furore in Congress and forced Clinton's hand, the Act becoming law in March 1996. However, a presidential decree waived for an initial six months the US rights under the Act's most contentious part, Title III, which extended the embargo to third-party countries by giving US citizens the right to sue (in US courts) any foreign enterprises operating in Cuba in or through property once owned by those citizens. That waiver responded to widespread anger abroad, several allied countries threatening international legal action against a restraint of their trade; moreover, the waiver was repeated every six months by subsequent presidents, until 2019.

Nonetheless, the legislation did deter some new investment which Cuba's recovery desperately needed, threatening to undermine the rising popular confidence. It was therefore partly to boost that confidence that the Cuban government laid greater emphasis on an international strategy initiated in 1992, in answer to the Torricelli Act: an annual autumn campaign in the UN General Assembly to garner increased international support from member states for a Cuban motion condemning the US embargo as an act of genocide and a breach of Cuba's sovereignty. While that strategy appeared rhetorical, with little immediate effect (other than generating a small degree of well-being in Cuba), it had a legal function, given the Assembly's role in establishing international law over time (White 2019). Time was certainly necessary and the favourable votes grew very slowly. In 1992, only fifty-nine states supported Cuba (although including Canada, France, Mexico and Spain), with three opposing (United States, Israel and an aid-hungry Romania) and seventy-nine abstentions (including Britain and the rest of the European Community, and Russia). However, the numbers in favour grew steadily: the EC (and then EU) moved from abstentionism to support, and by the early 2000s around 180 states were supporting Cuba. Finally, in 2016, the vote was 191 countries to zero, the US (under Obama, having recognized Cuba) and Israeli delegates abstaining. Hence, by then, the embargo's international illegality was firmly established.

The change in international thinking about, and sympathy with, Cuba's position was substantially helped by Latin American political shifts from the mid-1990s, with the so-called pink tide of elected leftist and anti-imperialist nationalist governments, most notably in Venezuela, Bolivia and Ecuador. Those governments' attitude to Cuba had been shaped decades before when many of the new leaders (Chávez and Morales, for example) were young radicals, admiring what Cuba represented for them, but it was now enhanced by both a continuing interest in Cuba's experience of surviving and a critical suspicion of globalization and US policies towards the region (Kapcia 2012).

DEBATE V: BUT WHAT DO WE MEAN BY 'THE REVOLUTION'?

The economic improvement however, which the post-crisis reform programme generated, together with signs that the political crisis might have been averted, led to a new internal debate which proved more difficult, more contentious and longer-lasting than the 'last-ditch' concentration of minds in 1991. This new debate followed directly from the reform programme, at a time of relative relief and space for reflection addressing a searching new question. Given that the first 1990s debate had focused on 'how to save the Revolution?' (often implying 'at all costs'), the question now posed asked: 'But what do we mean by 'the Revolution' and what have been the costs which have either resulted or should be avoided?' That went to the heart of the old discussions about, and definitions of, 'the Revolution', and was now characterized by a remarkable degree of openness and public involvement. Indeed, it really only became clear several years later that it had actually been a kind of debate: this became retrospectively clear because of the unusually broad scope allowed to individuals (usually intellectuals who were PCC members) and periodicals to discuss issues, people, historical experiences and ideas that had hitherto been considered taboo or at least sensitive. In the latter case, that often meant that there had previously been no real consensus about how to consider or theorize something or where to fit it into any existing narrative or way of thinking. At the time, few considered it a 'debate' but more as a wide-ranging rethinking of a great many hitherto unchallenged questions. Indeed, from that point of view, this particular 'debate' tells us much about the whole nature and scope of any 'debate' within the Cuba system – namely, that it often does not argue about issues between opposing poles but feels its way cautiously towards new approaches.

The lead was partly given in 1994 by the decision (notably by the influential minister of culture, Abel Prieto) to encourage the creation of new magazines, tasked with exploring the parameters to address the question of the Revolution's 'essence' and find a degree of consensus on future directions. Three magazines (*Temas*, *Nuestra América* and *Debates Americanos*) led the debate, reflecting the CEA roots of many of the contributors and, further back, the influence of *Pensamiento Crítico*. Beyond these, however, the debate was simultaneously encouraged in a range of university, ministerial and PCC research centres and was even reflected in the topics broached in the daily newspapers, and in the monthly *Temas*-organized Último Jueves (Last Thursday) open public forum. That this debate included the PCC was demonstrated when the scheduled 1996 congress failed to materialize on time, postponed until October 1997.

By 1997, some consensus had been achieved although still contested. The majority opinion seemed to be that the basis of 'the Revolution' to be preserved was found in the original revolutionary project from 1953 and through the programme, reforms and mobilizations of 1959–61, suggesting that, along with its benefits (security, economic support, social reform models and expertise and a level of ideological certainty), Cuba's insertion into the Cold War had also constrained definitions. Indeed, the major differences of opinion still focused on the Soviet link. Those admiring the Soviet model before the 1960s and those formed ideologically and intellectually in the Socialist Bloc retained a deep affection and nostalgia for what had been lost in 1989–91; they remained reluctant to reject some of that old model's 'pluses', and often saw the Revolution's 'essence' in the 1975–85 'golden age' of comfort, certainty and stability. Against them, some of the radical ex-guerrillas seemed occasionally to prefer the 'heroic' years of 1962–8, which, despite inefficiencies and errors, seemed a time of intellectual and ideological sovereignty. Meanwhile, influential voices in economics advocated a very different future, the neoliberal model offered by either post-1989 Eastern Europe or the state-led communist market model offered by China.

In many respects, the latter position reflected the continuing undercurrent of demoralization and dissent outside the institutions of the state and system: once crisis had seemed terminal (in the early 1990s) and once the US Interests Section began supporting organized resistance, dissident groups had proliferated, although they rarely collaborated with each other and most remained small, isolated and unknown to most Cubans. Even when one church-protected group began to voice open dissent, formally advocating change within the Constitution, that enterprise remained largely beyond most Cubans' awareness. That enterprise was Oswaldo Payá's Proyecto Varela which, in 2002–3, organized a 25,000-signature petition to demand constitutional reform and a more pluralist system; it was tolerated sufficiently to allow him to submit his constitutional proposal, until the judiciary decided against accepting it for formal Assembly debate.

As for debate within the system, specifically over the responses to the questions about the Revolution's meaning, the vast majority of those debating (including most of Cuba's leaders and many Cubans over forty) overall seemed to prefer a balance between the first and the third options, seeing the Revolution's essence and preferred future in both the original 'project' of 1959–61 and the 1980s 'golden age'.

THE BATTLE OF IDEAS: 2000–2005

Out of that intellectual and ideological ferment came a new campaign, helped by the boost to collective confidence by the January 1998 visit of Pope John Paul II. The invitation offered to him said much for the leadership's own confidence: aware that a hitherto vehemently anti-communist Polish pope might well condemn many aspects of the Cuban system, they reasoned that he might also share many Cubans' moralistic attachment to basic values and perhaps even condemn the US embargo (both of which he did during his visit). Moreover, the invitation and the visit might signal a degree of national celebration, and even implicit admission, that the 'Special Period' was over.

That moment was then followed by another unexpected manifestation of national unity: the curious and absorbing episode which, over seven months from November 1999, saw daily or weekly nationwide rallies calling for the return to Cuba of a six-year-old child Elián González. He had been rescued in the Florida Straits by the US Coastguard when the raft on which he and his mother were travelling to the United States broke up, drowning his mother; as the rescued Elián was technically a 'wet-foot' refugee (obliging the US authorities to repatriate him to Cuba and his father, who had been unaware that of the mother's plans), the US authorities adhered to the 1994 agreements. However, Elián's Miami relatives (looking after him after the rescue) mounted a campaign against his return, which then generated popular protests in Cuba against the family, rapidly becoming a vast coordinated campaign absorbing everyone's attention: rallies and protest marches were organized daily, mostly run by the youth bodies UJC and FEU, and Cuba was covered in billboards trumpeting the issue while the media gave wall-to-wall coverage and Cubans wore specially printed T-shirts proclaiming a determination to return Elián to his 'Cuban family' (an ambiguous term which implicitly included the whole population). The campaign was actually pushing at an open door since the US government (represented by Attorney General Janet Reno) sought Elián's return, culminating in the armed storming of Elián's family's Miami house by US Immigration and Naturalization Service officials to enforce the court's decision for repatriation by seizing the boy. This action generated angry street protests by Cuban-Americans in Florida, including some burning of the US flag, to many Americans' disgust. On 28 June 2000, Elián was indeed returned to Cuba to great acclaim.

However, for the Cuban leaders that episode was the start of a totally new campaign, the 'Battle of Ideas'. For the Elián campaign had rapidly convinced a previously dubious leadership that the system's ability to energize and rally Cubans in ways not seen since 1991 had survived the crisis and the 1990s demoralization (Kapcia 2009). More importantly, they had become convinced that young Cubans, often written off in the past and more recently as less revolutionary than their parents and grandparents and less likely, or willing, to be mobilized politically, could actually become a force for a revival and reinvigoration of 'the Revolution'.

That belief now created the 'Battle', which Fidel Castro declared as having started already on 5 December, that is, in the first days of the Elián campaign. It was fought against the combined effects of the Special Period's demoralizing austerity and the worrying effects of some reforms to address the crisis, increasingly seen as corroding a hard-earned equality and collective sense of solidarity. Those directing the campaign sought to achieve this by re-energizing young Cubans in a renewed ideological commitment to the Revolution's basic values. In this, they were encouraged by the UJC and FEU activists' discovery (during their efforts to rally young people for the Elián campaign in Cuba's poorest neighbourhoods) of a hitherto unrecognized pool of potentially discontented youth, marginalized and even forgotten by the system. This neglect had arisen from the selectivity of the university system which, because they had failed to be selected for a university-based path to a prestigious job, left those young Cubans on the margins in a period of austerity. The activists confronting this reality rapidly identified this youth sector as a potential time bomb but also as a wasted resource, which could be rescued and mobilized to good effect. Hence, the 'ideas' of the Battle were clear: an emphasis on moral values, and on education and culture, recognizing the seminal role of both in socializing and mobilizing young people in the 1960s, through experiences such as the Literacy Campaign and the *instructores de arte*.

Most visibly, the main focus of the new education campaign was that pool of neglected young Cubans: they were now the target of a nationwide drive to recruit them into a series of ad hoc *emergente* (emergency) training schools with three specific purposes. The first was to fill gaps that had emerged in the system, as labour drifted from the peso-earning public services to the hard currency-earning opportunities associated with tourism, leaving areas of those services depleted of the necessary teachers, doctors and nurses; these new students would now be trained as the new 'shock troops', echoing the Literacy Campaign's *brigadistas*, but now as *emergente* primary school teachers, nurses and *instructores de arte*. Secondly, a key part of this *emergente* generation was the totally new role of social worker, new because after 1959 the government had never recognized any need for such people, given the Revolution's social benefits. After the Special Period, however, their need was admitted, and these new quasi-professionals were sent out into the community to find evidence of poverty and neglect, and, by integrating those they found affected, contributing positively to the Revolution's rebuilding, echoing the politicizing effect of the 1961 campaign on the *alfabetizadores*. Thirdly, they offered those volunteering for such jobs and training priority access to higher education, allowing them to follow both routes (intensive professional training, followed by targeted employment, along with part-time wider study) over several years. Overall, the hope was that a new generation would be created, echoing the 1960s commitment and social effects and bringing young Cubans more systematically into the social structures, through the self-developing, as well as practical, benefits, of education.

The implications of this new campaign were considerable. Not only was a considerable investment needed to create the specialist training schools, with adequate provision of food and transport for the thousands involved, but the existing university system was also unable to cope with the sudden mass influx. The solution was simple but operationally challenging and expensive: a branch of an existing university would be opened in every one of Cuba's 169 *municipios*, using school premises in the evenings and weekends, and, echoing the old voluntarism of the construction *microbrigadas*, seconding university teachers from the relevant and possibly overstaffed departments, or inviting retired teachers to return briefly to employment, to teach there. The favoured subjects focused on the immediate needs perceived, such as sociology, computing and business studies. As with the new quasi-*brigadistas*, this 'massification' again echoed the university expansion of 1959–60 and, while hugely expensive at a time of budget scarcity and although many *emergente* recruits would prove to be inadequately trained to cope with the specialist demands of high-quality nursing or primary teaching (with deleterious effects on quality), the energy released proved exhilarating for many of those involved in teaching, organizing and learning. Subsequent research has demonstrated that the campaign did succeed in rescuing ideologically some, though not all, of the new students, with lasting effects (Smith 2016).

However, alongside this youth focus, higher education was also expanded to include the old, defying the former requirement to link training to specific guaranteed employment. This new focus was achieved by two mechanisms: the television-based *Universidad para Todos* (University for All) and the University of the Third Age, both targeting and enthusing many of the Revolution's most loyal and committed supporters. Clearly, education was again being valued for its intrinsic person-shaping capacity, rather than pragmatically geared to specific work.

However, the 'ideas' also included culture, and, once again, the enthusiasm of the *piratería* campaigns of the mid-1960s was copied in what was a new mass focus on reading, with UJC-led reading campaigns and with a startling and remarkable nationwide expansion of the biannual Havana Book Fair (which eventually reached around half of Cuba's population in over thirty places across the island) (Kumaraswami and Kapcia, 2012: 215-32). To support this, the Battle also expanded the facilities for printing, every province being given its own publishing house (Ediciones Territoriales), albeit printing much-reduced print-runs, mostly an average of only ten titles a year for each press, with runs of 500–1,000 copies. There was also a remarkable expansion of access to sociocultural training in local universities for a newly expanded workforce under the Ministry of Culture, now the Battle's main ministerial driver, accompanied by an equally impressive expansion of the provision of computer technology to all *municipios*, especially in hitherto neglected and isolated mountain regions.

There was one further dimension to the Battle: taking internationalism to a new level, to address and resist the effects of globalization on the developing world. This meant dispatching cultural workers, as well as the usual educators, to developing countries, but it also fed into the new Venezuelan-led initiative of the Bolivarian Alliance for Latin America (ALBA), which sought to channel the 'Pink Tide' energy and ideological commitment into an alternative to the free-trade mantra of the neoliberal orthodoxy, stressing instead cooperation, social welfare, international solidarity and trade in kind. Indeed, ALBA's energy arose from the close

relationship between Fidel Castro and the Venezuelan leader Hugo
Chávez, who looked increasingly to Cuba as a model and who proved
willing to enter a long and fruitful exchange of Cuban (human and
medical) aid for much-needed Venezuelan oil at low prices, substantially
helping to overcome the decade-long absence of Soviet oil supplies.

REFLECTIONS ON POWER, AUTHORITY AND THE STATE, 1990–2005

What, then, did all this mean for the character and effectiveness of the
state, power and authority? By 2005, what was clear about these key
elements of the system was that the state, so seemingly stable and strong
in 1985, had come close to collapse in 1991–5, deprived of the basic
resources to make it function properly or efficiently. However, those years
had also seen an unexpected ability and willingness of local activists and
ordinary Cubans (usually local activists from the PCC, People's Power
assemblies and Mass Organizations) to work collectively to rebuild a
new state in the ashes of the crisis. Therefore, partly replicating the Mass
Organizations' state-substituting efforts of 1959–68, the grassroots
activists did ensure adequate distribution of goods and communications,
ensuring that ordinary Cubans retained a sufficient degree of commitment
to, or at least tolerance of, the system. In that respect, therefore, it was
the People's Councils which most proved to be the instruments of state-
rebuilding, providing networks of supply and communications at the
vital, and long-neglected, *barrio* level between the street (CDR) and the
municipio, adding a new (*comunitario*) level to the state structures, one
that would prove more flexible than those already in existence. That
success, in turn, gave those new structures, as well as the individuals and
organization running them, a new authority, enjoyed because of their
effectiveness in achieving what was needed at that time of deep crisis.

   As for decision-making, decision-executing and decision-debating
powers, they had also been reshaped by the decade and a half of crisis,
being reallocated, often substantially so. At the top, real decision-
making power had noticeably changed. While Rectification might have
strengthened the hand of the ex-guerrilla 'inner circle' in decision-
making, a new power was emerging by 1993: the leaders of the Grupo
de Apoyo, noticeably Carlos Lage (secretary to the Council of State from
1993, who de facto acted as an unofficial prime minister, overseeing
the reform programme), Roberto Robaina (Foreign Minister in 1993–
7) and his successor Felipe Pérez Roque. This was because, with the

priority unquestionably given to the need to 'save the Revolution' by whatever means necessary, including introducing hitherto unthinkable economic policies, those younger (ex-UJC) leaders championing reform, untrammelled by a traditional commitment to the Revolution's traditional principles from 1953–75, now saw their real economic decision-making power increase significantly, and, as the economy began to show visible signs of improvement from 1994, also their authority.

Among the historic leadership and leading group, however, there were differences of opinion. On the one hand, the priority given to the urgent need to ensure the Revolution's survival was accepted without question by Raúl, whose authority rose commensurately (as the reforms' effects began to be felt) and who now gave those reforms his clear ideological and political imprimatur, enjoying both historic authority (as one of the two remaining historic leaders) and also the authority arising from the trust which many Cubans, even while nervous of the reforms, were willing to invest in him, aware that he could be relied upon not to throw out the baby with the bathwater. In retrospect, it also seemed likely that Ramiro Valdés (another leading survivor from 1953, once crucial in the security structures and twice Interior Minister) shared Raúl's commitment to both the Revolution's agreed essence and the need for urgent modernization. The fact that he was willingly seconded out of day-to-day access to decision-making to start an overhaul of Cuba's IT programmes, education and expertise suggested that shared commitment. Again, if he saw the need to go outside the normal parameters of policymaking thinking, then he too could be trusted to keep faith as he embraced reform.

However, the need to think the unthinkable was, at best, only accepted reluctantly by Fidel, persuaded by his brother. It seems likely that he saw the new measures (including increased tourism and access to the dollar) as a short-term 'fix', to be abandoned once recovery were achieved, given that he saw the long-term threats to ideological commitment if the measures had few limits. However, he was more willing to reform than others in the historic 'inner circle', most obviously represented in many Cubans' eyes by two ex-guerrillas, whose star had clearly risen and who steadily worked to build a base of their own, principally hoping to limit the scope of reform: José Ramón Machado Ventura and José Ramón Balaguer.

That base was clearly inside the PCC. Once the 1991 party congress had decided on the reform programme, the two individuals were given authority for national organization, ensuring ideological 'purity' among members, mostly through a diligent process of attending as many as possible of the several provincial PCC plenums, overseeing (and thus potentially containing and regulating) discussions of policy and principle and the election of personnel. That was clearly one of the possible explanations of the year-long delay in holding the scheduled 1996 (fifth) PCC congress, which to a large extent confirmed the outcome of the post-reform debate on what 'the Revolution' meant. However, the resistance to all-out reform became more a case of personnel than policy, through the PCC's gradual reshaping at all levels. While historically loyal members were preferred and promoted, a slightly younger ('middle') generation was also advanced: those who in their youth had been trained in Soviet and Socialist Bloc institutions, often referred to scathingly after 2000 as 'the Talibans' (although, as we will see, that term was also used for other political militants).

However, once again, this was not a case of 'factions' being formed, as there were at least five discernible lines of thinking visible within the PCC's upper reaches. The first were the ex-Grupo reformists who saw an opportunity to build their base at the top (rather than from the grassroots), relying on the popularity of reform ideas and practice, and on their authority as effective politicians; for them, the PCC was something of an anachronistic irrelevance, part of a growing shared view that the days of the 'historic generation' had passed. The second line of thinking was the Raúl-Valdés axis, believing in the need for a strong but accountable PCC, but also knowing that reform and modernization were urgent and that the ideas of the 1950s and 1960s were no longer pertinent.

The third 'group' was probably one person alone, Fidel: a reluctant but obstinately conditional reformer, who recognized the need for modernization but hankered after the spirit, if not the actual policies, of the 1960s and who was prepared to bide his time. Fidel had perhaps never shared his brother's commitment to the PCC as a concept: while Raúl always saw a properly organized single-party as a necessary means of structural communication and institutional accountability, but only if genuinely filled with committed and thinking members, Fidel had often tended to find it a useful tool for policy execution at best and more often a tiresome obstacle to the kind of mobilization-based 'permanent revolution' that he always espoused. For him, the atrophy of the late 1970s (requiring the 'surgery' of Rectification) and the PCC's use in 1962 and 1968 by those close to Moscow confirmed his suspicion about a large, close-knit and disciplined PCC. However, although notionally alongside him, the Machado Ventura-Balaguer axis held a very different view to Fidel: they saw the PCC as the basis of loyalty to the Revolution's origins and principles, prepared to use its structures to ensure resistance to the 'dangerous' reforms proposed. The fact that the scheduled 2002 (sixth) PCC congress repeatedly failed to materialize confirmed both the refuseniks' influential base within the structures and the party's new and conservative role in the decision-making and political power structures.

This became evident as the Battle of Ideas developed. There seems little doubt that the Battle was Fidel's brainchild, reading the public mood well in 1998–9 and seeing a new 1960s-style mobilization as the means for both reinvigorating the Revolution and ideological commitment, and bringing a new generation into the political fold. The latter issue was because, rather than using the existing PCC structures for his preferred acolytes, he used the UJC and FEU leaders as the Battle's political base, bypassing the PCC completely and harnessing the energy of a new generation to effect a necessary campaign. In this, he clearly enjoyed an authority even greater than that enjoyed by Raúl, who probably watched the Battle unfold with some distaste, suspicious of its cost, its unaccountable processes and structures and even its anachronistic methods.

But this array of different lines of thinking (the UJC-FEU 'axis' being yet another one for a few years) had one clear effect: the non-convening of the scheduled 2002 PCC congress. Fidel perhaps felt that it was not needed (as had often been true); the anti-reform leaders perhaps saw a congress as threat to their resistance and, although not sharing Fidel's enthusiasm for the Battle (possibly influenced by seeing the next generation of UJC/FEU bypassing them), continued to consolidate their base. Meanwhile, the Grupo had no interest at all in such a congress, seeing the Battle as anachronistic, harebrained and possibly clipping their political wings. Hence, since debate continued with no clear consensus (either emerging or imposed) and with only Raúl calling for the long-overdue congress, the congress had failed to emerge by 2005.

By then, however, Fidel's own authority was beginning to be questioned, but not so much because of policy mistakes, although many older Cubans (especially in Havana) saw the Battle's cost and scale as somewhat exaggerated and unnecessary; certainly, the *trabajadores sociales* (social workers) were often resented, especially during their short-term mobilization as 'shock troops' to 'intervene' in petrol stations and eliminate petty corruption. It was Fidel's health rather than his policies which was beginning to undermine that long-standing authority: the visible signs of his somewhat meandering speech-making and a public fall in 2002 led to growing fears that his hand on the national tiller might not be as assured as was necessary, not least against a rampantly hostile Bush administration. This, in turn, led some to see the Battle as embarrassing joke, significantly undermining Fidel's traditional authority. Hence, by 2005 the Cuban political decision-making structures were at a critical juncture, traditional authority being questioned but the state having grown in stature and authority: a mismatch requiring urgent attention.

Meanwhile, uncertainties about the leadership had increased confidence and visibility (although still not to most Cubans) among Cuba's dissidents, a challenge met by clampdowns on public protest. That reached a climax in April 2003 when seventy-five activists were arrested, tried and sentenced, departing from recent patterns which had seen a limited tolerance and mostly short-term detentions. When global media publicity (and political shifts in Europe) led the EU to start a period of diplomatic isolation, trenches were dug on both sides which would remain for a few years.

Institutionally, however, the system of governance seemed stronger and more confident: it was becoming clear that the Special Period had significantly reshaped and reinvigorated the matrix of power and authority at all levels. In large part that was precisely because the early 1990s experience of positive local collaboration between the PCC, Mass Organizations and People's Power activists to rebuild the state from grassroots had helped to formalize and legitimize the validity, effectiveness and necessity of the constant horizontal processes of negotiation, communication and collaboration. The damaged state would not have been rebuilt so swiftly and successfully without such processes, since each local agreement over what was needed and how best to achieve that had always demanded the greatest possible extent of horizontal consultation between local bodies and their representatives, but also often involving new stakeholders in the decision-making and the reshaping, such as locally relevant professional associations, recreational groups or even religious groups where they were significant or especially representative. Therefore, the reality was that the horizontal processes of consultation and negotiation within the matrix were strengthened in ways that had been true before 1990.

How then had the whole post-1989 experience reshaped the already variable uses and meanings of the term 'revolution' (or 'the Revolution')? In 1989–90 (after the Berlin Wall came down but before Comecon imploded), the Revolution had suddenly become an entity to be defended rather than extolled (as in the 1980s); enough doubts had crept in to create a level of fear, but were still largely overshadowed by an underlying sense of defiance, an ability to resist (based on three decades of survival) in ways that the more problematic and less flexible Eastern European states had not possessed. By 1991, however, that had given way to a much greater and deeper fear, especially after the Soviet Union's sudden collapse and disappearance. The Revolution was now something less capable of defending itself through defiance and its innate qualities and was now something whose achievements, basic values and sense of independence had to be defended by the whole population. While the ubiquitous image of *un eterno Baraguá* had captured the mood of 1989–90, people were now needed to contribute to its defence, with talk of the Option Zero 'trench warfare'.

By 1993–4, however, a significant shift had taken place: *el pueblo* (the people) of the more ideologically orthodox 1980s had now once again become more consistently the *nación*, and *La Revolución* was equated everywhere with *La Patria*. Hence, 'save the Revolution' was now phrased in terms that meant 'save the *Patria*'. This was reflected in the two conferences (1994 and 1995) called *Nación y Emigración*, bringing together, in Havana, emigrants and island residents in an attempt to use emigrants' basic patriotism and the more recent (largely economic) emigrants' residual sympathies for the Cuban system to save the Revolution's (earlier) achievements and in the process save the health and well-being of the emigrants' Cuba-based families.

As already seen, this also went much further in other areas, such as in the post-1994 emphasis on national history and celebration, confirming that the 1992 constitutional amendment to incorporate and reaffirm the Revolution's *martianismo* was real and permanent, and that the 1968 declaration of 100 years of revolution was still extant. Historiography, too, was driven to address Cuban history's key moments, episodes or protagonists of the non-socialist traditions of rebellion. Meanwhile, the détente with the churches stressed that national unity, and not ideological purity, was the key to survival. Indeed, while the debates over 'what *is* The Revolution?' had not clarified much by the late 1990s, the apparent consensus over the 1959–61 nation-building project as its essence seem to prevail and be confirmed by the pope's welcome and the revival of religious practice, as well as the whole tenor of the Battle of Ideas.

Meanwhile, abroad and among some disenchanted intellectuals and artists on the island, however, a further view of *La Revolución* was being expressed: as a failed project and an anachronistic phenomenon, in which the once lauded 'New Man' ideal reflected that failure, articulating a symbolic mythic representation of that anachronistic character.

9

FROM FIDEL TO RAÚL

The last chapter?

By around 2005, it was therefore becoming clear to most Cubans that something of a milestone, or even (according to some) a turning point, was approaching. On the one hand, while the Battle of Ideas was still in full swing, even succeeding in regenerating some Cubans' levels of ideological commitment, there were already serious concerns among economic managers about the disruptive and costly campaign, reviving memories of 1968–70. Those probably included Raúl himself, who, probably frustrated that the post-1991 reforms had not been extended, was still arguing within the leading decision-debating circles for a more sustained strategy of a 'bringing up to date' (*actualización*) of Cuba's socialist project, rather than (as some critics saw it) seeking to repeat the euphoria of the 1960s. However, the real cause for wider concern was Fidel's own health and age: he was provoking growing worries that his previously robust and seemingly indomitable energy were beginning to decline, with an equally growing concern among many Cubans at a possible risk of drift in the leadership.

On 31 July 2006, two weeks before his eightieth birthday, it was his health which surfaced most evidently and, for many outside Cuba, most dramatically: it was announced that he had been taken seriously ill (later deemed diverticulitis), requiring urgent surgery. At once, the evidently well-prepared emergency contingency plan was enacted: Raúl Castro (as senior vice-president) became interim president, while a small group of the most trusted leaders (including Ramiro Valdés and Machado Ventura) took responsibility for groups of defined areas of government.

This caught everyone by surprise, generating a range of very different responses. In Cuba, the overwhelming reaction mixed personal concern (for the health and well-being of the *Comandante en Jefe* (Commander in Chief), hoping that the man who had led the Revolution so distinctively for forty-five years would survive and return to health) with a degree of relief that under Raúl (widely respected for his historic authority, but positively associated with the 1990s reforms that had 'saved the Revolution', and widely reputed to have an impatient belief in efficiency and good government) the risk of drift in government would disappear. For a year, however, inertia reigned, as it remained unclear to many within the governing structures and within the many bureaucracies, who was actually taking the long-term decisions, what was the firm direction which might be decided and whether Fidel was, or would be, well enough to take back the reins of power; that affected decision-making at all levels, with officials and ministers alike being uncertain, especially on Fidel's favoured Battle of Ideas or on the reform and modernization long favoured by Raúl. Hence, the drift became more pronounced and real.

The outside world was certainly taken by surprise, especially in Washington, where Cuba policy had long been based on its focus on the person of Fidel: not only had the Helms-Burton legislation specifically identified the end of his rule and power as a prerequisite for ending sanctions, but when the Bush administration talked in 2004 of the 'biological solution' to the Cuban problem (i.e. the leader's death), it was clear that the traditional academic and political US focus on personality when interpreting the Cuban political system and future was more fundamental than the public rhetoric which many European observers had assumed it to be. Hence, when the unthinkable happened, US policymakers were in shock: other than dismissing Raúl as 'Fidel lite', in the words of Tom Casey, a State Department spokesman in 2008 (CBS News 2008), Cuba's inertia was fully matched by a parallel inertia in Washington and a dangerous inability to judge Cuban politics without Fidel at the helm. The 'unthinkable' of course was that Fidel should choose to retire from power, rather than dying with his boots on, which had always been assumed in US policymaking circles; that expectation had even reputedly led to the US Coastguard's long-standing plans to mount a naval barrier off the Florida coast the moment that Castro's death was announced to prevent the mass exodus escaping the inevitable unrest in Cuba.

However, since inertia could not be tolerated for long, Raúl seized the initiative in 2007. Having announced in February that Fidel's health was improving and later that he was being involved in discussions, he evidently decided by June that Fidel's return to active politics was becoming less likely, given the slow recovery. Hence, to prevent further drift and aware of the urgency of determined decision-making, on 26 July 2007 he startled Cubans in the annual and usually ritual speech to commemorate the 1953 Moncada attack by listing a string of unprecedented and fierce criticisms of the Cuban system's recent failings, especially condemning the lack of efficiency, productivity, discipline, commitment, honesty and purchasing power.

That was startling enough for most Cubans, both in the vehemence of Raúl's wholesale critique and in his confidence and freedom to deliver it while still only acting president; however, he followed that in September by calling for a nationwide consultation (inevitably to be effected through the PCC structures and Mass Organizations) to discuss those criticisms, as a way of identifying a consensus for reform and modernization. The result was yet another debate, but this time on an unprecedented scale and without clear parameters, although his criticisms (largely reflecting those expressed and heard daily by most Cubans) suggested that he fully expected the outcome to be a consensus for the very reforms which he intended to enact; indeed, the innumerable meetings to discuss this, within the PCC and Mass Organizations, were usually chaired by someone with a clear brief to shape (or at least regulate) the scope of discussion, most probably based on that person's PCC membership. Hence, the debate's breadth and depth in all the relevant organizations not only covered Raúl's scathing criticisms but also allowed whatever other complaints ordinary Cubans were willing to share with their fellow citizens; moreover, every Cuban had at least one channel through which to be involved (in whichever Mass Organization to which they belonged), but most had two or three, since, with most Cubans belonging to their local CDR (even if not necessarily actively so), any employee probably also belonged to a union (within the CTC) and half of the population belonged to the FMC: thus, a working woman within the PCC could actually have four opportunities to be involved. Furthermore, just as the meetings to discuss (at all levels) followed clear patterns and had clear 'tramlines', the outcomes of those debates were duly channelled upwards within each organization and then, to the PCC, which then channelled them upwards to the highest echelons of the *Buró Político*.

Generally, the consensus was precisely (and predictably) what Raúl had expected: a widespread demand for greater economic efficiency and increased material satisfaction, for greater openness and honesty in the much-criticized media, and for greater freedom for Cubans to travel. In other words, most collective responses suggested a substantial and sustained improvement, without any widespread evident demand for fundamental political change; this was partly of course because the consultation had been 'within' the system, but also because, while most people wanted rapid improvement in living standards and spending power, relatively few wished to 'throw the baby out with the bathwater' by reforming enough to threaten some of the Revolution's values and *logros*. Raúl had hence been given the ammunition that he needed for a programme of reform.

In the following months he went further, extending his criticisms of existing patterns of thinking and action: what he called Cubans' dependency culture (relying passively on a benefactor state rather than investing time and energy in improving things with initiative) and even inadequate wages and salaries. However, he was still partly operating within a vacuum, since he still only enjoyed interim authority, given Fidel's continuing occupation of the presidency and the continuing uncertainty over his health and political future. The approaching National Assembly elections (February 2008) could end that uncertainty, confirming Raúl's position, although a similar uncertainty applied to Fidel's PCC leadership until the next party congress, long overdue.

On the presidency, uncertainty remained until the last minute: with Fidel once again nominated for election as a deputy by Santiago voters, the possibility existed that, once elected to the Assembly, he might then be re-elected as president, if only by default. Yet his health remained unclear: in April 2007, his first post-operation appearance on television suggested some recovery but continuing frailty. Ultimately, on the eve of the election he confirmed that, although willing to be elected deputy, he would not stand for election as president, which opened the door to Raúl's presidential election by the new Assembly and Council of State.

Thus, Cuba passed overnight but peacefully from a Fidel-led Cuba to a Raúl-led Cuba and began a less certain but somehow also more confident path to some sort of reform – more confident because, given Raúl's record since the 1970s, most Cubans associated him with a desire for efficiency and material rewards. The general feeling was that, while lacking Fidel's penchant for passionate speech making and improvisation, Raúl's feet were firmly on the ground as a family man, focused on getting the job done rather than 'rallying the troops'. In fact, there was another dimension to his political principles which now came into play: his belief in the principle and practice of full internal accountability through properly constituted structures (with the regular congress acting as the forum for such accountability to be institutionally visible) and in the need for the PCC, above all, to listen to ordinary Cubans and act accordingly, and for the party rank-and-file to be listened to by those above, and not, as so often in the past, ignored without any possibility of questioning at any level.

That meant the parallel need now to tackle the vacuum in the PCC. If the question of Fidel's presidency remained unclear until February 2008, the parallel uncertainty over the PCC was even greater. After all, in the familiar pattern of some previous congresses (where lack of consensus postponed scheduled congresses), the 2002 congress remained un-convened, reflecting either a lack of consensus (over further reform) or Fidel's preference for operating without the encumbrance of formal accountability to a difficult party. Hence, one of Raúl first public announcements as president was the urgency of a new congress to debate, agree and legitimize reforms, coincidentally also legitimizing his own PCC leadership.

That task proved much more difficult, taking three years to be achieved. The obstacle was still many PCC members' resistance to change, a view still shared by many older Cubans outside the PCC who feared the proverbial 'baby' and 'bathwater' outcome. Hence, the ideological and political debate continued, Raúl and others around him advocating speedy and often deep reform against the imagined 'old guard', perhaps looking to Fidel.

Raúl himself indicated the 'battle lines': after being elected, he countered some domestic critics' fears that his aim was to dismantle the Revolution by declaring to the National Assembly on 8 January 2009 that he had not been elected to allow the Revolution to be destroyed (Cuba Solidarity 2009). This inevitably raised the question of what he meant by 'the Revolution', since he did not then refer to 'socialism'. However, in his famous 2007 criticisms of the system's failings he had stressed that he rejected a spurious and utopian egalitarianism, believing instead in equality of treatment and opportunity, for which he referred implicitly to the Soviet Constitution's definition of socialism, which added to Marx's 1875 definition of communism (in the *Critique of the Gotha Programme*), 'from each according to his abilities, to each according to his needs' (Marx and Engels 1970: 321), the definition of socialism as 'from each according to his abilities, to each according to his work'. In other words, Raúl stressed that Cuba was still very much in the pre-communist and necessarily 'messy' and contested stage of socialism.

Hence, Raúl now seemed to be saying that the time for seeking an impossible communism had long ago passed, and that Cubans should be aiming for a down-to-earth transition to socialism, suggesting that he intended to aim for the original 1959–61 project and not simply a manageable and pragmatic version of utopia. He further clarified that by defining his reform programme as *actualización* (updating), suggesting that, however relevant and feasible one version of 'socialism' might have been in the 1960s, global realities now dictated updating what was possible within a more globalized and free-market world. In other words, he remained faithful to the Revolution's original project.

That interpretation of Raúl as a possible Gorbachev was curious in one key respect: the 'reforming' Raúl, urging Cuba's updating away from a partly anachronistic and partly failing definition, was the same person who in the first two decades (once the outside world had stopped dismissing his role as simply attributable to family favour) had routinely been assumed to be the system's 'hard line' ideologue, seemingly committed to a Soviet-style vision of communism and determined to clamp down on any dissent. Indeed, as late as 1996, when he voiced criticisms of maverick thinkers inside the PCC CEA (Giuliano 1998), it seemed that the 'hard line' image was still relevant, despite having led the post-1992 reform programme. Was he therefore a 'reformer' or a 'hardliner', pragmatist or ideologue? And how accurate was that interpretation of his understanding of 'the Revolution'?

That question as ever goes right to the heart of the trajectory outlined here, with the possible answers (there being no one single simple answer to 'explain' the Revolution) reflecting the process's unique combination of factors, pressures, decisions, ideals and practical priorities which have always shaped it. In this, Raúl was no different from Fidel, although their styles and personalities did undoubtedly differ.

For, in understanding 'Raúl's Cuba', we are best advised to remember that his 2008 presidential election (being re-elected in 2013, albeit – at his insistence – for one time only) and his 2011 election as the PCC's leader (also re-elected once in 2016) were not because he was Fidel's younger brother: whatever foreign media might have thought, the Cuban system was never simply a personalist autocracy or a dynastic structure. Instead, Raúl was elected because he was (literally) 'the last man standing' of the three historic leaders of the 1956–8 guerrilla-led insurrection and therefore of the whole dramatic post-1959 transformation. Thus he enjoyed both popular legitimacy and the loyalty of the leading group, especially among ex-guerrillas, but, being also widely associated with the successful reforms of 1992–5, he also enjoyed the respect and support of 'modernizers' in the leadership and many ordinary Cubans, especially those with fears for Cuba's future under an evidently ageing and ailing Fidel. Hence, it is useful here to assess Raúl's particular place in Cuban history before the Special Period to discover the origins of the confusion about his character or politics.

The starting point is probably his induction into the murky and confusing world of Havana student politics, where he cut his political teeth in the early 1950s. Following his brother's footsteps would not have been easy, given the shadow that Fidel already cast over those around him; hence, Raúl soon seemed to take his own path at the university as his own political ideas radicalized. That path was towards the more orthodox PSP and its JS youth wing, where he formed enduring friendships with other members. That link certainly led to his inclusion in a youth delegation to the Socialist Bloc-backed World Youth Congress in Vienna in February 1953, which included a brief visit to Romania. Whether he was a JS member before travelling or after his return to Cuba in June or July 1953 (the date remains unclear), that association helped classify him for many later observers (including the CIA before 1959) as the Revolution's ideologue (Paterson 1994: 185–6).

Whatever the case, it was on his return from Europe in summer 1953 that he learned from Fidel of the Moncada plan, immediately joining the venture, although that automatically identified him with the more nationalist pole of Cuban radicalism rather than the PSP, which would soon condemn the attack as 'adventurism'. Raúl's late recruitment, however, meant that, lacking the others' military training at the university, he had no leading role; instead, he was second-in-command of the small unit detailed to seize the nearby hospital. There, he conducted himself with intelligence and bravery, and, escaping with Fidel and others after the attack, he shared their fate: arrest, trial, sentencing and finally imprisonment in the Isle of Pines' Model Prison. Therefore, whatever Raúl's previous affiliations or faith in communism, he had unquestioningly opted for the less orthodox and more nation-focused activism of the Moncada plotters.

Thenceforth, he moved to centre stage, becoming Fidel's trusted second-in-command, de facto if not yet formally. Once the rebels were released in Batista's May 1955 amnesty, establishing the 26 July Movement in Havana and leaving for Mexican exile to prepare the promised return, Raúl became increasingly influential in the group and its aims. Possibly his most influential role, however, was accidental: it was he who first encountered and befriended Che Guevara in Mexico City, introducing him to the group and, more significantly, Fidel (Anderson 1997: 173–4). However, Guevara only joined the *Granma* expeditionary force as their doctor and not yet in a leading role; hence, when they left Mexico on 25 November 1956, Raúl was already second only to Fidel in authority, having distinguished himself by his skills in training and his political acumen. Interestingly, while preparations continued, the PSP had sent messages via Raúl, asking Fidel to abandon the expedition and work with them; when Fidel characteristically rejected those overtures (realizing the political value of fulfilling promises), Raúl's support for him demonstrated his loyalty to the revolutionary project rather than the PSP. Indeed, although Raúl would always seem to prefer a less action-led dramatic approach to problems than Fidel, his loyalty to the rebellion perhaps already suggested that any admiration for the Soviet Bloc communism was based on its effectiveness, organization and structural internal accountability, for even then he probably believed more in those values than in head-on challenges within larger projects. Nonetheless, his rejection of the PSP line possibly reflected a distaste for their narrow interpretations of communism, seemingly already leading towards what many saw as pusillanimity.

During the 1956–8 insurrection, Raúl certainly came into his own as a guerrilla leader, strategist and tactician, as a thoughtful administrator who commanded personal loyalty, and as someone always aware of the political importance of effective structures. On 18 December 1956, after the expedition had been attacked and scattered bloodily at Alegría del Pío, his small group of stragglers met Fidel's group at Cinco Palmas, a moment later commemorated as the point when confidence was restored, Fidel famously echoing Céspedes's 1868 declaration about twelve men being enough to win the war (thereby accidentally creating the misleading myth of twelve guerrillas surviving) (Franqui 1967; Kapcia 2014: 48–9). After that meeting, Raúl became increasingly influential and respected, and in mid-1958 he was logically given command of the new Frank País Second Front in eastern Oriente's Sierra del Cristal to spread the rebellion geographically and take the offensive. There, Raúl grew in stature, his zone becoming significant for the administration and politicization among both the guerrillas and the local population, more than for military successes, since fighting was still concentrated in the Sierra Maestra and, increasingly, from August in the areas affected by the two westward columns of Cienfuegos and Guevara. That was when Raúl began to create a loyal group which, after January 1959, would become significant in the emerging apparatus of security, policing and military defence (Kapcia 2014: 122–6). It was also when he willingly worked alongside local PSP activists, recognizing their political and organizational talents and discipline.

The area of military expertise was where Raúl was given real authority after the rebel victory, named in July 1959 as head of the newly formed FAR, a decision triggering Matos's outright opposition, less against Raúl's personal qualities than against his close collaboration with the PSP. Thereafter, Raúl's FAR significance would be seen as much in its development as a military force as in any advocacy of close Soviet links, economically and ideologically; his association with the emerging security apparatus, while seeming to confirm his 'hard line' reputation, was also a logical adjunct to that FAR preoccupation.

Certainly, his good relations with the Soviet military (Klepak 2005: 45) contributed significantly to the Revolution's future, reinforcing the FAR's place at the centre of the system: not only did they, together with local militias and the nationwide CDR network, defeat the Bay of Pigs invasion, but they also kept regular soldiers and reservists in constant readiness for any new invasion. Equally, while it was mostly the militias (rather than the army) which defeated counter-revolutionary rebels in the Sierra del Escambray, Raúl oversaw that campaign, both aware of the need to pair military responses with the battle for peasants' hearts and minds and deciding on their large-scale transportation to isolating encampments. While Cuba's safety from invasion after 1961 was ultimately attributable to the 1962 US-Soviet agreement, the FAR's and security forces' readiness and effectiveness certainly helped. After the Soviet Union's disappearance in 1991, the FAR remained as sufficient deterrent to any US ideas of ending 'the Cuban problem': periodic Pentagon studies of the feasibility of any invasion of Cuba always concluded that, given the FAR's strength and guerrilla strategy, it would be politically unpalatable to the US public, given likely US casualties (Klepak 205: 250).

Meanwhile, the FAR proved their mettle spectacularly in the military campaigns in Angola (1975–89) and Ethiopia (1977–8), both involvements successfully resisting external threats to those countries' new and ideologically sympathetic governments. In all, over 200,000 Cuban troops were deployed in Angola over the years and the involvement's wider political significance was paralleled by its military effectiveness. Although Fidel often led the campaign's decision-making, Raúl was always, quietly and efficiently, at the helm and it was clearly *his* FAR that proved successful.

Hence, Cuba's military effectiveness was always paramount in Raúl's thinking after 1959, making any Soviet links more important in that respect than any ideological affinity. Once the threat of invasion and sabotage had dissipated by the 1970s, he concluded that the FAR would have to adapt, becoming a more recognizable military apparatus (without losing their historic legitimacy and identity as a guerrilla-based force): those years saw a sustained programme of close relations between the FAR and the Soviet military, including the purchase of, and Cuban training in, Soviet armaments, the FAR's reconfiguration along Soviet lines (of hierarchy and ranks) and a constant exchange of ideas, planning and education between the two militaries. Therefore, while a still guerrilla-based FAR had defeated the 1961 invasion, it was a Soviet-influenced but guerrilla-conscious FAR which defeated the South African troops in 1988.

Raúl's third major point of significance after 1959 was related to this FAR role: his contribution to economic debates inside the leadership. His attention to the FAR's structure and efficiency enabled him to convince the wider leadership to give the FAR its own economic infrastructure: both a military decision (ensuring a reliable supply of goods and agricultural produce for troops and operations) and a growing mistrust of the questionable efficiency of Cuba's economic production systems and structures (Klepak 2005: 75–102). The economic role grew, feeding into Raúl's 1980s drive to streamline the FAR's economic and commercial operations with Japanese experts. It seems likely that Raúl may have influenced the leadership's move away from the 1960s ad hoc mobilization-based approach towards a more conventional institutionalization after 1972. Yet, this did not necessarily reflect continuing admiration for the Soviet Union; before Rectification, he probably shared Fidel's growing distaste for the Cuban system's loss of ideological consciousness that the PCC's growth and a growing 'consumerism' had begun to produce. Hence, as already seen, Rectification was not simply a nostalgic return to the 1960s emphasis on ideological rather than pragmatic motives, but included Raúl's drive for economic streamlining (partly influenced by the FAR's recent experience), in preparation for the predicted Comecon crisis.

Therefore, it was consistent that, after 1989–91, it was Raúl who led those advocating an economic reform programme to save the Revolution, enabling it to survive in a Soviet-less world. Certainly, of all the leading decision-makers then, his was the most respected voice for what became the agreed strategy, giving the lie to the commonly held external assumptions that the Revolution's leadership was always about Fidel's autocratic rule, brooking no opposition or alternative to his preferences: as in the early 1970s, Fidel proved willing to be persuaded by Raúl and others about the need for a hitherto unacceptable strategy.

We can therefore see that two common assumptions about the post-1959 system are questionable, if not inaccurate and misleading. The first is that the political system was essentially a personality-based autocracy until 2006, with Fidel determining all decisions and policies and centralizing all authority in himself: as already argued, although he always commanded greater personal loyalty and affection than Raúl through his personality, he was always subject to the same structural and institutional checks, balances and internal pressures as Raúl after 2007. Both had to compromise much more than was assumed outside Cuba and, certainly, in US policymaking circles. Indeed, that reality was partly what persuaded the political advisers of Barack Obama to consider the time right to begin dialogue with Havana and end Cuba's isolation.

The second assumption was that, as was common in outside interpretations of many pre-1991 Socialist Bloc polities, the Cuban leadership was formed by a series of factions, often subsumed under the headings of 'idealists' (or 'ideologues') and pragmatists, or conservatives and reformers, or radicals and moderates – those categories often being new forms of older ones, 'radicals' becoming 'idealists' and then, decades later, 'conservatives' and (liberal) 'moderates' becoming 'pragmatists' and then finally 'reformers'. As already seen, whatever truth there may have been in those depictions, they generally misread the complexity and contradictions of a constantly changing series of debates (whose nature and scope varied widely) inside a much wider leadership than outsiders had usually believed. Hence, Raúl's apparent transformation from an exponent of one 'camp' in 1953–9 to being an exponent of another camp in the 1990s was not that surprising, since his understanding of what had to be done was always close to Fidel's and that of the other ex-guerrillas, but his belief in the ways to achieve that often differed. Whatever the case, once the internal battle had begun (between at least two different perspectives of means, rather than ends), in 2008 Raúl was determined to follow through his desired *actualización*, a process that would prove difficult, with reverses, a frustrating degree of hesitation and a constant need for cajoling and negotiation.

In fact, Raúl had already started to prepare the ground for that process, even while only serving as interim president in 2006–7: even before he took hold of the reins of power in 2007 (with his July speech and the following consultation), he had already initiated a cautious and unseen reshaping (including a slow rejuvenation) of the PCC's lower and middle levels. Over that first year, for example, the costly Battle of Ideas was quietly shelved, many of those leading activists associated with it being quietly replaced by more efficient and reliable people; this happened in several national bodies and crucial research centres but was also echoed less visibly outside Havana, through a slow process of promoting younger and more effective PCC cadres to key positions. After February 2008, therefore, he had the formal authority to embark on a similar process of renewal within the government itself. Several older government figures were steadily retired (through ill-health or age) or demoted, replaced by a new, much more female, generation of efficient operators, with authority to push through restructuring – not yet *actualización* – within their areas of responsibility, and to build a more efficient apparatus of decision-making. Simultaneously, a national drive was launched to rid the system of the pockets of the low-level corruption that had grown up (not least in those areas more susceptible to the attractions of hard currency, such as foreign trade and tourism) and also to eliminate the corrosive culture of pilfering and perquisites which had long characterized the bureaucracy and most workplaces. For all that Raúl seemed a 'systems' man, focused on efficiency, he evidently shared Fidel's moralistic imperative for 'correct' behaviour within a socialist system.

This new focus on the government also had another dimension. Given the prolonged struggle with the entrenched PCC elements, Raúl knew that to reform he had to find an alternative channel for decision-making and change. That turned out to be the People's Power system and, at the top, the Council of Ministers (i.e. the government and cabinet). This therefore meant cultivating a close relationship with the National Assembly (under the open-minded Alarcón) and using that body as the alternative to the still elusive 2002 PCC congress, proposing and debating reform proposals in government and the Assembly, rather than within and through the PCC structures, particularly using the Assembly's Standing Commissions as alternatives to the PCC Central Committee departments for discussing, shaping and refining proposals and policy. Unusually, it thus became possible for the Assembly to launch proposals, passed to the PCC for formal ratification, rather than the other way round: a totally new role for the Assembly and the government which gave both bodies greater credibility and authority, partially sidelining the PCC.

However, it was not just the PCC where Raúl had to negotiate. Soon after his election, he announced a draconian (seemingly Thatcherite) plan to cut one million jobs from the public sector within six months. The aim reflected his known preferences for efficiency, visible accountability and legality: to remove from the state sector those 'undisciplined' workers (estimated by some to be 200,000) who, while receiving state salaries, were working informally in a hidden self-employed sector. Hence, his estimates of the desirable size of an expanded *cuentapropista* sector (between 500,000 and a million) reflected the knowledge that that sector already included double the 200,000 legal operators. He was determined to end this unacceptable anomaly.

Faced with the plan, it was not just the PCC which looked askance but, more importantly, the CTC, whose leaders immediately – knowing full well that their credibility now depended on their effectiveness – began to negotiate with the government, insisting on a slower pace and fewer cuts, together with checks and guarantees for the process of identifying those at risk of unemployment and protecting their income. Eventually, the original proposals were negotiated down to fewer job losses and a much slower time frame – something that Raúl had probably expected, knowing well the essential importance of the principles and practice of constant negotiation within the political system.

Hence, the final agreement was still remarkable, given past expectations and the established principles of employment, but more importantly (on the question of power), what Raúl had achieved by this long and ponderous process was not just legitimacy (for his plan, himself and the CTC), but also authority for all three. Within the system's ethos, that counted for much, not least in Raúl's further battles with the PCC. While the CTC leadership knew the limits of their objections (they could not reject the plan outright, but could only negotiate better terms and greater protection), the PCC stalwarts knew that, given the party's 'leading role', they had no such limits. Moreover, as long as Fidel had not yet confirmed his retirement from the PCC's leadership (despite having the opportunity while announcing his effective retirement from the presidency in April 2008), not only did Raúl still lack the formal ideological authority which such an election would give him within the PCC decision-making structures but the possibility also remained that Fidel might use his authority to block reforms. Hence, PCC resistance enjoyed some vicarious assumptions of authority.

Hence, with the CTC now on board, Raúl had now to address the PCC problem, which included confirming his own position and authority by being elected to Fidel's remaining post. As already seen, he had already started the process of outmanoeuvring resistance through the back door, because, although lacking the formal authority to make such changes nationally, he could use his limited authority and links to effect those changes, as he had done in the government: replacing older and more conservative elements by younger, more effective and more forward-looking activists with proven ability, loyalty and reliability in the lower (municipal) levels and the smaller provinces. One clear case was the promotion to the leadership of the Santiago provincial PCC (the PCC's second most important provincial body) of Lázaro Esposito, who had demonstrated his open-mindedness and effectiveness in Granma province.

Finally, Raúl's frustration became visible and public. In early 2011, he announced that, if the long-overdue sixth congress continued to be delayed (he had publicly identified its convening as one of his most urgent priorities on being elected president in 2008), he would have little choice but to use the PCC's internal rules to call a Special Conference to make 'generational changes'. The targets were clear, and that finally unlocked the resistance: the PCC leadership duly announced that April 2011 would see the nine-year delayed congress convened.

That assembly did give Raúl most of what he wanted. It was preceded by Fidel's last-minute declaration that he had always intended his 2008 resignation as presidential candidate to include resignation from the PCC leadership, which allowed Raúl to be duly elected, giving him the necessary authority. Secondly, the congress approved in principle the reform programme, as outlined in the extensive *Lineamientos* (guidelines), after being subjected to a remarkably long process of popular consultation via all the usual vertical structures and channels.

However, to many outsiders' and Cubans' surprise, the congress elections showed the continuing need for compromise by electing Machado Ventura to replace Raúl as the PCC's Second Secretary. Given the etiquette of the Cuban system, Raúl clearly needed to reassure everyone who feared 'the baby' being thrown out with the bathwater, so compromise may have reflected that. Equally, it may have reflected continuing resistance: given Raúl's historic authority, he was never going to be challenged for the leading post once Fidel had vacated it, but anti-reform resisters could perhaps make a point by electing someone widely assumed to be their leading exponent, if only to restrict Raúl's freedom of action.

Hence, when Raúl eventually called a Special Conference in 2012, no longer to make urgent generational changes but to clarify and even change the PCC rules determining its systemic role, this seemed a further battle. What emerged from the conference was of some significance: the standard reference (in the former Socialist Bloc) to the party's theoretical 'leading role' was now expressed more as *rector* (guiding), rather than *dirigente* (directing), and the event seemed to stress that the PCC's (still systemically fundamental) purpose was to give ideological guidance, and not to interfere in the mechanisms and processes of governmental decision-making, although such guidance would still been viewed as essential for the ideological authority for any crucial decisions.

Hence, on that front, any significant long-term change would still have to wait until the next (seventh) PCC congress, scheduled for April 2016. Meantime, the process of debate and reform continued, the latter enacted by presidential decree or National Assembly voting. One such was the January 2012 decision to allow Cubans the freedom to travel abroad without the previously requisite 'exit visa' (a past source of much frustration), providing that the country of destination allowed them entry; furthermore, the length of time that Cubans could stay abroad was extended. Another welcome reform was the decree allowing the sale and purchase of housing, moving away from the decades-long system of swapping housing (the *permuta*), which had often involved an illegal payment, given that the two dwellings exchanged were rarely of equal value or quality, perhaps being exchanged because of death or family convenience.

A further significant change was less a decree than a shift in behaviour: greater tolerance of dissident activists. One easy move here was for Raúl to decree the freeing at last of the remaining activists of the seventy-five who had been controversially imprisoned in 2003 during the clampdown, which had originally generated internal protest, led by the high-profile Damas de Blanco (Ladies in White), mostly wives or girlfriends of those imprisoned; those protests were protected by the Catholic Church until the protesters extended their campaigning beyond their narrow aim. The clampdown had also attracted much international condemnation in human rights forums, leading to a freeze in relations with the EU, which thereupon developed a 'common position' to make better relations conditional on progress on human rights.

Mention of the church brings back the always revealing issue of church–state relations. To recap, since the early 1960s the Catholic Church experienced a rocky relationship with the evolving Revolution. Already socially weak even before 1959 (more than anywhere in Latin America), its base being strongest in the white urban (and even Spanish-origin) middle class, the church tended to be doctrinally and politically conservative, making its initial welcome for the Revolution somewhat fragile. By 1961, welcome had turned to hostility, as the middle class rejected the political radicalization and as the church's influential foothold in private education was threatened (Kirk 1989: 68–71); school nationalization eventually came in June 1961. Antagonism grew as some radicals' developing Marxism included Marx's (misused) dictum about religion being 'the opium of the people', making them hostile to all religion, even though many of the Revolution's leaders were more ready to tolerate those Protestant churches whose working-class members unquestionably supported the Revolution. In this anti-religion posture, the PSP and the main ideological journal *Cuba Socialista* took the lead (Cuba 1962; Roca 1963), albeit focusing more on the political postures and US links with the Catholic hierarchy, Jehovah's Witnesses and Pentecostalist churches. By the late 1960s, therefore, the Catholic hierarchy had retreated from cooperation to a kind of internal exile, adopting the Eastern European church's self-image of a victim of communist oppression.

Eventually, Vatican diplomatic and spiritual priorities persuaded greater cooperation, helped by the 1980s rise of Liberation Theology bringing Latin American radical clergy to Cuba that was puzzled by the Cuban church's continuing conservativism (Kirk 1989: 127–71). In the late 1980s, the PCC opened an office for religious affairs, suggesting détente, and, as seen earlier, the early 1990s crisis brought both sides together more pragmatically and even morally, after the hierarchy's brief flirtation in the early crisis with the idea of copying the Polish church's anti-communist activism. Thereafter, the relationship continued to develop, with the tacit understanding about tolerating church-linked dissidence, something which determined the authorities' attitude to Osvaldo Payá's Proyecto Varela campaign in 2002–3, which focused on changing the Constitution (to allow his demands) rather than seeking to end the system, as some US-linked dissidents advocated. This understanding served both sides: it gave the church valuable space (hitherto denied) and much-needed prestige, lost in the earlier decades by its stance and social character; on the authorities' side, the security forces were more able to clamp down on the US-linked activists on the grounds that they had chosen to work against the system, even conspiring with, and taking aid from, the government whose long-standing hostility and embargo were intended to end a system from which, it was argued, many Cubans benefited socially. Therefore, while attracting criticism from human rights organizations abroad for continuing to harass or supress many dissidents, the Cuban state could claim to be tolerant with those who chose not to flout the law and worked *dentro*.

This new relationship brought other benefits. In late March 2012, Cuba hosted a three-day visit from Pope Benedict XVI, who followed the success of his predecessor's 1998 visit: John Paul II had won a Cuban government undertaking to allow the celebration of Christmas, but Benedict now exacted a commitment to allow Good Friday to be a public holiday. Moreover, like his predecessor, Benedict condemned the US embargo. The greatest advantage came with the shock US–Cuban détente in 2014, which had been smoothed substantially by the Vatican's mediation, as a 'backchannel' of communication between the Cuban government and the church, in exchange for the government's freeing of the remaining 2003-arrested prisoners (LeoGrande and Kornbluh 2014). It was, therefore, only a matter of time before the next pope (Francis I) was invited to Cuba, in September 2015, demonstrating the complete normalization' of church–state relations.

The US–Cuban détente was indeed a shock. Just when many were bewildered by the pace of change under Raúl (although others, especially the Havana young, were frustrated by the lack of speedy change), the greatest shock to everyone's expectations came on 17 December 2014 when Obama and Raúl simultaneously announced to their citizens and the world that both countries intended as soon as possible to resume full diplomatic relations. The shock was great because, although Obama publicly considered the embargo anachronistic and a failed policy, damaging to US interests, there had been little hint of relations changing any further than the generally warmer atmosphere since 2008. However, it later transpired that the intervening six years had seen a slow cautious process via various third-party channels (the Vatican and the Swiss and Canadian embassies in both capitals) to build mutual confidence and explore the possibilities of détente. Hence, the two presidents were able to declare confidently that within a few months the two countries' missions (Interests Sections since 1977) would be upgraded to full embassy status. Those embassies duly opened in 2015: the Cuban in April and the US (opened by Secretary of State John Kerry) in August.

The motives behind the decision were revealing. On the Cuban side, the basic intention was to normalize Cuba's external environment as much as possible (knowing that the embargo could not be ended by Obama alone but only – under the terms of the Helms-Burton Act – by an almost impossible two-thirds majority of both houses of the US Congress), which might help attract investment and external economic interest to support Raúl's reforms. But it was also driven by the determination to end the use, since 2000, of the existing US Interests Section for supporting dissident activity, which would be more difficult once upgraded to an embassy. From the US perspective, Obama's desire was to remove what had become a running sore and a growing irrelevance in US foreign, and especially Latin American, policy, and perhaps to undermine the electoral importance of Florida's Republican-voting Cuban-American constituency. However, there was another urgent motive: to counter the explicit and potentially embarrassing threat by Latin American and Caribbean countries to boycott the April 2015 Summit of the Americas if Cuba was not invited. Once the Democrats lost control of the US Senate in November 2014, Obama knew that he had to act on Cuba by January 2015 if he hoped to create a momentum for change that might eventually unlock the constitutionally bound congressional impasse on the embargo.

That latter drive on the embargo began on 17 December when Obama issued three presidential decrees: allowing US IT firms to start negotiating for Cuban purchase of much-needed modernized equipment (at both state-enterprise and individual levels), allowing US banks to back their credit and debit cards in Cuba and restoring the pre-Bush levels of remittances allowed to Cuban-Americans. While the remittance measure was designed to help ordinary Cubans (and small businesses), the first two were clearly designed to aid US enterprises regain some of the ground lost over preceding decades to European, Asian and Latin American countries. However, only the last of the three decrees ever really took shape: the first two were delayed and eventually shelved by US banks and companies' fear of falling foul of the US Treasury for embargo breaches. Hence, apart from changing the tenor of US–Cuban relations (and reducing the US mission's role in Cuban dissidence) and, worryingly for the Cuban leadership, raising Cuban expectations to unrealistic levels, nothing really changed. Donald Trump's surprise 2016 election as president did indeed restore much of the old hostility, as he sought to tighten the embargo (initially by small measures and threats, sufficient to halt further business interest in Cuba, including non-US businesses) and halted the growing flow of US visitors, with tighter conditions on their permission to travel. This certainly frustrated many Cubans' expectations in 2017, often wasting Cubans' small-scale self-employment investments.

Finally, Raúl's presidency ended when, as promised in February 2008 and confirmed in February 2013, he declared his non-candidacy (for the presidency) in the April 2018 elections. This was widely seen as ending the era of 'the Castros', although Raúl (re-elected party leader in April 2016) would continue to lead the PCC until April 2021, thereby allowing pro-embargo US interests to argue that a Castro was indeed still in power. Certainly, it opened up the presidency to a new leader, Miguel Díaz-Canel Bermúdez being duly elected by the new National Assembly on 18 April 2018.

What then had Raúl's 2008–18 presidency achieved? Most obviously, he had succeeded in enacting and defending more wide-ranging reforms of the Cuban system's policies than most observers had thought possible in 2007. Besides furthering the stalled reform processes of 1992–3 in terms of *cuentapropismo* (trebling the sector's size) and opening the door to further foreign investment, he had completely changed official attitudes towards dissent (easing the pressures on many (though not all) dissidents), foreign travel, the loss of Cuban citizenship by those emigrating illegally in previous decades, property ownership and sale and private farming. By 2018, Havana –especially – could boast a much higher level of access to hard currency, a greater range of self-employed activities, a more effective approach to increasing tourism and greater material improvement.

He had also, of course, overseen a major change in Cuban–US relations. Although the embargo remained in force, with Trump soon reversing Obama's détente, Cuba and the United States were at least now talking formally to each other in ways not visibly possible before 2014, creating the necessary mechanisms ready for an eventual full 'normalization' in a future relationship.

THE STATE AND THE MEANING OF 'THE REVOLUTION'

The developments, however, were simply the more visible and eye-catching aspects of the changes which Raúl had overseen, for below the surface he had also succeeded in steadily reshaping the structures of political decision-making, decision-enacting and decision-advising, and had done so by a subtle but determined mix of the usual slow process of constant vertical and horizontal negotiation, with political manoeuvring and alliance building.

Most crucially, he had succeeded in shifting the balance of decision-making power between the PCC's vertical structures and the National Assembly and government: by 2011, he had outwitted the most

recalcitrant of the middle and upper PCC structures, using the Assembly
and government as forums for presenting, debating and deciding policy,
before PCC ratification. Equally, he had reshaped government in both
purpose and personnel, bringing in younger, more female, more effective
and less politicized executors and decision-makers: the government's
job was now to govern, deciding policy collectively and acting with
autonomy. Hence, his changes in 2012, confirmed partly (albeit still
through compromise) in the 2016 PCC congress, saw the latter dragged
back slowly towards a role that would see it interfere less directly in
government decisions, acting more in what Raúl saw as its ideologically
guiding role, advising with authority but not power, on the necessary
decisions.

That latter process was not yet complete by 2018, since the internal
PCC compromises inevitably meant much slower progress than the
changes in governance and government. However, one crucial reality
of the post-2018 Cuban system was that Cuba was still not entering
a period of 'Cuba without Raúl Castro' since he remained PCC First
Secretary until 2021. That gave Raúl the opportunity to concentrate on
using those three years to effect the same scale of changes inside the PCC
that he had achieved inside the structures of government and governance,
suggesting that, as the crucial years of debate and difference would come
in the build-up in 2020–1, he had two years to effect an overhaul of PCC
personnel at all levels.

Of course, it also raised an interesting question: having argued since
2008 that the PCC had to withdraw from the day-to-day involvement
in decision-making and act as an overseeing ideological authority, would
he stand by and watch his presidential successor take decisions with
which he disagreed, or would he use his formal authority and new base
to prevent such decisions? His historical authority gave him considerable
scope to do so. However, the early indications after Díaz-Canel's election
suggested that he would refrain from such interference, insisting on
the PCC's guiding (not governing) role, while using the opportunity to
change the PCC's personnel and thinking. Indeed, his role in chairing the
2018–19 discussions for the much-promised new Constitution indicated
a Raúl still prepared to make structural reforms that his previous 'old
guard' image would not have led us to expect.

Another aspect of his reforms which escaped outside notice was his
strengthening of the decision-making powers of local governance, with
his policy of giving municipal assemblies the freedom to develop their
economic decisions to suit their local needs. While that began as a desire

to cut their funding to stimulate them to develop their own sources of local income, the characteristic processes of consultation soon saw the assembly structures object forcefully to that somewhat draconian policy (based on their awareness that not all *municipios* had the equal natural, economic or tourist resources to find such sources of income) and amend it to a decision to distribute a portion of local funding on an equal basis and give *municipios* greater autonomy (Espina Prieto 2017). As already seen, this development was part of a wider strengthening of the political authority and governance power of the whole People's Power system, including the Council of Ministers and the National Assembly, with the latter's Standing Commissions steadily acquiring more authority to propose policies and determine decision-making, hitherto the monopoly of the PCC Central Committee departments.

On balance, therefore, the long-term judgement of Raúl's 'Revolution' may well be that he succeeded in using his authority, power and capacity for negotiation to keep 'the Revolution' largely intact and the population mostly tolerant and patient, while continuing to effect the changes which he deemed urgent or necessary for the process's future. As he put it, *sin prisa pero sin pausa* (without haste but also without pausing), a line which might have frustrated many but which may have guaranteed enough continuing support among those wary of the corrosive effects of reform.

This brings us back once again to the question of the meaning of the term 'the Revolution', an issue which Raúl himself had of course broached publicly in 2008, countering mutterings about the possibly fatal damage that reforms might cause; overall, his success may well have been in doing precisely what he said: ensuring the Revolution's survival by modernizing it and not, as was feared, destroying it. However, by the time he retired as president, there were two promises that remained unrealized: the long-promised fusion of the two currencies and the long-overdue rewriting of the Constitution. In 2018, the former still seemed elusive, although further steps towards the fusion had been taken, and the purchasing power of the peso had steadily increased, bringing fusion closer. Meanwhile, the Constitution seemed to have been left to Raúl's successor to achieve, thereby giving him a basis for authority of his own.

Meanwhile, Raúl's whole post-2007 approach had spectacularly confirmed how much the new matrix, confirmed and legitimized in the early 1990s process of rebuilding the damaged state, really did work. While he engaged in the battles with different vertical structures of the matrix (strengthening the governance and electoral structures to force the ideological structures to fulfil their historic and formal role and not control), using allies in different places, he always operated as he knew he had to, through complex and multilayered processes of negotiation. Whether it was the negotiation with the CTC, the PCC or the Catholic Church, he negotiated and consulted throughout. Partly this was something of a device, to be seen to be consulting when he knew that the likely outcome would confirm his decisions, but it was also partly recognizing that the horizontal processes of inter-structure were crucial and had to be respected.

Hence, this raises a fundamental truth about the Raúl years which explains much. When Cubans, especially the young, complained about the slow pace of reform (while their elders occasionally complained about precisely the opposite), many of the delays arose from those horizontal processes of negotiation, necessary to get consensus and thereby keep a majority of citizens and key groups 'inside' the Revolution. Equally, when ordinary Cubans complained about the slow pace of all local decision-making, what seemed wilful bureaucratic time-serving or procrastination, or even power-exercising, was often a reflection of the whole system's growing complexity, a characteristic which, curiously, may well have contributed substantially to saving the beleaguered Revolution in the 1990s. Although, for example, government decisions might be passed down through the vertical structures of governance (via the different elected assemblies or provincial and local ministerial offices), the reality on the ground was that every such decision had to be the subject of consultation and even adaptation with all the relevant vertical structures at that level, in case a vital issue had been overlooked or the particular locality needed to question some aspect or other. Hence the proliferation of committees, meeting and consultations, while slowing down (and even preventing) decision-making, also ensured institutional participation of key groups at all levels, perhaps ensuring that the key element of the 1990s rebuilding (local collaboration and negotiation) became permanent in what seemed increasingly like a quasi-corporatist system.

EPILOGUE: CUBA UNDER DÍAZ-CANEL.

For many, Cubans, and outsiders alike, Díaz-Canel had emerged somewhat unseen before his surprise election as vice-president in 2014. This was largely because he had come up through the provincial ranks of the system: born (in 1960) and educated in Las Villas province (which largely became Villa Clara after 1976), he had a scientific, rather than humanities or law, training, graduating as an engineer in the province's Universidad Central (1982). Having already been politically active as a student, he joined the UJC 1987 and made his mark there as a quietly efficient and open-minded activist. In 1993, he moved up to the senior PCC and was immediately elected (in 1994) as both the provincial PCC's first secretary and to the national PCC's Central Committee. It was a rapid rise indeed, suggesting that others locally and nationally saw his talents, especially as he was eventually (in 2003) moved to Holguín to lead its provincial PCC, being simultaneously elected to the national PCC's Political Bureau. That posting was indicative, since Holguín was clearly seen by the national leadership as an economically crucial area for the future (based on tourism and mining); he was evidently being trained in the provinces for higher things. Indeed, in 2009, as Raúl Castro reshaped the PCC, Díaz-Canel was unexpectedly named Minister of Higher Education, again a post seen as strategically important to Cuba's intellectual, professional and ideological development. His impressive and rapid rise was confirmed, firstly, in March 2012 when he was elected one of the Council of State's vice-presidents and then (February 2013) elected surprisingly to succeed Machado Ventura as Cuba's senior vice-president; he evidently had Raúl's backing, seeing him as young, quietly dynamic, broad-minded and effective, but ideologically sound: the ideal choice to succeed his own drive for steady progress to reform. Moreover, he was from the provinces, suggesting an ear closer to the ground (indeed, he was famed for his ability and willingness to listen) and far from the political 'hothouse' of Havana.

In fact, in the first few months as president, Díaz-Canel showed himself to be as much of his own man as he could, given the external and internal constraints on his power of decision-making. These constraints included Trump's reversal (from 2016) of Obama's détente, with no prospect of easing hostility until at least 2021; the continuing resistance from the 'historic generation' to any further deep systemic reforms, and the accompanying need to balance continuity and change; and the simple fact that Raúl remained as PCC head until April 2021, suggesting the possibility of political interference or incoherence within a dual leadership. However, his position was substantially supported by Raúl's early decision to absent himself from high-level meetings to review government policies.

Díaz-Canel was also limited by another problem: lacking Raúl's historic authority, he knew that his authority depended on his ability to deliver something that would give Cubans some of what they increasingly wanted, bearing his stamp. That stamp soon proved to be based on two things: listening as widely as possible to ordinary Cubans, and at last starting rapid work on the promised new Constitution. The latter task was soon achieved, as the necessary Assembly commission to debate the ideas and provide an initial draft was created within a few months of his election. Interestingly, its chairmanship was given to Raúl. While some presumed that this meant his continuing control over sacrosanct aspects of the post-1959 ideas, ethos and structures, it actually turned out to mean yet further reform, with longer-term implications.

The most evident change came in the opening pages when the statutory preambles about the country's ideological principles showed a significant discursive change. Besides the same historic references as in 1976 to Cuban heroes and events of the past, those pages introduced a new element, adding Fidel to the previous duo of Marx and Martí as ideological influences whose ideas were being followed. In addition, Marxism–Leninism seemed to have more or less disappeared as a concept (and historic symbol), seemingly replaced by a reference to *marxismo y leninismo*, the separation of the two '-isms' suggesting significantly that Marxism–Leninism (the usual past shorthand for the Soviet thinking and for legitimizing stances) was no longer as relevant, although Marxism (on its own) was present, underpinning many of the ideas, while Leninism was included, but probably more for its role in shaping post-1920 notions of imperialism and anti-imperialism and notions of a necessary political vanguard, something that had long resonated with both Castros and Guevara, the latter seeing that in his theory of 'subjective conditions'.

Beyond those preliminary pages, there were some other meaningful shifts, most predictably perhaps (given the impulse of recent years) confirming the importance of, and right to, private enterprise, but always subordinate to the state and cooperatives. One potentially significant shift had been excluded, or finessed, after the fierce and public opposition from several of Cuba's churches: the effective legalization of same-sex marriage as of equal value and rights as more traditional male-female unions. The whole campaign had been a defeat for Mariela Castro's ardent advocacy (in her role as director of the influential CENESEX, National Centre for Sex Education), which had successfully championed homosexual rights, changing official and popular attitudes and thereby removing a blot on Cuba's external image. Now, while same-sex marriage was implicitly allowed (as had long been true) there was no explicit constitutional reference to it as a norm.

Another absence was any hint of either competitive elections (whether between parties or between individual candidates) or the direct election of the country's president. For many, this was a disappointment, although such hopes were probably unrealistic in the continuing context of active, and now intensified, US hostility: the reality still was that, while the embargo remained active and the US embassy under Trump (its functioning already reduced to a shell over the mysterious 'sonic attacks' of 2017–18) returned to supporting dissidence, a single party and no electoral competition would continue to be justified on the grounds that a country at war cannot afford to open up a breach in the defensive walls.

On the continuing political structures and system, however, the new Constitution included perhaps significant changes. First, the provincial People's Power assemblies would be abolished (they were finally ended in January 2020), replaced by a governor elected by all municipal delegates and working with a provincial advisory council composed of the municipal presidents and vice-presidents. While the justification for this measure was as much administrative as a matter of principle (echoing the People's Councils), the motivation seemed to be to rid the system of a cumbersome and bureaucratic level of administration which had blocked change downwards and consultation upwards, perpetuating some time-serving officials' powers. However, it also paved the way for a more sustained and explicit emphasis from late 2019 on local development as the basis for Cuba's future, with the *muncipios* as the engine for any future growth.

The changes further up the system, however, seemed to have a clearer intent. First, in an evident drive to separate more clearly the Council of State and Council of Ministers, the members of the latter were no longer permitted (for the first time since the 1970s) to serve on the former; meanwhile, the Council of State was henceforth to be presided over by the elected president of the National Assembly, instead of by the nation's president, the latter being still elected indirectly by the National Assembly, but with only one vice-president instead of the previous six or seven Council of State vice-presidents. The Council, reduced in size and now answerable to the National Assembly, seemed to have lost authority, becoming an advisory body for the Assembly and an executive committee of the Assembly between sessions. It too would henceforth have only one vice-president instead of the traditional six or seven, many of the latter often being former inner- or outer-circle members whose authority was institutionally preserved by their posts. Finally, the new

Council of Ministers would be presided over by the restored post of prime minister (not seen since Fidel moved from the prime ministership to the presidency in 1976), responsible for directing and executing the day-to-day running of national governance, with one deputy, but, strangely, with six vice-presidents of the Council. Overall, it seemed also to confirm Raúl's intention in 2012 of separating the PCC and government.

All this raised several interesting prospects. First, it raised the real possibility of up to four different leaders or politicians sharing between them the national task of leading decision-making, or at least decision-enacting: the national president, the prime minister, the president of the National Assembly and the PCC leader. On the presidency, its character and power were fully confirmed with the necessary re-election (by the existing Assembly) of Díaz-Canel in October 2019, with the 74-year-old former CTC head Salvador Valdés Mesa elected as his single deputy. The powers of the prime minister (confirmed in December 2019 as the long-standing Tourism Minister, Manuel Marrero Cruz) were still unclear: Marrero was evidently trusted for his effectiveness in Cuba's most important ministry and seen by Raúl, Díaz-Canel and the FAR as a safe and reliable pair of hands, but the national president would constitutionally (and probably ceremonially) preside over Council of Ministers meetings, while day-to-day running of government would be determined by Marrero. The president of both the National Assembly and the Council of State (the latter showing a revealing range of twenty-one representatives of Mass Organizations, key educational and scientific institutions and other significant posts, but without any of the usual 'historic generation'), already confirmed in 2018 as Esteban Lazo, the long trusted PCC provincial operator who had successfully run the Havana party after the 1994 unrest, evidently enjoyed as much authority as Raúl had ensured during his battles with the PCC. As for the latter, that would all become clearer after the scheduled 2021 congress.

Given those changes and the internal and external uncertainty until 2021, it was widely expected that 2018–21 would see a degree of stasis as people got used to 'Cuba without the Castros' in government and decision-making, while 2021 might be the moment for Díaz-Canel to decide things more in his preferred direction, possibly generating significant shifts in personnel and various institutions in the matrix. However, that remained speculation.

While this expectation reigned, it was all overshadowed by the reality of a Trump-led United States. Starting in June 2017, his administration proceeded to enact a stream of measures to tighten the embargo: by March

2020, these had amounted to 191. By late 2018, his administration, strongly influenced by the Cuban-American lobby (and especially Florida's senator Marco Rubio), reversed Obama's changes still further, restoring the old restrictions on US citizens' freedom to travel to Cuba (thereby hopefully weakening Cuba's tourist economy); finally, in April 2019 Trump decreed the most dramatic change to the six-decade long embargo by refusing the follow the post-1996 pattern of all US presidents (Republican and Democrat) of waiving the enactment of Title III of the Helms-Burton legislation. Despite the prospect of international legal challenges by angry governments, Trump seemed to have reasoned that, given the state of the global economy and internal EU divisions, the EU and Canada were unlikely to act on their threats. Either way, the effects on the Cuban economy were immediate, with a discernible fall in US-origin tourism to Cuba, seriously undermining Cuban income – of both government and ordinary citizens in the private tourist accommodation and catering sectors – and plans to sustain the recent growth in tourist numbers, reaching over four million in 2018. More worryingly in the short term, the interconnected nature of international banking and finance operations soon persuaded even those European and Canadian banks and investors already operating in Cuba to end their activity, deterring much new external capital from entering the Cuban economy. This, in turn, seriously affected the capacity of trading entities to operate without the ability to pay any Cuban counterparts. Hence, in early 2020 it seemed likely that any significant improvement of the Cuban economy's performance would have to await the outcome of the 2020 US elections.

In spring 2019, Trump had also ended the 2000 presidential decree to allow US food sales to Cuba (especially chicken and grain) on the condition of Cuban pre-payment in cash: the 2019 move immediately created a shortage of some foodstuffs for most Cuban consumers. He then decreed a series of measure to tighten sanctions on third-party vessels and airlines working with Cuba, changing the embargo's formal justification yet again, now that being Cuba's continued support for the Maduro government in Venezuela. Whatever the justification, the effects on most Cubans' daily life were substantial, albeit not on the scale or with the effects of the Special Period (despite popular fears). This raised a real prospect of rising discontent (presumably the purpose of the new measures), but now without a Castro in power to give people a familiar sense of confidence to survive the worsening. Díaz-Canel was indeed in something of a dilemma in late 2019, with little prospect or opportunity of being able to find short-term ways out of the situation.

10

REFLECTIONS ON THE CUBAN MATRIX OF POWER, GOVERNANCE AND DECISION-MAKING

The preceding narrative, having traced the complex and constantly challenged evolution of 'the Revolution' and its political system, has followed the process through its many periods, phases, debates and crises. As a result, we have seen both how much the original project from January 1959 has changed, in response to internal discussions and pressures and to changes in the external context and also to what extent we can detect any underlying continuity between that original project and the recent developments, a continuity which does not depend on, nor refer to, personnel alone.

The latter question, that is, the person and the personality of the leader of the evolving system at any one time (Fidel, Raúl or (now) Díaz-Canel), brings us back to one crucial point that was made clear from the outset: that the tendency of so much of the literature on post-1959 Cuba – and certainly of so much of the media coverage and treatment of modern and contemporary Cuba – to focus attention on Fidel, and then Raúl, has been unhelpful, misleading and ahistorical. As we have seen, this tendency has gone through several stages since 1959: from Fidel as the 'typical' Latin American *caudillo*, seizing power through armed rebellion and then ruling with a mixture of authoritarianism and charisma (Draper 1965; Gonzalez 1974), then as an equally 'typical' personalist communist leader, ruling through a single-party structure under his firm control (a view perpetuated for two decades, even when his actual power was constrained by the greater influence of pro-Moscow elements in the ruling circles), and then, after 1990, a Fidel that mixed the first and second versions, as the most common explanation of how and why the seemingly doomed Cuban system survived against all the odds (Oppenheimer 1992).

This survival, as we know, was generally attributed (in the academic literature as much as in the media) to a set of explanations, usually varying according to the political position of the one explaining: the extent and effectiveness of coercion, the population's fatalism and passivity (also argued to explain Fidel Castro's lasting popularity or the resigned acceptance of authoritarianism), the effect of decades of indoctrination (via the strictly controlled media, publicity campaigns and education texts) and simple fear of the unknown alternatives, or the depth of the long-standing Cuban nationalism which, given US hostility expressed immediately after the onset of the crisis in the tightening of the embargo, was perhaps inevitably strengthened, drawing on Cubans' reserves of radical interpretations of Cuba's historical struggle for national independence.

Some of these popular explanations offered may well have proved wide of the mark or less convincing in the circumstances: Could the weakened army and police really have coerced a whole population effectively in those initial years, and was it likely that, in the depths of a seemingly terminal crisis, passivity would dominate people's thinking enough to make them accept fatalistically the prospect of such a collapse of the system they had known for decades? Other explanations have pointed to the combination of factors that made a difference at a crucial time and among crucial groups. For example, innate nationalism (of a wide range of imperatives, from Marxist-influenced radicalism to simple but visceral national pride and anger at US antagonism) was undoubtedly reinforced by the seemingly vindictive approach of the Bush administration in 1992 (Kapcia 2000); a pragmatic adherence to the system's determination to keep key social expenditure as high as possible undoubtedly helped persuade many Cubans that, to avoid going down the route of precipitate disintegration of welfare and security witnessed in post-1989 Eastern Europe, they should continue to place their faith in the leaders who had built that social edifice, keeping Cuba safe for so long; and, as we have seen, the structures of popular participation did indeed prove crucially effective and all-inclusive at a time of disaggregation and demoralization, and local-level cooperation and state-reconstruction did ensure some degree of minimal systems of supply and delivery (Collins 2017). Furthermore, as this author and others have argued elsewhere, the depth, effectiveness and breadth of the system's basic ideology (beyond the 'official' Marxism–Leninism) did probably continue to keep a sufficient degree of popular faith in the system and its leaders (Rosendahl 1997; Kapcia 2000; Gordy 2015).

However, this narrative and its focus on the complex and interlocking structures and processes of power, participation and governance over the decades, and the simultaneous processes of constant negotiation and consultation, have perhaps begun to demonstrate yet another dimension and factor in the system's survival: the simple effectiveness of what has been described elsewhere as a semi-corporatist, post-colonial and decolonization project (Kapcia 2014). For the narrative given here has traced the whole Revolution's system not as one of distinct and countervailing 'phases', or changes of direction, but as a rarely seamless and often baffling empirical evolution of several simultaneous and overlapping systems of vertical structures (of power, governance and decision-making) and processes of horizontal communication and involvement, to produce a matrix as complex and confusing to the outsider as could be imagined, but one that has also seemingly played a significant part in the preservation of loyalties, commitment (or toleration), and conviction. Indeed, those same structures and processes that might have helped cement loyalty over the years have often also contributed to the frustrating (not least for most Cubans) slowness of decision-making, contributing in turn to a bewildering slowness in responding to crisis or the unexpected. For, if (as argued here) debate has always been a crucial and characteristic element in the shaping and evolution of the Cuban system and 'the Revolution', then it must necessarily mean that, for debate to be real or at least functionally useful and convincing, and for all that a given situation might seem to demand a rapid decision, the underlying need to carry at least a significant part of the population along with any such decisions, debates must take time to be spread beyond the confined quarters of small parties, groups or decision-making circles. In a very clear sense, this responds to the quasi-corporatist nature of the system, needing always to include rather than exclude, and to do so more or less convincingly.

In fact, if we turn our attention once again to each of the earlier periods, crises, periods of change and so on traced in this narrative, we can perhaps see that the six decades of the Revolution have seen a slow, gradual and often simply empirical (rather than ideologically determined) process of the steady construction and compilation of several parallel, and sometimes overlapping, vertical structures of power (decision-making or decision-influencing), participation at different levels and with different effects, and governance, again at different levels and for different purposes. Of course, within that matrix one crucial element (and even cement) has always been the central question of political authority, which has generally been interpreted (outside and inside Cuba) as simple power, but which has often been more subtle, more complex and thus more convincing on a day-to-day and longer-term basis, akin to Gramsci's notion of hegemony (Gramsci 1971: 12–13). Moreover, as we have seen, all the different elements of the evolving system have developed their particular character and purpose over time, and have tended eventually and cumulatively to interlock with each other via at least three different levels of crosswise and horizontal processes of consultation and negotiation.

The essential points that have been made throughout this narrative are firstly that the Cuban political structures have variably (i.e. not uniformly, in their character or effectiveness) been either (or both) top-down decision-communicating processes or bottom-up processes of some sort of feedback. In the best of circumstances, these complaint- or observation-communicating processes have seen decisions taken after having been passed down constantly through all the different structures and levels, probably within several different structures, but all for the specific purposes of consultation and (perhaps limited) debate. Where successful, the results have then been passed back up the structures for final consideration at the top, and perhaps final decision-making.

The second essential point made has been that each of the separate vertical structures of communication and decision-transfer has had to engage in a simultaneous and constant process of sideways negotiation with the other parallel structures, at each appropriate level. Therefore, because of the necessary scope of the inclusion of each of those other parallel structures, the resulting process of debate, which has always slowed down decision-making (often with stultifying effect) has also perhaps served to ensure that the decision-makers are at least aware of the many and contradictory concerns, complaints, sentiments, pressures and demands from the grassroots, not least as the structures between them all include most people at some stage, apart from those who have explicitly chosen to refuse to be included. Hence, passivity may actually have played a part, not so much in creating a resigned acceptance of awfulness as in accepting by custom and practice that some sort of consultation (not necessarily, or even, to be equated with democratic input) is part and parcel of the system to which they have become accustomed.

This is, of course, not to say that dissent has either not been significant or has not been repressed; to argue that would be to ignore convincing evidence of a consistent institutional intolerance of dissent (dating from Fidel's famous intolerable *contra* category of 1961), periods of harsh authoritarianism (especially at times of external threat or internal crisis, such as 1965–76, which saw the UMAP camps and *quinquenio gris*) and a thread of exclusion alongside the surprising degree of inclusivity argued here. However, the precise nature of any repression has often been difficult to gauge, thanks to the polemics that have always bedevilled the literature on Cuba, with axes to grind and political point-scoring often overwhelming calm assessment. What we can say with any degree of certainty is that, while it might be possible to argue that, at any one time, maybe a quarter or a third of the population had historically tended to accept the system come what may (varying of course with any major crisis or period of hardship), possibly the same percentage can be assumed to be un-mitigatingly against the system, albeit rarely openly (not least because of the effectiveness of the CDRs and the lack of institutional spaces to express that opposition). Here, however, we must observe that, with the 'safety valve' of permitted and even occasionally encouraged emigration (1965, 1980 and 1994), that percentage may well underestimate the scale of would-be and unexpressed dissent. However, if these assessments are in any way accurate (they were made in 1995), it also means that between one-third and a half of the population potentially can be assumed to be in the middle, complaining and desiring economic change above all, but prepared to tolerate and accept, often given benefits that are seen to outweigh the problems.

To recap finally, therefore, what have those structures and processes been and how have they evolved? Taking firstly the vertical structures of power, governance and participation, we need to address primarily those focused on what we have called political power (decision-taking) and political (decision-shaping) influence.

Essentially, these have consisted of two structures. The first are the concentric circles of power and influence (Kapcia 2014), namely the inner, intermediate and outer circles of power and influence, and consisting from the outset in 1959 of key participants in the 1953–8 rebellion, with the slow inclusion of trusted individuals from the pre-1959 communist PSP and a handful of others included for their representation (the DR's Faure Chomón), prestige (Raúl Roa, in foreign affairs) or cultural significance (ICAIC's Alfredo Guevara). Ultimately, it was only age and death which would change the personnel within those circles, which otherwise remained in existence, with lasting authority until the 2000s. Those circles therefore constituted and guaranteed a significant continuity of ideology, commitment and loyalty (both to the group and its leader, and to the whole revolutionary project) and a pool of talent and capacity, seen as ideologically reliable and enjoying historic legitimacy for enough Cubans to ensure residual loyalty and trust. Some of the members of those circles were clearly individually powerful in their survival, their ability to shape decisions and the continuing trust placed in them by either of the Castro brothers (notably people like Ramiro Valdés, Almeida, Alarcón and Machado Ventura), but others were perhaps more 'ceremonially' included over the decades, typically within either or both the PCC's Central Committee or as deputies in the National Assembly. Essentially, therefore, the former Rebel Army continued to represent (as late as 2019) the most lasting vertical structure, wielding an unquestioned authority at all levels: nationally, it shaped the continuity of some key individuals (and within the FAR a continuity of leadership after 2008, as Raúl moved to centre stage), but locally it gave authority to surviving *combatientes*' opinions, to their version of the historical narrative, and to their regular ceremonial importance. In that respect, the ACRC, while never really exercising power, continued (now under Víctor Dreke) to enjoy authority; with wider generational changes since 2016, the ACRC may indeed be the only institution representing that authority and legitimacy. In a sense, the 'civic soldier' role of the early decades remained intact.

Alongside those circles and individuals, the next important vertical structure of decision-making and decision-influencing political power is, of course, the single party, since 1965 the PCC. However, as already seen, a single party did not emerge until PURS in 1962, preceded by the preparatory ORI; neither enjoyed a clear-cut, authoritative and fully-fledged national structure until at least 1965, and thereafter was not as effective as the PCC would become after 1975. Crucially (unlike all the Mass Organizations), the single parties were always selective in membership, based on workplace-based nomination by fellow workers and then acceptance by existing members. This pattern was repeated in the UJC, the training ground for the 'senior' party. In late 2019, both organizations' memberships were approximately the same size (around 500,000), which meant that their combined total represented less than one-tenth of the population. Between late 1962 and 1975, the single party was mostly identical with the concentric circles, its governing bodies mostly matching the three circles (Kapcia 2014: 115–31). Hence, it was never clear until 1975 if the party was simply a vehicle for the inner circle, a formalization of their authority or a body with a life and authority of its own, although retrospect suggests the former rather than the latter. This was equally true at the grassroots, although for a while (1961–2) the emerging party seemed to be a vehicle for local PSP cadres, presumably aiming for it to have that life and authority. From the mid-1970s, however, this changed as the PCC grew, becoming more powerful (and not just authoritative) at all levels, but perhaps especially at the base where membership could sometimes bring real power in local decision-making and, more controversially, access to material benefits.

The 1990s then ate significantly into that emerging power, as members left (either demoralized or, reading the runes, seeing membership as no longer a route to local power and benefits), but the residual body thereby regained some of its old authority, since only the fully committed were likely to be members, and given also the local members' seminal role in the process of rebuilding the state. Finally, after 2011 and the gradual settling of the internal battles over party power and reform, the PCC seemed to be changing significantly, perhaps returning to its official role of (ideological) guidance and, after 2018 (as Raúl's only institutional source of power), re-establishing itself as a parallel (but necessarily more powerful, i.e. influential) source of authority to the ACRC.

Before moving on to the next category of organizational power (the Mass Organizations), any historical overview of the post-1959 polity has to consider, even if only briefly, the role of the Rebel Army and FAR, always alongside the party (in whatever form). This is because, as argued already, the historic 'circles' have until recently been coeval with (and, like the Mass Organizations, actually preceding) the single party. Certainly in 1959–60, it was demonstrably true at all three levels (local, provincial and national), although the Rebel Army's hegemony was certainly being contested at top and bottom, firstly by the growing counter-revolution (in the Escambray), but most subtly by the PSP. At the top, the ex-guerrillas constituted the most legitimate and popular element of the governing alliance, trusted by all around and above them, and trusted equally by most Cubans, simply because of their heroic and historic role since 1953 or 1956. That role gave them a legitimacy which no other group could match.

At the bottom, that was equally true, ex-*combatientes'* local prestige giving them a louder voice in the ways that local entities were shaped; however, while the upper echelons saw a steady movement of PSP cadres into positions of influence, the grassroots bodies experienced a more overt, and therefore more resented, movement of the disciplined PSP cadres, whose organization and ideological confidence (e.g. in the EIR contestations) helped them influence the shaping of the base. The only area where the Rebel Army's hegemony was uncontested early on was the provincial governorships, almost all governors being Rebel Army *comandantes*, enjoying a degree of unchallenged autonomy, which allowed Matos in Camagüey to act as he did.

After 1962, with the 26 July-PSP battles settled, the Rebel Army and the PURS/PCC reigned supreme, being one and the same at all levels. However, by then the army as a separate entity (other than for its historic prestige) had been overtaken by the three-service FAR, a change which (under Raúl) ensured the army's hegemony alongside and within the party. Indeed, the strength of the party's base in the FAR (continuing until today) dates from that fusion of the two bodies, party membership being seen as the badge of ideological firmness within a national body with clear historic prestige, after Playa Girón, the Escambray and, eventually, Angola (Klepak 2005). Moreover, the FAR's remit and power would soon expand into other related areas, the CDRs' and militias' operations being partly subsumed by FAR leadership, while the development of conscription (in 1963), including the labour-focused Ejército Juvenil de Trabajo (EJT, Youth Labour Army) ensured that the whole defence infrastructure became identified closely and universally as part and parcel of the Revolution as a historic entity and ethos. The conscripts and labour brigades were soon partly presented to the public as recruits in the Revolution's defence. Then the FAR moved into the economy, especially after 1991, a move designed to ensure that, while the state could not guarantee sufficient investment to fund Cuba's full defence, the FAR's ingenuity and dedication could cover the gap and ensure survival. Moreover, when the FAR was moved into the tourist sector in the late 1990s, specifically to counter emerging corruption, it was a popular and effective measure, the FAR again guaranteeing the 'purity' of what had now become Cuba's economic mainstay. Equally, the FAR's monthly (and now even weekly) markets offered in each *municipio*, selling their surpluses directly to the needy public at low prices, enhanced their prestige. By then, the FAR had ceased to be coeval with the PCC, given the massive reductions of manpower, but this curiously increased the FAR's relative autonomy, now economically capable of operating outside the formal governmental state structures and surviving on the basis of its own separate economy. Indeed, for many Cubans and outside observers, the FAR economic power had created something of a state within a state, potentially reducing its accountability, which led many to see the FAR as key players in Cuba's post-Castro future and any transition to capitalism, with FAR leaders akin to the ex-Soviet *apparatchik*-turned-oligarch class in post-1991 Russia. Mostly such external observations (often repeating rumours on 'Radio Bemba', the popular grapevine, and echoing suppositions in Miami) were expressed by visiting and US-based journalists, but some established researchers began to see evidence of such a pattern.

Returning then to the second type of power within the Cuban system, which, as already argued, has long been what we might call participatory power and mobilization, we address the power exercised at all levels by the seven Mass Organizations: especially the CDR, FMC, CTC, FEU and ANAP, but also, more formally, the 'junior' FEEM Federación de Estudiantes de la Enseñanza Media (FEEM, Secondary Students' Federation) and the Unión de Pioneros José Martí (UPJM, Union of Pioneers) for pre-secondary level students. As we know, five predated any of the successive single parties: the CTC and FEU existed before 1959, the CDR and FMC were created in 1960 and the ANAP followed in 1961. That is not simply a chronological curiosity but of more significance in the Cuban matrix: not only were they 'mass' organizations, that is, available without selection to all who qualified through residence (CDR), gender (FMC), work (CTC and ANAP) or study level (FEU, FEEM and Pioneros), thus potentially including all Cubans in one or more of them, but they were also created with a double purpose. The first was to ensure the maximum involvement of citizens in the processes of mobilization (for a range of purposes), political socialization and activity, and communication upwards and downwards, thereby capitalizing on, and developing further, the majority's commitment and active support, and all before the formal political structures were agreed and established. The second purpose, as already argued, was to stand in for the emerging but still weak and fluid state, providing the mechanisms and human infrastructure for local administration, provision, organization and information. In other words, the Mass Organizations in the 1960s were the means through which the series of laws, measures and projects were realized on the ground. Thereafter, as they grew in size and scope, they performed another function: to continue, deepen and normalize the ethos of the individual's role and identity within the collective, since, for most Cubans (apart from the PCC and UJC members) and apart from the regular People's Power mechanisms, they were the only formal and active institutions for any individual to belong to the collective.

Beyond these historic uses of the Mass Organizations, we should also consider one further, invaluable, purpose which they have always served: as mechanisms for institutional representation in higher decision-taking or decision-enacting bodies, and therefore potentially also acting as sounding boards for gauging grassroots opinion, sentiment and complaints, presuming that the processes of upward feedback actually operate effectively. Both functions apply especially to the CDR and FMC, whose (still appointed, rather than elected) presidents have, since the early 1990s, automatically been de facto members of the PCC's *Buró Político* and are now (under the 2019 Constitution) equally on the new Council of State, allowing them formally a seat at one of the top tables of both ideological authority and governance. Moreover, one should remember not only the Mass Organizations' role in nominating candidates for the elected assemblies, effectively giving them a degree of corporate membership of those bodies, but also that, during all of the national processes of consultation and dissemination (especially after 2007), all Mass Organizations have been the primary mechanisms for ensuring anything like a full discussion of the issues.

One might observe therefore that these Organizations' sectional character (for women, for workers and for residents) suggests a quasi-corporate element in the Cuban structures, raising the question of those sections of the population not so far thus included and represented. These include the retired and old (usually subsumed into the CDRs, FMC or CTC), the black population (not least given the sensitivity of race as an issue over the years and the growing evidence of resurfacing racial inequality with the arrival of remittances) and the urban *cuentapropistas* (the rural private farmers already having ANAP) after 1993, and, alongside them, the new urban cooperatives allowed and encouraged after 2012 (Jiménez Guethón 2017). On race, there are three major explanations usually offered for the lack of a national body to represent and mobilize the black population. The first is (in the eyes of some activists) a residual racism in the institutions and structures, perhaps enhanced after the early 1990s (Moore 1988). The second is that, precisely because race has long been a sensitive issue, a measure of 'colour blindness' has operated for decades, often citing Martí's well-known phrase *Cubano es más que blanco, más que mulato, más que negro* (a Cuban is more than white, mixed-race or black). Such a view was very prevalent in the 1960s when, allegedly in the interests of national unity and fearing the divisive effects of any colour-based institution, the authorities clamped down on attempts by black activists to propose a Cuban Black Power movement, inspired by the US movement which Cuba did support enthusiastically. The third explanation is the complexity of the definition of colour in Cuba: censuses have repeatedly confirmed that officially around 20 per cent of Cuba's population is black and 65 per cent white, but black academics in Cuba have pointed to the importance of colour rather than race, of racial mixing over centuries, of tendencies in censuses to cautious self-identification and of the prejudices or subjective judgements of census-takers. Instead, they argue, the real figures should refer to Cuba's non-white (rather than black) population, estimating that at around 65 per cent (Morales 2013).

As for the absence of a *cuentapropista* Mass Organization the most likely explanation seems to be that, when self-employment was legalized in 1993 as an identified economic sector, several key decision-makers in the PCC (possibly Fidel himself) saw that sector as a short-term emergency measure to battle against the crisis, rather than a permanent element of the system. Hence, to recognize them formally by their own separate organization would be to recognize their long-term presence. That attitude certainly prevailed until the 2010–19 decade, resulting in a lack of discussion of the sector's organizational character in preparation for the 2019 Constitution. If such an attitude did exist, we can probably assume that Raúl did not share it, seeming always to have believed that Cuba needed such a sector, and in office worked to increase and empower it. However, that delay in formal institutional recognition has led to the anomaly whereby, since the *cuentapropristas* have been formally represented by the CTC, even though they have no employer (already an anomaly in itself), the decision eventually to allow them to employ others, increases that anomaly. The final point here about the Mass Organizations is, of course, to remember their key role in the early 1990s providing the human capital and mechanisms locally for rescuing and rebuilding the damaged state. Even then, therefore, despite the challenges of transport, resources and belief, they proved capable of re-enacting their 1960s role and importance.

The penultimate category of power and authority to be discussed here is what we might call legislative power, governance power and representative power. As we have seen, before 1976 this dimension was the subject of successive experiments (notably JUCEI and Poder Local), alongside the serious attention paid to making more of the CDR. Since 1976, however, this has meant solely the People's Power structures, until 2020, consisting of the three levels: municipal, provincial and national, with the credibility of the latter two being partly undermined by the indirect nature of their election (until 1992) and, for the National Assembly, the brevity and infrequency of the Assembly's meetings. The 1992 changes certainly allowed the national body to gain greater legitimacy in ordinary Cubans' minds, while the growth and semi-permanent nature of the Standing Commissions, together with the role which the combined forces of the Assembly and Commissions played in developing Raúl's reforms, bypassing the party on occasions, have added to their importance. Now, the 2019 Constitution seems to have suggested even more authority, as well as decision-making power, with a presidency which is clearly separate from the national presidency suggesting greater autonomy. As already observed, of course, for some (perhaps many) Cubans, the Constitution's failure to allow competition in any elections has seriously undermined its credibility.

The final category is, of course, the executive power exercised by government itself, through the Council of Ministers and the different ministries. Generally, one might accurately observe that, during the Revolution's first two decades, most ministries were more executive than decisive, with the prominent exception of MinFAR, the Ministry of Education (under Hart) and the Foreign Ministry under Roa, the latter given considerable leeway to shape Cuba's new 'Third World' strategy beyond the MININT-based insurrectionary Liberation Department (Kapcia 2014: 107–10). By the late 1970s, with institutionalization under way, the ministries' growing organizational strength increased their governance authority, especially as each ministry developed offices at both provincial and municipal level and as institutionalization bred a greater bureaucracy in all of Cuba's nationwide bodies. Hence what was governance authority at the top (each minister executing decisions taken by either the presidency, the Council of State or the PCC leadership, and benefiting from their authority) became governance power at the lowest levels, the precise interpretation and execution of decisions handed down through the system being left to the local bureaucracy to actually enact (Bengelsdorf 1994: 87–8, 131–3).

While that ministerial pattern, power and authority would then go on to suffer, as with all institutions, during the state's traumatic unravelling after 1991, when most national bodies became weakened and lost authority, from 2008 (as Raúl sought to outmanoeuvre PCC resistance), the government as a body of individuals and (by virtue of their separate areas of responsibility) as a collective was gradually strengthened in authority, especially becoming Raúl's key power base in those battles, in the process making it a much more decision-making, rather than executing, body. That, in turn, meant that each ministry's provincial and municipal structures thereby wielded more real power (and not just authority) at those lower levels too.

From that point of view, therefore, the changes arising from the 2019 Constitution, separating government more clearly, under its own presiding prime minister, seem to be legitimize that new power and authority, making government (and its ministries) a more significant separate element of the vertical structures of power and authority than was ever true between 1959 and 2008, alongside and equal to the PCC, FAR and the Mass Organizations.

However, to complete the picture of the Cuban matrix which has evolved since 1959, we need now to consider the other, equally crucial and often overlooked, dimension which is central to its operation and legitimacy: the many layers of horizontal processes of negotiation, consultation and inclusion of all these parallel structures at each of at least three levels: national, provincial (after 1976) and local. Repeating observations made at different stages earlier in the narrative outlined, we can say that there have been moments when neither Fidel nor Raúl were able to wield absolute power of decision-making and get their own way, but also we have seen whole periods, some long, when 'the leader' was forced to negotiate sideways (to ensure a degree of compromise), and even to consult downwards (usually for greater legitimacy or ammunition), not forgetting the several times when a PCC congress failed to meet its statutory five-year schedule, on each such occasion the scale and length of the delay reflecting deep or at least bitter internal divisions. Of the eleven congresses that should have taken place since 1965 (when the current PCC was established at its predecessor party's last congress), only seven have actually materialized: three were convened and met on schedule, five years after the preceding congress (1980, 1991 and 2016), but the other four were delayed by five years (1970), four months, followed by a further ten-month suspension (1985), one year (1996) and finally nine years (2002).

The statistics alone suggest that the idea of the Cuban system being monolithic, without debate or disagreement, is wide of the mark. Indeed, as has been argued here in detail, defined processes of debate (some open but other more closed in nature) have been identified: in 1959–61 – over the direction of 'the Revolution'; in 1961–2 – between the 26 July and PSP leaders and cadres; in 1962–5 – the 'Great Debate'; in 1970–5 – over how to address the crisis of 1968–70 and how to proceed; in 1986–9 – 'Rectification'; in 1990–1 – over how to save the Revolution; in 1993–8 – over the essence and meaning of 'the Revolution'; and from

2007 – over the nature, extent and speed of reforms. In other words, of the Revolution's sixty-one years of existence, only around twenty-seven years have seen little or no internal discussion, and, even then, discussion and disagreement were clearly continuing under the surface of an apparent consensus, certainty and consolidation. Clearly, debate, disagreement and discussion have not by any means been exceptions. Instead, they have always been at the heart of the process and, therefore, at the heart of any explanation of the political system's (i.e. the Revolution's) survival.

Returning to the horizontal processes of debate, therefore, the important thing here is to see how exactly it works, not just at the top but also at the bottom, that latter level not simply being at the stratum of the 169 *municipios*. For, as has been seen and argued here, while the 1960s created the unique mechanism for involvement in the form of the street-level CDR, the 1990s saw the nationwide spread of the experimental 1980s idea of the People's Councils, crucially at the intermediate level between the highly participatory CDRs and the more distant municipality, and, as a result, the emergence of what became increasingly called *lo comunitario*, the *barrio*-level mechanisms, units, centres and workshops which, between them, ensured the state's reconstruction and the effective revival of enough processes of basic involvement.

Essentially those different levels of operation have seen all of the vertical structures of governance, power and authority develop a necessary and ultimately automatic set of processes of discussion, negotiation, communication and debate, to ensure that, when a decision is finally reached at the top, it is passed down through the vertical structures for implementation but filtered through those horizontal processes for local enactment. Moreover, given the constantly growing complexity of the whole matrix, the top-level decision-makers have been forced more and more to be accountable to those below them in whatever vertical structure, in some form or other.

In the rapidly changing political environment of the 1960s, the most effective form was the somewhat rhetorical 'direct democracy' which included the basis for the official Declarations of Havana of 1960 and 1962, supposedly decreed by the People's Assembly in the Plaza de la Revolución (Castro 2008). Instead, any feedback was processed through the workings of the emerging Mass Organizations, asked constantly to spread the word, discuss locally and gauge reactions. More importantly, each Mass Organization increasingly felt the need to communicate and exchange ideas and practicalities with the other Mass Organizations in the relevant district, to ensure that the best possible coverage was achieved, an ethos of effectiveness which continued to shape the growing matrix, as (still developing) ideology played second fiddle to empiricism (Collins 2017). At the top, horizontal communication and discussion could often be less systematic and increasingly limited to negotiations and cooperation between the different partners in the governing alliance, something which, by 1965, had ceased to be all-encompassing, being instead somewhat haphazard or selective.

In the 1970s and 1980s, as growing institutionalization and bureaucratization created an inevitably reduced ability to respond productively, grassroots frustration with the non-comprehending *burócratas* and *funcionarios* who invariably seemed to obstruct ordinary Cubans' daily needs or complaints or demands led to something of a decline in active expressions of support. However, the horizontal discussions and cooperation which had emerged in the 1960s continued to develop, albeit more slowly, with the municipal assemblies and elected authorities needing constantly to share discussions on local decision-making or decision-enacting with Mass Organizations and also with any other 'civil society' professional organizations of relevance to the issue, as part of the permanent need to ensure maximum coverage. Meantime, in the upper national and provincial echelons, that similar sharing of discussion was often, but not always, less evident, given the underlying tensions between different competing discourses of what was meant by the newly institutionalized 'socialism', which excluded the perspectives adopted by those associated with what we might call 'Guevarism'. Hence, what horizontal consultation there was at the highest level was never as all-encompassing as it had been, not to mention the obstructions (and occasional obstructionism) built into the more institutionalized structures. Indeed, it was precisely that absence and its effects which conspired to produce the debates of the 1980s which led to Rectification and its drive to reassess and return to some aspects of the former ethos.

In the 1990s, of course, those discussions helped shape the much wider and more urgent debates and consultations which produced some consensus over, firstly, the means to save the system, and then the meaning of 'the Revolution', although, as already seen, disagreement over the scope or permanence of the reforms continued well into the 2010–19 decade. At the grassroots, however, now acquiring an unprecedented importance as ordinary Cubans struggled to find their own ways of surviving, negotiation and cooperation became the order of each and every day. That meant constantly negotiating, but more importantly cooperating, with neighbours, families, officials, transporters, relatives abroad and so on to ensure some vestige of normal life and some vestige of material satisfaction in the grim days of shortages and darkness. In that context, the familiar watchwords of *inventar* (inventing), *resolver* (resolving) and *luchar* (battling) – the three metaphors most commonly used with a degree of black humour among the majority of the population as euphemisms of illegal access to services or goods – always had a collective context; for, as we have seen, it was never simply true (despite some accounts) that survival was based on a savage individualism, but rather on vastly expanded family networks, on neighbourhood collaborations and communications and on local knowledge of ways of, and materials for, resolving and inventing. Moreover, the fact that, for many, if not most, Cubans, those strategies involved living with the contradictions between their moralistic ideology and their practical needs to resolve shortages meant constant internal negotiation. After all, even hardened PCC members needed occasionally to dip into a black market where goods had either been siphoned off from the state supplies (especially the *bodega* rationing provisions) or had made their way into the cities through contraband between farmers and middlemen. In part, the old *solidarismo* had taken a new shape, as a means of individual survival through the collective.

Meanwhile, however, more official ways of surviving collectively were becoming increasingly evident and effective, through the whole *comunitario* experience; the People's Councils were based on the ethos of getting all relevant local organizations cooperating together to ensure provision and rebuild the state from the bottom up. In the workplace, however, formulaic and even quasi-corporatist they may have been, the *parlamentos obreros* (workers' parliaments) of the early 1990s involved a degree of discussion, and therefore partial ownership, of reform proposals during the debates.

That same duality (formulaic consultation and a degree of willing participation and quasi-ownership) would be seen after 2007, when nationwide consultations became more frequent and systematic as Raúl sought to push his reforms through, and then to legitimize them through the *Lineamientos*. Throughout those consultations, individuals' multiple membership of different Mass Organizations, and even for some the PCC or UJC, also ensured a degree of cross-fertilization and discussion, and the level of editing of proposals which resulted showed some degree of effective and thus unusually real debate, that is, changing proposals or at least their wording to accommodate different views. Hence, the very person (Raúl) who had shared in the collective leadership of the original Revolution in 1959 and set in motion the development of the Cuban matrix eventually ensured that, as the whole process prepared for an unknown future without any of the three historic leaders, the matrix would be strengthened sufficiently to ensure continuity and a level of tolerance either passive tolerance or active support, regardless of the internal dissent and external pressures and threats.

As a footnote to this discussion, Cuba's response to the Covid-19 pandemic after March 2020 is worth comment, highlighting the very processes and matrix outlined here. On 11 March, Cuba saw its first cases (three Italian tourists); then, as cases rose slowly (either connected to that initial outbreak or, increasingly, tourists and returning Cubans), the systemic response began. Borders were soon closed (despite the cost to an economy heavily reliant on tourism), as were schools and many workplaces, leaving many unable to work (lacking home-based internet). The many vertical and horizontal structures and networks immediately geared up, partly following a well-worn model against health crises (as in the 1981 dengue epidemic) and all hurricanes; Cuba's substantial healthcare workforce was mobilized (including medical students) to identify and monitor cases. After that, all cases were subjected to rapid hospitalization and treatment with existing Cuban anti-viral drugs, a process focused on speedy recovery. Thereafter, as new cases were identified, local quarantines were imposed and strictly controlled by police, civil defence and local mass organizations. As a result, by early June numbers of both cases and deaths were falling rapidly, from a peak of fifty per day down to ten. By late June, the borders were ready to reopen to limited package-holiday tourism; by 10 July, official statistics showed 2,403 cases in total and 86 deaths since 11 March, with several successive days without deaths. While outside commentators either questioned the statistics or attributed this success to Cuba's authoritarian structures (forcing Cubans to obey strict controls), the reality seemed to be simply that, alongside a much-ingrained sense of civic responsibility, all the national and local structures (vertical and horizontal) had slipped into gear rapidly, ensuring both a comprehensive and grassroots coverage. The system seemed to have worked in one key role: protecting well-being.

BY WAY OF CONCLUSION: THE CHANGING AND UNCHANGING MEANINGS OF 'THE REVOLUTION'

In Chapter 1, one of the essential threads of this narrative was laid out: the perhaps revealing changes in the evolving use and meaning of the terms 'revolution', 'the Revolution' and *La Revolución*. Hence, at each major stage of this narrative, we have returned briefly to update those meanings and uses, reflecting on their possible meaning at any one time. To conclude the narrative and the overall analysis, therefore, it is appropriate to return again to that thread and, by retracing and reassessing, reflect on the history of the Revolution through that same prism: the meanings of those terms.

Overall, those changes and that continuity can be best expressed by framing them all within three historic uses of the term. The first came after January 1959, in the thereafter statutory and unthinking reference to *el triunfo de la Revolución* as the moment when a preceding process of rebelling to overthrow Batista and enact an intentional transformation, which had implied both a recent past (the increasingly popular insurrection) and a hopeful present towards a better future, or, when used over the subsequent decades (as it became the standard way of referring to January 1959), as the start of the whole post-1959 process. The second came in June 1961, with Fidel's outline of the parameters of cultural expression: *dentro de la Revolución . . . . todo*. This use had assumed that by then *La Revolución* had become more than a process and was now something *within* which one could exist and operate, and even belong to, that is, it had substance and a collective identity. The third came in 2008, with Raúl Castro's promise not to destroy 'the Revolution', a use implying that, after five decades 'the Revolution' had become, or had constructed, something that could be destroyed rather than just ended, and that needed to be preserved actively, and was not just a historical artefact or museum piece.

Within the parameters of those three uses (one continual and the others at specific moments of crisis or danger), we can therefore trace the changes in the way in which Cubans on the island – and also both non-Cubans (academic experts, journalists and politicians) and Cuban émigrés – have used the term. The starting point, as was pointed out in Chapter 2, was the amorphous and vague concept of 'revolution' which had been so loosely used (and therefore steadily abused) over the six decades of the independent Republic as to lose any real meaning beyond a violent and armed challenge to a disliked government, including the complex and contradictory combination of several parallel rebellions, protests and actions in the 1933 '100-days' revolution', and the historic referent through the adjective *revolucionario* which thereafter was widely used to gain historic credibility, often claiming legitimacy from Martí's 1892 PRC. It was precisely the term's vagueness which enabled a wide range of Cubans to join, support or welcome the 26 July Movement's insurrection and victory, and then, as the process radicalized, to condemn Castro's betrayal of 'the revolution', whose character had not universally been defined before 1959 and about which there was little clear consensus even within the emerging rebel alliance. Hence, in 1959–60, the adjectives *rebelde* (assuming rebellion *against* something) and *revolucionario* (assuming either an intentionally radical transformation in the immediate future or a transformation process already established or under way) were often used interchangeably (as in the *Ejército Rebelde* and the *Asociación de Jóvenes Rebeldes*, on the one hand, and the *Fuerzas Armadas Revolucionarias*, the *Milicias Nacionales Revolucionarias* and the *Policía Nacional Revolucionaria*).

By September 1960, however, the creation of the CDRs implied that 'the Revolution' was already an entity and a process which could, and needed to, be defended, with some concrete *logros* (achievements) or future plans now under threat. It was, therefore, that use which Fidel referred to in his June 1961 mention of *dentro* and *contra*. By then, however, a concrete definition had implicitly been added to the term, with Fidel's passing reference in April 1961 to the making of a 'socialist revolution' under the noses of ' the imperialists', which assumed – as did most of those listening to the speech or reading it the next day in the newspapers – that a revolution with such a character was indeed already under way. As argued earlier, few among the process's supporters disagreed with that definition, given the traditional use of the adjective by many (often far from socialist) parties. The only question then, and subsequently, was 'what type of socialist was it'.

By 1962, that had, of course, been clarified, for better or for worse, by Cuba's insertion into the Cold War, which introduced the notion of a revolution heading towards communism, although, as we have seen in detail, there was little consensus then – neither inside Cuba nor outside – over what exactly that meant. The US government's point of view, shared to a large extent with many in Cuba (notably the Catholic Church hierarchy and clergy and many in the old elite and middle class) already equated 'socialism' (and, it should be said, nationalization) with 'communism'. However, the PSP included prominent voices against the idea of Cuba's revolution being even socialist, let alone communist, in orthodox Marxist terms making the Revolution underway a 'bourgeois revolution' at best, although few dared to express that view openly. What the external interpretation meant was, as we know, Cuba's isolation and eventual expulsion from the OAS, specifically on the grounds of the

Revolution's communism; what the internal differences meant was the Escalante affair and the acceleration of moves towards the first single party with its explicit reference to *la Revolución Socialista*, more than just implicit rejoinder to the PSP. In 1965, that rejoinder went further when the party became the Cuban Communist Party, implicitly declaring the Revolution to be communist, faithfully following the theoretical precepts identified by Che Guevara: achieving communism through subjective conditions, which meant aiming for a classless and stateless communist society but, in the process, seeking to create communism in the here and now through *conciencia* and the active involvement of the *masas*, the *pueblo*, resurrecting the guerrilla ethos by 'doing' and not theorizing, and by transforming on the hoof. By then, of course, isolation and an ideological and political distancing between Havana and Moscow meant also that 'the Revolution' was a *pueblo* under siege, a siege mentality which demanded positive unity and (an at times stultifying and paranoid) more negative conformity.

The year 1968, however, saw a further dimension of *La Revolución* being emphasized when, on 10 October, Fidel called attention to '100 years of revolution', redefining the Revolution once again, but this time with a clear historical base in Cuba's heroic and rebellious past, in Cuba's search for nationhood rather than just in a scientifically based class struggle for an egalitarian future. In other words, the Revolution was already several things at one and the same time: a class struggle, a fulfilment of a historic mission to create a free Cuban nation (revolutionary nation building) and the fulfilment of the dreams and sacrifices of Céspedes, Maceo and Martí by freeing Cuba and building an equal and independent Cuba on Cubans' own terms. That immediately gave a new depth and meaning to *el triunfo*, seeing the present transformation as the culmination of decades of popular struggle and not just the 1950s' insurrection.

Just seven years later, institutionalization ushered in yet another version of 'revolution': as a stable and fair system, rather than a bewildering and exciting process, that is, as an entity to which a good citizen could belong. Indeed, the use of *buen revolucionario* to mean 'good citizen' dated from the end of that period (Smith 2016), now through systemic and institutional means rather than through passionate mobilization (Fernández 2000; Kapcia 2009). In a sense, if one can indeed say that at any time 'the Revolution' stopped being evidently 'revolutionary' in the speed and depth of the constant transformation it was in the 1975–85 years, when stability meant more to most Cubans than the 1960s' mobilizations now did. By the end of the 1980s, however, events in

Eastern Europe had cast a cloud over this positivity, leading to the first suggestions that this stable and seemingly long-term socially fair state might be under threat, a sense of danger which, of course, intensified as the collapse of Soviet and Soviet-backed communism unrolled with bewildering and traumatic speed. The discourse of 'Special Period in Peacetime' and 'Option Zero' spelled a different view of 'the Revolution', not as anything to celebrate but, rather, as something to save, defend and preserve at all costs. Indeed, by 1994, that redefinition took a very Cuban turn, as *La Revolución* began to be coterminous and synonymous with *La Patria*, whose defence and deliverance would be achieved not just by short-term emergency measures but by the combined efforts of *la nación*, which now included those Cubans who lived abroad (*la emigración*) and who were enjoined to add their contribution to the collective patriotic struggle, a redefinition whose scope was ever wider, moving into all manner of aspects of the system and the discourse.

Meantime, as we have seen, outside Cuba (and even among some Cuba-based intellectuals and artists), *La Revolución* was being proclaimed dead, a historical anachronism and a failed project, along with its symbolic representation in the unattainable myth of the 'New Man'. At the same moment, however, on the island, other intellectuals and artists (outside and inside the PCC) were being urged to explore and express what they felt should be preserved of *La Revolución*, establishing what that term now meant and perhaps should have meant over the last three decades.

As already observed here, while the hegemonic discourse that resulted – inferred from the evidence of the literature emerging and the tenor of the media and public celebrations, rather than understood explicitly – defined that essence as 'the project' of 1959–61 (i.e. before the Cold War complicated, and partly constrained and even distorted it), that conclusion was not uncontested, given that others found it in 1975–85 or 1962–8. Finally, of course, we have seen already that the Battle of Ideas from 2000 took 1959–61 as the basis for new mechanisms of mobilization and regeneration, directed at a future Cuba based on a new generation of young and committed Cubans. Then, as Fidel died (2016) and Raúl partially retired (2018), *La Revolución* took on a totally new connotation for many younger, and not so young, Cubans, as something now definably in the past, as a heroic period which firmly belonged to a past that no longer held much appeal for them, however genuine their grief at Fidel's passing. Meanwhile, a quiet change had been underway since 2018 when Raúl stressed in 2008 that the focus was on socialism rather than communism. He set in train a pattern of thinking and discourse which continued, to the extent that it became increasingly common to use the term 'socialist' rather than 'communist' to define Cuba's political character. Indeed, by 2020, more reference was being made to the Revolution being 'in transition towards socialism', thereby forgetting the past aims and definitions but actually returning to the 1959–61 purpose.

To conclude therefore, it may be revealing and appropriate to give the final word to Fidel, whose passing seemed so much to represent for some a moment of real closure. On 1 May 2000, he had given a speech which, although noted at the time (and effectively being a closing speech for the post-1994 debate on the meaning of 'the Revolution'), went on to acquire greater meaning for many, especially as, after his death, a significant quotation from it began to appear on billboards and posters all over Cuba, began to be recited by schoolchildren, and to appear on tablets. The extract in question defined the meaning of 'revolution' in these terms:

Revolución es sentido del momento histórico; es cambiar todo lo que debe ser cambiado; es igualdad y libertad plenas; es ser tratado y tartar a los demás como seres humanos; es emanciparnos por nosotros mismos y con nuestros propios esfuerzos; es desafiar poderosamente fuerzas dominantes dentro y fuera del ámbito social y nacional; es defender los valores en lo que se cree al precio de cualquier sacrificio; es modestia, desinterés, altruism, solidaridad y heroísmo; es luchar con audacia, inteligencia y realism; es no mentir jamás ni violar principios éticos; es convicción profunda de que no existe fuerza en el mundo capaz de aplastar la fuerza de la verdad y las ideas. Revolución es unidad, es independencia, es luchar por nuestros sueños de justicia para Cuba y para el mundo, que es la base de nuestro patriotism, nuestro socialism y nuestro internacionalismo. (*Granma* 2000: 4)

[Revolution is a sense of a historical moment; it is changing what needs to be changed; it is full equality and liberty; it is being treated and treating others as human beings; it is freeing ourselves by our own efforts; it is forcefully challenging powerful forces inside and outside our society and nation; it is defending the values we believe in at any cost; it is modesty, disinterest, altruism, solidarity and heroism; it is fighting with bravery, intelligence and realism; it is never lying or violating ethical principles; it is the deep conviction that no power exists anywhere in the world capable of destroying the power of truth and ideas. Revolution is unity and independence, it is fighting for our dreams of justice for Cuba and the world, which is the basis of our patriotism, our socialism and our internationalism.]

Why finish on this note? The reason is not because Fidel's words were correct in any way; we can be sure that many Cubans disagreed with aspects of that quotation, and that many – outside and inside Cuba – saw them as fine words betrayed by the reality of the last six decades. It is because in those words he managed to encapsulate much of the complexity and the multilayered meanings of 'the Revolution', reflecting many Cubans' ability over the years to pick and choose (and customize) those parts suiting their own interpretation and way of living 'the Revolution', but doing so in ways that enabled them to have enough of a belief and investment in 'the whole' (despite the parts that they did not accept) to continue tolerating, supporting or acting *within*. After all, any successfully enduring ideology must mix principles, ideas, moral codes, beliefs and a sense of belonging in ways that can be customized, adapted, reshaped to suit, enabling the basic principles to survive as guides to action. In that sense, 'the Revolution' has indeed become something of an ideology in its own right over six decades, possibly the current conclusion reached by many Cubans and the leadership after decades of evolution, definition, debate and negotiation. Interestingly, when Díaz-Canel issued his statutory 1 January speech in 2020, he outlined Cuba's four priorities, the first of which stood out clearly: the need to defend and study the Revolution's ideology. Had Fidel or Raúl said that earlier, few would have been surprised, but the new (non-Castro) president's emphasis said much for the tradition which shaped his role and government, and the Cuba he wanted to emerge. In 2020, only time will tell how that panned out.

Notes

PREFACE

1 Leverhulme Trust-funded project: *Interaction between literature, politics, and the reader in revolutionary Cuba.*
2 Leverhulme Trust-funded project: *Beyond Havana and the nation? Peripheral identities and literary culture in Cuba.*

CHAPTER 2

1 'Revolución' is the name of the daily newspaper; 'Lunes de Revolución' therefore means 'Revolution on Monday', since, as used to be common in Spanish-speaking countries, the normal daily edition did not come out and was replaced by a dedicated cultural supplement.

Bibliography

Abreu Cardet, J. M., and Michel E. Cordero (2009), *Dictadura y revolución en el Caribe: las expediciones de junio de 1959*, Santiago de Cuba: Ediciones Oriente.

Adair-Toteff, Christopher (2005), 'Max Weber's Charisma', *Journal of Classical Sociology*, Vol. 5, No. 2: 189–204.

Aguiar Rodríguez, Raúl (2000), *El bonchismo y el gangsterismo en Cuba*, Havana: Editorial de Ciencias Sociales.

Alcántara Janeiro, Andrea (2019), 'Fulgencio Batista (1901–1973): Cuba a través del personaje', PhD thesis, Universidade de Santiago de Compostela.

Álvarez Batista, Gerónimo (1994), *Che: Una Nueva Batalla*, Havana: Editorial Pablo de Torriente Brau.

Álvarez Blanco, Ernesto A. (2009), *Subiendo como un sol la escalinata. Biografía de José Antonio Echeverría*, Havana: Abril.

Ameringer, Charles D. (2000), *The Cuban Democratic Experience. The Auténtico Years, 1944–1952*, Gainesville: University Press of Florida.

Andaya, Elise (2014), *Conceiving Cuba: Reproduction, Women, and the State in the Post-Soviet Era*, New Brunswick, NJ: Rutgers University Press.

Anderson, Benedict (1983), *Imagined Communities: Reflections on the Origins and Spread of Nationalism*, London: Verso.

Anderson, Jon Lee (1997), *Che Guevara: A Revolutionary Life*, London, New York, Sydney, Toronto, and Auckland: Bantam Press.

Arendt, Hannah (1951), *The Origins of Totalitarianism*, Berlin: Schocken Books.

Argote-Freyre, Frank (2006), *Fulgencio Batista. From Revolutionary to Strongman*, New Brunswick, NJ: Rutgers University Press.

Ariet, María del Carmen (ed.) (1992), *El Pensamiento del Che*, Havana: MININT.

Artaraz, Kepa (2009), *Cuba and Western intellectuals since 1959*, New York and Basingstoke: Palgrave Macmillan.

Azicri, Max (1988), *Cuba. Politics, Economics and Society*, London: Pinter.

Bain, Mervyn J. (2008), *Russian-Cuban Relations Since 1992. Continuing Camaraderie in a Post-Soviet World*, Lanham, Boulder, New York, and London: Rowman & Littlefield.

Bain, Mervyn J. (2017), 'Havana, Moscow, and Beijing: Looking to the Future in the Shadow of the Past', *Social Research: An International Quarterly*, Vol. 84, No. 2, Summer: 507–26.

Bain, Mervyn J. (2019), *Moscow and Havana 1917 to the Present: An Enduring Friendship in an Ever-Changing Global Context*. Lanham, Boulder, New York, London: Rowman and Littlefield.

Barreto, Jesús (1984), *No hay tregua con la delincuencia*, Havana: Gente Nueva.

Beckford, Luis Salomón (1986), *La Formación del Hombre Nuevo en Cuba*, Havana: Ciencias Sociales.

Bengelsdorf, Carollee (1994), *The Problem of Democracy in Cuba: Between Vision and Reality*, New York and Oxford: Oxford University Press.

Blight, James G., and Peter Kornbluh (eds) (1998), *The Politics of Illusion: The Bay of Pigs Invasion Re-examined*, Boulder, CO: Lynne Rienner Publishers.

Brown, Jonathan C. (2017), *Cuba's Revolutionary World*, Cambridge, MA and London: Harvard University Press.

Brundenius, Claes (1994), 'From Growth to Crisis', *Cuba Business*, Vol. 8, No. 7, September: 2.

Buch, Luis M., and Reinaldo Suárez (2009), *Gobierno revolucionarios cubanos. Primeros pasos*, Havana: Ciencias Sociales.

Cabrera, Olga (ed.) (1974), *Antonio Guiteras. Su Pensamiento Revolucionario*, Havana: Ciencias Sociales.

Cairo Ballester, Ana (ed.) (2010), *Eduardo Chibás: imaginarios*, Santiago de Cuba: Ediciones Oriente.

Cantón Navarro, José, and Martín Duarte Hurtado (2006), *Cuba: 42 años de la Revolución. Cronología histórica 1959–1982*, Havana: Editorial de Ciencias Sociales.

Carpentier, Alejo (2004), *La Música en Cuba*, Havana: Letras Cubanas.

Castro, Fidel (1961), *La Historia me absolverá*, Havana: Imprenta Nacional de Cuba.

Castro, Fidel (1973), Discurso pronunciado por Fidel Castro Ruz, presidente de la República de Cuba, en el acto conmemorativo del XIII aniversario de los Comités de Defensa de la Revolución. 28 September. Accessed

10 February 2020 at: https://www.biobiochile.cl/noticias/internacional/america-latina/2016/11/26/las-frases-que-marcaron-el-discurso-de-fidel-castro-tras-la-muerte-de-salvador-allende.shtml.

Castro, Fidel (2008), *The Declarations of Havana. Presented by Tariq Ali*, London and New York: Verso.

Castro Ruz, Fidel (1980), 'Palabras a los Intelectuales', in Varios, *Revolución, Letras, Arte*, Havana: Editorial Letras Cubanas: 7–30.

Castro Fernández, Silvia (2008), *La masacre de los Independientes de Color en 1912*, Havana: Ciencias Sociales.

Centeno, Miguel A. (2009), 'El estado en América Latina', *Revista CIDOB d'Afers Internacionals* No. 85/86, Los Retos de América Latina en un mundo en cambio (Mayo): 11–31.

Chomón, Faure (1969), *El Asalto al Palacio Presidencial*, Havana: Editorial de Ciencias Sociales.

Clayfield, Anna (2019), *The Guerrilla Legacy of the Cuban Revolution*, Gainesville: University of Florida Press.

Colectivo de Autores (1989a), *Pensar al Che. Tomo I: Desafíos de la Lucha por el Poder Político*, Havana: CEA and Editorial José Martí.

Colectivo de Autores (1989b), *Pensar al Che. Tomo II: Los Retos de la Transición Socialista*, Havana: CEA and Editorial José Martí.

Collier, David (ed.) (1979), *The New Authoritarianism in Latin America*, Princeton, NJ: Princeton University Press.

Collins, Lauren (2017), 'The Dense Web: Local Governance and Popular Participation in Revolutionary Cuba', PhD thesis, University of Nottingham.

Cuba, Santiago (1962), 'El clero reaccionario y la Revolución Cubana', in *Cuba Socialista*, Año II, No. 10: 8–29. cuba-solidarity.org.uk/news/article/1676/raul-i-wasnrsquot-elected-to-restore-capitalism-in-cuba. Accessed 2 March 2020.

Cushion, Steve (2016), *A Hidden History of the Cuban Revolution: How the Working Class Shaped the Guerrillas' Victory*, New York: Monthly Review Press.

Daigle, Megan (2015), *From Cuba with Love: Sex and Money in the Twenty-First Century*, Oakland, CA: University of California Press.

Díaz, Clara (1994), *La Nueva Trova*, Havana: Letras Cubanas.

Díaz Vázquez, Julio A. (1985), *Cuba y el CAME: integración e igualación de niveles económicos con los países miembros*, Havana: Editorial de Ciencias Sociales.

Domínguez, Jorge I. (1978), *Cuba: Order and Revolution*, Cambridge, MA and London: Belknap Press of Harvard University Press.

Domínguez, Jorge I. (1989a), 'The Cuban Armed Forces, the Party and Society in Wartime and during Rectification', in Richard Gillespie, *Cuba After Thirty Years: Rectification and the Revolution*, London: Frank Cass: 45–62.

Domínguez, Jorge I. (1989b), *To Make a World Safe for Revolution. Cuba's Foreign Policy*, Cambridge, MA: Harvard University Press.

Domínguez, Jorge I., María del Carmen Zabala Argüelles, Mayra Espina Prieto, and Lorena G. Barberia (eds) (2017), *Social Policies and Decentralization in Cuba: Change in the Context of 21st-Century Latin America*, Cambridge, MA and London: Harvard University Press.

Draper, Theodore (1965), *Castroism: Theory and Practice*, New York and London: Praeger Publishers.

Duany, Jorge (2011), *Blurred Borders: Transnational Migration Between the Hispanic Caribbean and the United States*, Chapel Hill, NC: University of North Carolina Press.

Dumont, Rene (1970), *Cuba. Socialism and Development*, New York: Grove Press.

Espina Prieto, Mayra (2017), 'Municipalization and Social Policy in Cuba', in Jorge I. Domínguez, et al., *Social Policies and Decentralization in Cuba: Change in the Context of 21st-Century Latin America*, Cambridge, MA & London: Harvard University Press: 87–114.

Fagen, Richard R. (1965), 'Charismatic Authority and the Leadership of Fidel Castro', *Political Research Quarterly*, Vol. 18, Nos. 2-1: 275–84.

Fagen, Richard R. (1969), *The Transformation of Political Culture in Cuba*, Stanford, CA: Stanford University Press.

Feinsilver, Julie M. (1993), *Healing the Masses. Cuban Health Politics at Home and Abroad*, Berkeley, Los Angeles, CA and London: University of California Press.

Fernandes, Sujatha (2006), *Cuba Represent! Cuban Arts, State Power, and the Making of New Revolutionary Cultures*, Durham and London: Duke University Press.

Fernández, Damián (2000), *Cuba and the Politics of Passion*, Austin, TX: University of Texas Press.

Franco, Jean (2002), *The Decline and Fall of the Lettered City: Latin America in the Cold War*, Cambridge, MA and London: Harvard University Press.

Frank, Andre Gunder (1967), *Capitalism and Development in Latin America*, New York: Monthly Review Press.

Franco, Jean (1967), *The Modern Culture of Latin America: Society and the Artist*, London: Pall Mall Press.

Franco, Jean (2002), *Decline and Fall of the Lettered City: Latin America in the Cold War*, Cambridge, MA and London: Harvard University Press.

Franqui, Carlos (1967), *El Libro de Los Doce*, Havana: Instituto del Libro.

Fuller, Linda (1992), *Work and Democracy in Socialist Cuba*, Philadelphia: Temple University Press.

Gallardo Saborido, Emilio (2009), *El martillo y el espejo: directrices de la política cultural cubana (1959–1976)*, Madrid: CSIC.

Giuliano, Maurizio (1998), *El Caso CEA: Intelectuales e Inquisidores en Cuba. ¿Perestroika en la Isla?*, Miami: Ediciones Universal.

Gleijeses, Piero (2002), *Conflicting Missions: Havana, Washington, and Africa, 1959–1976*, Chapel Hill, NC and London: University of North Carolina Press.

Gonzalez, Edward (1974), *Cuba under Castro: The Limits of Charisma*, Boston, MA: Houghton Mifflin.

Gonzalez, Edward (1976), 'Political Succession in Cuba', *Studies in Comparative Communism*, Vol. 9, Nos. 1–2, Spring-Summer: 80–107.

Gordy, Katherine A. (2015), *Living Ideology in Cuba: Socialism in Principle and Practice*, Ann Arbour, MI: University of Michigan.

Granma (2000): 2 May; Año 36; No. 87; Havana.

Gramsci, Antonio (1971), *Selections from the Prison Notebooks* (edited and translated by Quintin Hoare and Geoffrey Nowell Smith), London: Lawrence and Wishart.

Grau San Martín, Ramón (1934), *La Revolución Cubana ante América*, Mexico: Ediciones del Partido Revolucionario Cubano (Auténticos).

Guerra, Lillian (2005), *The Myth of José Martí: Conflicting Nationalisms in Early Twentieth-Century Cuba*, Chapel Hill, NC: University of North Carolina Press.

Guerra, Lillian (2012), *Visions of Power in Cuba: Revolution, Redemption, and Resistance, 1959–1971*, Chapel Hill, NC: University of North Carolina Press.

Guerra, Lillian (2018), *Heroes, Martyrs, and Political Messiahs in Revolutionary Cuba, 1946–1958*, New Haven and London: Yale University Press.

Guevara, Ernesto Che (1965), 'El socialismo y el hombre en Cuba', https://www.archivochile.com/America_latina/Doc_paises_al/Cuba/Escritos_del_Che/escritosdelche0078.pdf.

Guevara, Ernesto Che (1977), 'Mensaje a los pueblos del mundo a través de la Tricontinental', in Ernesto Che Guevara, *Obras, 1957–1967*, Havana: Casa de las Américas: 584–98.

Helg, Aline (1995), *Our Rightful Share: The Afro-Cuban Struggle for Equality, 1886–1912*, Chapel Hill, NC: North Carolina University Press.

Hennessy, Alistair and George Lambie (eds) (1993), *The Fractured Blockade. West European-Cuban Relations during the Revolution*, London: Macmillan.

Hernández Otero, Ricardo Luis (ed.) (2002), *Sociedad Cultural Nuestro Tiempo. Resistencia y Acción*, Havana: Letras Cubanas.

Hernandez-Reguant, Ariana (ed.) (2009), *Cuba in the Special Period: Culture and Ideology in the 1990s*, New York: Palgrave-Macmillan.

Hoffmann, Bert, and Laurence Whitehead (eds) (2007), *Debating Cuban Exceptionalism*, New York and Basingstoke: Palgrave Macmillan.

Horowitz, Irving Louis (2008), *The Long Night of Dark Intent: A Half Century of Cuban Communism*, New Brunswick and London: Transaction Publishers.

Hurtado Tandrón, Aremis A. (2005), *Directorio Revolucionario 13 de marzo*, Las Villas, Havana: Editora Política.

Ibarra Cuesta, Jorge (1967), *Ideología Mambisa*, Havana: Instituto del Libro.

Ibarra Cuesta, Jorge (1980), *José Martí: Dirigente Político e Ideólogo Revolucionario*, Havana: Editorial de Ciencias Sociales.

Ibarra Cuesta, Jorge (1992), *Cuba, 1898–1921. Partidos Políticos y Clases Sociales*, Havana: Ciencias Sociales.

Ibarra, Guitart, and Jorge Renato (2000), *El Fracaso de los Moderados en Cuba. Las Alternativas Reformistas de 1957 a 1958*, Havana: Editora Política.

Jessop, Bob (2002), *The Future of the Capitalist State*, Cambridge: Polity Press.

Jessop, Bob (2007), *State Power*, Cambridge: Polity Press.

Jessop, Bob (2016), *The State: Past, Present, Future*, Cambridge: Polity Press.

Jiménez Guethón, Reynaldo, and Niurka Padrón Sánchez, 'Nonfarm Cooperatives in the Current Cuban Context: Challenges and Perspectives', in Jorge I. Domínguez, et al., *Social Policies and Decentralization in Cuba: Change in the Context of 21st-Century Latin America*, Cambridge, MA and London: Harvard University Press: 115–38.

Kapcia, Antoni (1995), *Political Change in Cuba: Before and After the Exodus*, Occasional Papers No. 9, London: Institute of Latin American Studies.

Kapcia, Antoni (2000), *Cuba: Island of Dreams*, Oxford and New York: Berg.

Kapcia, Antoni (2005), *Havana: The Making of Cuban Culture*, Oxford and New York: Berg.

Kapcia, Antoni (2008), *Cuba in Revolution: A History since the 1950s*, London: Reaktion Books.

Kapcia, Antoni (2009), 'Lessons of the Special Period; Learning to March Again', *Latin American Perspectives*, Vol. 36, No. 1: 30–41.

Kapcia, Antoni (2012), 'Celebrating 50 Years – But of What Exactly and Why is Latin America Celebrating It?', in Par Kumaraswami (ed.), *Rethinking the Cuban Revolution Nationally and Regionally: Politics, Culture and Identity*, Chichester: John Wiley and Sons: 58–76.

Kapcia, Antoni (2014), *Leadership in the Cuban Revolution: The Unseen Story*, London: Zed Books.

Kapcia, Antoni (2018), 'What's in a Name? Emigrant Cubans since 1959 and the Curious Evolution of Discourse', in Antoni Kapcia (ed.), *Rethinking Past and Present in Cuba; Essays in Memory of Alistair Hennessy*, London: Institute of Latin American Studies: 204–27.

Karol, K. S. (1970), *Guerrillas in Power: The Course of the Cuban Revolution*, New York: Hill and Wang.

Keuthe, Allan (1986), *Cuba, 1753–1815: Crown, Military, and Society*, Knoxville: University of Tennessee Press.

Kirk, Emily J. (2017), *Cuba's Gay Revolution: Normalising Sexual Diversity Through a Health-Based Approach*, Lanham, MD: Rowman and Littlefield/Lexington Books.

Kirk, John M. (1989), *Between God and the Party: Religion and Politics in Revolutionary Cuba*, Gainesville, FL: University Presses of Florida.

Kirk, John M. (2015), *Healthcare Without Borders: Understanding Cuban Medical Internationalism*, Gainesville, FL: University Press of Florida.

Klepak, Hal (2005), Cuba's *Military 1900–2005: Revolutionary Soldiers During Counter-Revolutionary Times*, New York and Basingstoke: Palgrave Macmillan.

Krull, Catherine, and Jean Stubbs (2018), 'Decentering Cubanidad. Commodification, Cosmopolitanism and Diasporic Engagement Shaping the Cuban Migration to Post-1989 Western Europe', in Antoni Kapcia (ed.), *Rethinking Past and Present in Cuba; Essays in Memory of Alistair Hennessy*, London: Institute of Latin American Studies: 183–226.

Kumaraswami, Par (2009), 'Cultural Policy and Cultural Politics in Revolutionary Cuba: Re-reading the *Palabras a los Intelectuales*', *Bulletin of Latin American Research*, Special Issue, Vol. 28, No. 4: 527–41.

Kumaraswami, Par (2015), *The Social Life of Literature in Revolutionary Cuba: Narrative, Identity, and Well-Being*, New York and Basingstoke: Palgrave Macmillan.

Kumaraswami, Par, and Antoni Kapcia (2012), *Literary Culture in Cuba: Revolution, Nation-Building and the Book*, Manchester: Manchester University Press.

Leimdorfer, Karen (2008), *Cultural Imperialism or Cultural Encounters. Foreign Influence Through Protestant Missions in Cuba, 1898–1959. A Quaker Case Study*, Saarbrucken: VDM Verlag Dr. Muller.

LeoGrande, William M., and Peter Kornbluh (2014), *Back Channel to Cuba: The Hidden History of Negotiations between Washington and Havana*, Chapel Hill, NC: University of North Carolina Press.

Lipset, Seymour Martin (1960), *Political Man: The Social bases of Politics*, Garden City, NY: Anchor Books.

Lipset, Seymour Martin, and Aldo Solari (1967), *Elites in Latin America*, Oxford: Oxford University Press.

Llerena, Mario (1978), *The Unsuspected Revolution: The Birth and Rise of Castroism*, Ithaca, NY and London: Cornell University Press.

López Civeira, Francisca (1990), *La Crisis de los Partidos Políticos Burgueses en Cuba: 1925–1958*, Havana: MES.

López Segrera, Francisco (1981), *Cuba: Capitalismo dependiente y subdesarrollo, Tomo II*, Havana: Editorial de Ciencias Sociales.

Loss, Jacqueline (2013), *Dreaming in Russian: The Cuban Soviet Imaginary*, Austin, TX: University of Texas Press.

Lowy, Michel (1973), *The Marxism of Che Guevara*, New York: Monthly Review Press.

Ludlam, Stephen (2018), 'A Mixed Economy of Labour in a Changing Cuba', in Antoni Kapcia (ed.), *Rethinking Past and Present in Cuba; Essays in Memory of Alistair Hennessy*, London: Institute of Latin American Studies: 123–48.

Luis, William (2003), *Lunes de Revolución. Literatura y cultura en los primeros años de la Revolución Cubana*, Madrid: Editorial Verbum.

Manke, Albert (2014), *El pueblo en armas. Die Revolutionären Natiionamilizen und die Verteidigung der kubanischen Revolution von 1959*, Stuttgart: Verlag Hans-Dieter Heinz.

Martí Martínez, Alberto (2017), 'An Archaeology of Counter-Insurgency: Exploring the Materiality and Memory of Cuban Re-concentration Camps (1895–1898)', PhD diss., University of Nottingham.

Martínez Heredia, Fernando (1988), *Desafíos del socialismo cubano*, Havana: Centro de Estudios sobre América.

Martínez, Milagros, et al. (1996), *Los balseros cubanos*, Havana: Editorial de Ciencias Sociales.

Marx, Karl, and Frederick Engels (1970), *Selected Works*, London: Lawrence and Wishart.

Mesa-Lago, Carmelo (1974), *Cuba in the 1970s: Pragmatism and Institutionalization*, Albuquerque: University of New Mexico.

Moore, Carlos (1988), *Castro, the Blacks and Africa*, Stanford: UCLA Press.

Morales Domínguez, Esteban (2013), *Race in Cuba. Essays on the Revolution and Racial Inequality*, New York: Monthly Review Press.

O'Connor, James (1970), *The Origins of Socialism in Cuba*, Ithaca and London: Cornell University Press.

O'Donnell, Guillermo (1973), *Modernization and Bureaucratic-Authoritarianism: Studies in South American Politics*, Berkeley, CA: Institute of International Studies & University of California.

Olson, James S., and Judith E. Olson (1995), *Cuban Americans. From Trauma to Triumph*, New York: Twayne Publishers.

ONEI (2019). Accessed 18 February 2020 at: http://www.onei.gob.cu/sites/d efault/files/servicios_informativos_no.12_turismodiciembre_2019.

Opatrný, Josef (1990), *US Expansionism and Cuban Annexationism in the 1850s*, Prague: Charles University.

Oppenheimer, Andrés (1992), *La Hora Final de Castro. La Historia Secreta detrás de la Inminente Caída del Comunismo en Cuba*, Buenos Aires: Javier Vergara.

Ortega, Gregorio (1989), *La coletilla. Una batalla por la libertad de expresión, 1959–1962*, Havana: Editora Política.

Paterson, Thomas G. (1994), *Contesting Castro: The United States and the Triumph of the Cuban Revolution*, New York and Oxford: Oxford University Press.

Pérez Jr., Louis A. (1972), 'Supervision of a Protectorate: The United States and the Cuban Army, 1898–1908', *Hispanic American Historical Review*, Vol. 52, No. 2: 250–27.

Pérez Jr., Louis A. (1976), 'Army Politics in Socialist Cuba', *Journal of Latin American Studies*, Vol. 8, No. 2, May: 251–71.

Pérez Jr., Louis A. (1983), *Cuba Between Empires 1878–1902*, Pittsburgh: University of Pittsburgh Press.

Pérez Jr., Louis A. (1986), *Cuba under the Platt Amendment 1902–1934*, Pittsburgh: University of Pittsburgh Press.

Pérez Jr., Louis A. (1988), *Cuba: Between Reform and Revolution*, New York and Oxford: Oxford University Press.

Pérez Jr., Louis A. (1999), *On Becoming Cuban. Identity, Nationality and Culture*, New York: The Ecco Press.

Pérez Jr., Louis A. (2008), *Cuba in the American Imagination. Metaphor and the Imperial Ethos*, Chapel Hill, NC: University of North Carolina Press.

Pérez Jr., Louis A. (2013), *The Structure of Cuban History. Meanings and Purpose of the Past*, Chapel Hill, NC: University of North Carolina Press.

Pérez Cruz, Felipe de J. (2001), *La alfabteización en Cuba: Lectura histórica para pensar el presente*, Havana: Editorial de Ciencias Sociales.

Peters, Christabelle (2012), *Cuban Identity and the Angolan Experience*, New York and London: Palgrave Macmillan.

Pichardo, Hortensia (1969), *Documentos para la historia de Cuba. Tomo II*, Havana: Editorial de Ciencias Sociales.

Pichardo, Hortensia (1986), *Documentos para la historia de Cuba, Tomo II*, Havana: Editorial Pueblo y Educación.

Pino-Santos, Oscar (1983), *Cuba: Historia y economía*, Havana: Editorial de Ciencias Sociales.

Pogolotti, Graziella (ed.) (2006), *Polémicas culturales de los 60*, Havana: Letras Cubanas.

Port, Lukas (2012), 'Hegemonic Discourse and Sources of Legitimacy in Cuba: Comparing Mariel (1980) and the *Maleconazo* (1994)', PhD diss., University of Nottingham.

Poulantzas, Nikos (1978), *L'Etat, Le Pouvoir, Le Socialisme*, Paris: Presses Universitaires de France.

Poyo, Gerald E. (1998), *Con todos, y para el bien de todos. Surgimiento del nacionalismo popular en las comunidades cubanas de los Estados Unidos 1848–1898*, Havana: Ciencias Sociales.

Revolución (1961), Año IV, No. 726, 17 April: 3, 12–3.

Roca, Blas (1963), 'La lucha ideológica contra las sectas religiosas', in *Cuba Socialista*, Año III, No. 22: 28–41.

Rosendahl, Mona (1997), *Inside the Revolution: Everyday Life in Socialist Cuba*, Ithaca and London: Cornell University Press.

Roy, Joaquín (2009), *The Cuban Revolution (1959–2009): Relations with Spain, the European Union and the United States*, New York and Basingstoke: Palgrave Macmillan.

Rueda Jomarrón, Hugo (2009), *Tradiciones combativas de un pueblo: las milicias cubanas*, Havana: Editora Política.

Shaffer, Kirwin R. (2005), *Anarchism and Countercultural Politics in Early Twentieth-Century Cuba*, Gainesville, FL: University Press of Florida.

Smith, Rosi (2016), *Education, Citizenship and Cuban Identity*, New York and Basingstoke: Palgrave Macmillan.

Soto, Lionel (1985), *La Revolución del 33. Tomos I, II, III*, Havana: Pueblo y Educación.

Story, Isabel (2019), *When the Soviets Came to Stay: The Soviet Influence on Cuban Culture, 1961–1987*, Lanham: Lexington Books.

Suárez Amador, José (2014), *De Las Villas a Oriente: Combatiendo el bandidismo (1959–1965)*, Santiago de Cuba: Editorial Oriente.

Sweig, Julia E. (2002), *Inside the Cuban Revolution. Fidel Castro and the Urban Underground*, Cambridge, MA and London: Harvard University Press.

Szulc, Tad (1986), *Fidel: A Critical Portrait*, London: Hutchinson.

Tablada Pérez, Carlos (1987), *El pensamiento económico de Ernesto Che Guevara*, Havana: Casa de las Américas.

Thomas, Hugh (1971), *Cuba: The Pursuit of Freedom*, London: Eyre and Spottiswoode.

Tone, John Lawrence (2006), *War and Genocide in Cuba, 1895–1898*, Chapel Hill: University of North Carolina Press. www.washingtonpost.com/archive/politics/1989/08/05/cuba-bans-2-liberal-soviet-publications/7ecc0ea2-9b75-4f29-9553-e7ff8e0e8e4c/. Accessed 2 March 2020.

White, Nigel D. (2019), 'Ending the US Embargo of Cuba: International Law in Dispute', *Journal of Latin American Studies*, Vol. 51, No. 1, February: 163–86.

Whitfield, Esther (2008), *Cuban Currency: The Dollar and "Special Period" Fiction*, Minneapolis: University of Minnesota Press.

Whitfield, Esther, and Anke Birkenmaier (eds) (2011), *Havana Beyond the Ruins: Cultural Mappings of the City after 1989*, Durham: Duke University Press.

Whitney, Robert (2001), *State and Revolution in Cuba. Mass Mobilization and Political Change, 1920–1940*, Chapel Hill, NC: University of North Carolina.

Wierzbicki, Agnes Martha (2005), 'The Cuban Black Market', MA thesis, University of California, Berkeley.

Yaffe, Helen (2009), *Che Guevara: The Economics of Revolution*, New York and Basingstoke: Palgrave Macmillian.

Zeitlin, Maurice (1970a), *Revolutionary Politics and the Cuban Working Class*, New York: Harper and Row.

Zeitlin, Maurice (1970b), 'Cuba – Revolution Without a Blueprint', in Irving Louis Horowitz (ed.), *Cuban Communism*, New Brunswick, NJ: Transaction Books: 117–29.

Zito Valdés, Miriam (2016), *Palacio Presidencial. Una acción sin retirada*, Havana: Editorial de Ciencias Sociales.

Index